Falling for Me

Also by **ANNA DAVID**

Fiction

Bought

Party Girl

Nonfiction

Reality Matters

Falling for Me

How I Hung Curtains,

Learned to Cook,

Traveled to Seville,

and Fell in Love . . .

Anna David

HARPER

NEW YORK · LONDON · TORONTO · SYDNEY

HARPER

HarperCollins books may be purchased for educational, business, or sales promotional use. For information please write: Special Markets Department, HarperCollins Publishers, 10 East 53rd Street, New York, NY 10022.

FIRST EDITION

Designed by Betty Lew

Library of Congress Cataloging-in-Publication Data

David, Anna, 1970–
    Falling for me / Anna David. — 1st ed.
        p.   cm.
    ISBN 978-0-06-199604-7
    1. David, Anna, 1970– 2. Novelists, American—21st century—Biography.
3. Single women. 4. Dating (Social customs) 5. Self-realization in women.
I. Title.
PS3604.A945Z46 2011
813'.6—dc22
[B]
                                                                                    2010054574

11 12 13 14 15   OV/RRD   10 9 8 7 6 5 4 3 2 1

Contents

Part One

CHAPTER ONE

Falling Apart

If you'd like to be loved, then love.

—*Sex and the Single Girl*

I'm not supposed to be here.

I don't mean "here"—standing in an unmoving line in the middle of Madison Square Park waiting for a cheeseburger I don't want on a hot June day.

I mean that I'm not supposed to be the 30-something with two cats, one toolset I don't know how to use, and zero prospects on the horizon.

I'm not.

And yet I am.

How in God's name has it taken me so long to see this?

Hey," he said as he sauntered over to where I was on my phone in the corner of a room. We were at a party in an L.A. warehouse and I was checking my voice mail. Thrown by his directness, by the way he walked right up to me even though I was busy, and then by how he looked at me—again, so directly—I hung up the phone even though I was in the middle of listening to a message I'd been waiting for. "You look stressed," he said. He appeared bemused.

This guy wasn't gorgeous; his brown hair was starting to gray, his face was a little pinched, he wore glasses and was neither rugged nor slim. But for some reason, I shook as I smiled at him. "And you look amused by that," I responded.

He laughed—a loud, guttural guffaw. "You were very focused on what you were doing," he said. "It made me want to see if I could break your focus." I noticed that stubble decorated his cheeks and chin.

"Mission accomplished," I said. Under normal circumstances, I would have been annoyed—being accosted by a stranger doesn't tend to bring out my good-natured cheer. But nothing about what was happening felt normal: the air was suddenly charged with energy from some otherworldly place.

We introduced ourselves. When he told me his name was Will, I suddenly realized he was the painter my friend had been telling me earlier was going to be at this party. Since my knowledge about art was somewhere between minimal and nonexistent, I'd only half listened when she'd talked about how he was a hero of sorts in the art world, credited with creating some new medium that enraged purists but was celebrated by modernists, and how his work sold for millions of dollars. But I didn't tell him that I'd just figured out who he was; by this point, I was focused on his eyes, which, now that he'd removed his glasses and tucked them into the front pocket of his white button-down shirt, I could see were swimming-pool blue. They contained vestiges of pain in the irises but they also looked simultaneously delighted and seemed to be pleading with me to stare back at them, a request that felt so overwhelming I had to look away. And when I glanced down, I noticed the wedding ring. *Of course*, I thought. *The first man to captivate me at first sight couldn't be single.*

We continued talking. I didn't understand what was happening—I'm a realist, practical and pragmatic, someone who believes in the right timing and compatibility, and not soul mates and Cupid's arrows. But I couldn't deny the fact that this stranger was eliciting something in me that I hadn't ever experienced instantaneously—a feeling that was simultaneously familiar and unfamiliar, like a song I used to love but had long since forgotten the words to. Our communication, I soon discovered, was just as unusual: words began coming out of my mouth as sentences before I had the chance to experience them as thoughts, and I had no desire to try to impress him or make him laugh or showcase my intelligence. Somehow, he—or the combination of the two of us—rendered my omnipresent self-consciousness obsolete. Time both slowed down and sped up. I wanted to crawl inside his eyes and take a swim. I wanted everything else to disappear. Within three minutes of being introduced to this man, I felt like he was the only thing in the world that mattered.

I tried to act normal. He was married—and, he told me, had two kids—and I wasn't going to go there. We made small talk, jokes. I pretended I wasn't having trouble breathing. But at the same time, there was only so much I could deny. A part of me knew, even then, that I was in serious trouble.

· · ·

The Shake Shack line continues not to move and tears stream down my face—something so common these days that it takes me at least a minute to even notice. They're certainly not my first tears of the day. Before I ventured out to get this burger, I'd actually been curled up in the fetal position sobbing for a good week straight, one sentence making an endless loop in my brain:

I'm going to be alone forever.

Then that thought elicited an endless stream of far more disturbing editions of it.

I'm going to be alone forever while the rest of the world is coupled off.

I'm going to be alone forever while the rest of the world is coupled off because there's something terribly wrong with me.

I'm going to be alone forever while the rest of the world is coupled off because there's something terribly wrong with me that's obvious to everyone but me.

Occasionally I'd switch to beating myself up for feeling this way while giving relationship advice on TV. It was shameful for someone who'd written so many articles on sex and dating, someone who'd been the relationship expert on a cable show, someone who regularly shared her thoughts on romance on major networks, to be in this state.

As I inch closer to the Shake Shack counter, I rationalize that it's okay that I offer relationship advice but can't seem to maintain a long-term one in my own life. How, I remind myself, could someone who easily found and married the man of her dreams early in her life help the lovelorn, the struggling, the confused, and brokenhearted? I can understand people's mistakes because I've made them myself. The fact that I've fallen in love with a married man and am now falling apart as a result will give me the experience and knowledge to be able to counsel someone else in the same situation.

But that still doesn't mean I'm supposed to be here.

Before my trip to L.A., I'd managed to keep depressing thoughts about my single status at a simmer whenever they bubbled to the surface. Through a combination of optimism, denial, and a collection of other single friends whose lives appeared to be exciting and glamorous, I walked with relative ease through every form that asked for my husband's employment information, every singles table at a wedding, every conversation about marriage. The "Have you met anyone special?" queries from my mom and other curious parties had, essentially, eased up, and I didn't ask myself if this was because everyone had given up on me or was just assuming I was gay and in the closet. In therapy, where I dissected my relationships, the conversations tended to focus on the particular guy I was involved with—the micro, not the macro—so I usually avoided seeing the big picture. Whenever a romance fizzled, an I'm-going-to-be-alone-forever mindset would set in and I'd agonizingly flip through people's happy family Facebook photos and wonder why I couldn't seem to do something that everyone—even the girl from my high school with the implacable body odor—had seemingly pulled off effortlessly. But those bouts tended to be ephemeral.

Of course, by the time I hit my 30s, I'd begun reacting to pregnant bellies and women or couples with children. I'd always smiled at, talked to, and played with children, but these activities took on a more panicked intensity once I started to pass through my prime childbearing years; a sensation that I'd better wave, smile, and coo at these kids since I might not ever have my own. I'd be struck with the feeling that the mothers of these children were much happier and better adjusted than I, no matter their circumstances. But I didn't experience this all that often and whenever I did, I never let the thoughts fester or cling to me: instead I'd turn back to the manuscript I was working on or keep walking to the gym or check to see if a stranger had written something nice about me on my blog, and the fear that I might not have a husband or be a mother would be replaced by whatever thought I'd slid in there.

Most of the time, I convinced myself that I'd be fertile well into my 40s, that I was simply someone who would not settle, and that when I did eventually commit to a man—a man whom I would of course feel had been well worth waiting for—our future children would never utter words like "dysfunctional family" or "I hate my mother" because I'd have worked out all of my issues during those long single years before I brought them into the world. I'd talk about this with friends, most of whom were childless and felt the same way. Phrases to explain my situation poured out of me almost subconsciously whenever necessary. *I'm happy being alone.* Or: *I haven't met the right guy.* Or my favorite, for when I was feeling particularly sanctimonious in the face of what I perceived to be smugness: *People think they need a relationship in order to be complete but I don't.*

And I really didn't think I did—until now. Interacting with Will had unearthed something so primal and overwhelming in me that not having a deep romantic connection suddenly feels unbearable. It's like a dam inside of me has tumbled down and I'm mourning all the years I've felt this way without ever allowing myself to know I felt this way. I'm in my 30s, in other words, and just finding myself in the state most girls enter when they're in their teens. I've never had a 10-year-plan or a must-be-married-by age and never worried about either of these things. Now it all feels like it's too late—like while I was off screwing around and building a career, the men I'd want to partner off with went and married younger girls who were happy to put their work lives second or possibly not even have them at all so that they could focus on a relationship. It's like coming out of a blackout and discovering that you're in the process of losing a game of musical chairs you didn't even know you wanted to play.

So how come you're single?" he asked as the DJ finally gave Lady Gaga a rest and put on a Rufus Wainwright song.

"How many weeks do you have to hear about it?"

He laughed as he leaned against the wall. "Actually, I tend to think of these things as easily explainable."

"Is that so?"

He shot his pointer finger up. "One: Dad issues—either you hate him or idealize him so much that no guy's ever going to measure up."

"Go on."

His middle finger joined the pointer. "Two: you're still not over a heartbreak you should have worked through a long time ago." Now the ring finger, with its gleaming wedding ring, united with the other two. "Option three: you have overly ideal-ized notions of what a relationship should be. You expect every moment to be like a romantic comedy—red roses, perfect sex, trips to the Eiffel Tower." I smiled and he looked pleased with himself. "Of course there's always option four, but I find that one to be rare."

"Let's hear it."

He cradled his left pinkie finger in his right hand. "Pure self-hatred. You don't think you deserve love."

"Not bad, Dr. Will," I said. My voice sounded normal, and not like I'd just had my precise issues accurately assessed by someone I'd known less than an hour. "I'd say I've done a decent job of covering all of those."

He gave me a sad smile before breaking into a grin. "Of course, there's always option number five: that you just think about this stuff too much and all you need to do is stop the analysis and pick a nice guy."

As Rufus switched to a U2 song about healing the world, I leaned against the wall next to him. "It's weird," I admitted. "I used to think marriage looked like giving up—accepting the fact that you probably weren't going to do much better. A commitment to endless nights in front of the TV."

He laughed. "Yeah, well, it does make you pretty comfortable with your remote."

A waitress walked by with a tray of bottled waters and we each grabbed one. "And see, that depresses me," I explained. "I'm like the girl from option two: I want excitement, fluttering hearts, embraces so impassioned that they could be captured on camera and displayed in college dorm rooms for decades to come."

"Ha, I had the Robert Doisneau print, too. But I think that was option three."

"Whatever." We smiled at each other as we sipped our water. "I don't actually know where things went awry for me in the relationship arena. I was the first girl in my class to have a boyfriend—in fifth grade! And there were a lot after that—so many that I think I assumed men came from a sort of bottomless reservoir." I gulped down the rest of my water and told myself that I should stop talking, that only an insane person would confess her entire romantic history to a complete stranger. Then I said, "I fell in love when I was 21 but a year later, I just sort of discarded him."

"You thought you were too young?"

"Yeah. The rest of your life sure sounds like a long time to spend with someone at that age."

"And then?"

"Well, then there was the other guy—the one from option two, I think?"

"He destroyed you?"

I nodded and ordered myself not to cry, the way I still sometimes did when I talked about Brandon. "I moved from San Francisco to L.A. to be with him."

"Oy."

"No, it was good—for a while. Before that, I thought relationships couldn't be balanced—that one person always loved the other more. But Brandon and I had this sort of mutually respectful worship for each other."

"Oy."

I laughed. "Will you stop doing that? You sound like a Jewish mother."

He smiled. "So what happened?"

"I don't know, exactly. I couldn't control my temper: I kept getting incredibly angry at him—like seeing-red angry—over anything I perceived to be a slight."

"I'll refrain from saying 'oy.'"

"He told me he'd leave if I couldn't stop losing my shit. And I couldn't. So he left."

"I guess in the end one of you did love the other more."

I nodded as our eyes met. To break the intensity of the moment, I said, "And then—what can I say? The reservoir dried up."

"Come on. Not entirely."

"Well, after that, I only seemed to be drawn to the ones who would disappoint me: these guys who would come on strong but cool significantly when my interest level matched theirs. And, you know, I got older. A 30-year-old just doesn't have the same options as a 20-year-old. And every year, there are fewer and fewer."

"Oh, save the I'm-too-old crap. Younger girls don't have anything on older women."

"Well, suffice it to say that not all men feel that way."

"The smart ones do." He took my empty water bottle from my hand and I felt a shiver through my body as our fingers touched. He smiled. "But good job on covering all the issues on my list."

"And I didn't even tell you about my dad yet."

"You don't need to. I'm no Freudian but your anecdotes revealed enough."

I laugh. "So what's your diagnosis, Doctor?"

He handed our empty bottles to a passing waitress, and then

turned to face me. "I think you need to be told that you're wonderful."

I felt embarrassed but pretended I didn't. "Thank you."

"And then you need to believe it."

'm so focused on my thoughts that I'm surprised to notice that
I've moved from the counter to a park bench and am now sitting and eating. I want to savor the burger I waited over an hour
to get but it's useless. I might as well be eating paste and not a
celebrated, much-written-about mixture of sirloin and brisket.
But I didn't come here for the culinary experience, really. I came
here because I've been engaged in a full-blown breakdown since
my birthday a week ago. And because I'd been hearing since I
moved to New York that I had to try Shake Shack—a recommendation that was always followed by a warning that the line
took at least an hour, which was then followed by my assertion
that I don't wait an hour for anything. So I'm here, really, to
prove to myself that I'm capable of change and can thus behave
differently from how I think I can. It sounds ridiculous, but the
way I dried my tears and got myself out the door of my apartment was by convincing myself that if it was possible for me
to do something small that was so contrary to who I naturally
was—to wait in a long line by choice—then there was at least
the slightest bit of hope I'd be able do something large that was
also contrary to who I was. Like be in a loving relationship with
a man who was available.

I watch a woman with a gleaming wedding ring and perfect French braid play with her even more perfect toddler on a
bench a few feet away and think back to how I used to believe

that falling for a married guy was one of those tropes it was almost my duty to stumble on, since I'd been single for so long and had made the pursuit of unavailable men into something of an urban hobby. I'd figured adultery was a rite of passage as elemental as a pregnancy scare or a one-night-stand. But somehow, like eating disorders and panic attacks, an affair with a married man was one of those experiences that I had long been able to cheerfully and surprisingly say had passed me by. I used to chalk this up to strong moral fiber; once I'd spent enough time on a shrink's couch to leave an indelible imprint, however, I reasoned it had more to do with the fact that I'd watched my dad cheat on my mom with the kind of determined consistency he'd been unable to display in so many other aspects of his life, and my role as the person who could make her feel loved enough to cushion and distract her from this left me certain I'd never be able to do to another woman what those women had done to her. I'd even said this, if not out loud then at least to myself, feeling a bit like Rosie the Riveter from the We Can Do It poster but without any of that eau de lesbian she seemed to emanate.

When other girls would tell me about falling for married men, I'd try not to judge but I always wondered why they didn't seem to notice the terrible tragedies that lurked right around the corner from extramarital affairs. Diaper-wearing astronauts. Late-night TV hosts turned late-night TV punch lines. Humiliated government officials having friends pretend they were the fathers of the out-of-wedlock babies or making incomprehensible apologies while their wives stood by them—the same wives that they had surely promised someone they were definitely going to leave. If unavailable was what these women were after, I'd wonder, why didn't they didn't honor the sort of time-honored traditions that I had, like dating actors or other simultaneously self-obsessed and tormented people? To me, married men were a turn-off; they represented rejection, solid evidence that another woman had gotten this man to commit.

I crumple my greasy trash and try to imagine what I could have done differently to avoid ending up here. Not assumed love was an ever-available commodity because it came along effortlessly at first? Run away from the charming bastards I'd spent most of my 30s dating? Been born with a different brain?

The French-braided woman feeds her daughter crackers as I reflect on my trip to Los Angeles. I've thought about it so many times that the scenes have already been worn down, like the 45s I'd play and replay in grade school until they wouldn't go up to full volume anymore. But instead of causing the experience to fade, this rehashing only seems to make the memories grow sharper. I have the feeling I'm shifting things a bit—adding nuances where there weren't any, maybe editing some dialogue— but at the same time I can't distinguish what happened from what I remember now. And I can't prevent my mind from going here. I may have quit drinking and doing drugs over eight years ago, but thinking about Will is my addiction now.

Look, I should tell you," he said the day after the party as we passed two gay men walking a teacup poodle at Runyon's Vista Street entrance, "I can't be physical with you."

"What?" I responded, stalling. He'd mentioned the night before that his wife was at her parents' house with their kids for the month. At some point in the evening, I'd decided to extend my trip an extra two weeks, figuring I could write from L.A. and telling myself it had nothing to do with him. When the party was ending, he asked if I wanted to go on a hike with him the next day and I'd said yes before I had time to consider that I shouldn't socialize with a married man or that if I was feeling what I was certain I was feeling, I needed to run in the other direction.

"I don't think it's fair—to any of us," he said as we continued up the mountain. "I'm pretty far down the hole already, so something like that might leave me at the bottom of it."

I was thrilled and terrified—I'd had no idea what he was thinking or feeling up until this point and was shocked, in a way, to hear that we were experiencing something similar. I also thought that falling down a hole with him sounded almost unfathomably appealing. But I simply said, "That makes sense." I acted like I hadn't been hoping he might pull me off somewhere at the top of Runyon and fuck me the way Michael Douglas had a pre-bunny-boiling Glenn Close, or at least try to kiss me while I gave him a halfhearted "No, we shouldn't" that I didn't mean and desperately wished he'd ignore.

"Good," he said, but he wasn't smiling. I told myself that I was relieved—that I didn't want to be a woman who got involved with a married man, didn't want to potentially cause this guy's daughter to see in her mom's eyes the kind of suffering I'd seen in my mom's. But a large part of me couldn't have cared less and was already compiling justifications in my head—coming up with lines about how everything was fair in love and war and how I hadn't made any sort of vow to his wife and how what she didn't know wouldn't hurt her and any number of clichés that wanton women have been uttering for years. And yet, because of his decision, I didn't need to know which side of the line I fell on—and for that I was grateful.

For the next two weeks, we spent most of our time together—going out for meals, taking walks, and seeing movies, essentially acting like people who were free to get to know each other—as if his wife and kids didn't exist and the only reason I hadn't been in a serious relationship for so long was that I'd been holding out for him. We talked about things I hadn't admitted to myself, let alone another person: my worry that I'd never be able to have a real relationship and that it was too late for me to have children. We talked about his art and about love, and were either silly or prescient enough to confess that we thought we were in it. We pretended that what we were doing was harmless because we weren't, after all, having sex. We weren't even kissing. We were strong enough to see the hole and dance over it. But the space between us crackled with lust and the sexual fantasies I was having whenever I wasn't around him were filled with multiple orgasms, sweat-soaked bodies, and constant declarations about never having been this turned on before. Despite the fact that we weren't so much as holding hands, it was the most sexual relationship I'd ever been in.

When we hugged good-bye outside Hugo's on Santa Monica Boulevard a few hours before I had to leave for the airport to go back to New York, our nether regions were perched as far from each other as our upper bodies allowed, almost as if a step closer on either of our parts might cause us to tear off one another's clothes and go at it on the street of West Hollywood boys' town.

"I'm only going to screw up your life if we stay in touch,"

he whispered. I nodded, my head moving up and down on his chest. "I want you to have everything you want and I'd only distract you," he added, as if I'd put up a fight. I knew I could argue—that there was a tiny door, a pet-size one, I could probably flip open, past his good intentions and determination to do the right thing. Instead I nodded again, got in my rental car, and looked back to see if he was still watching me. He was.

I wanted to feel excellent. We'd fallen hard—if it wasn't love, then it was the most piercing simultaneous attraction and comfort level I'd experienced—but we hadn't acted on it because it wasn't the right thing to do. Instead of being awash with pride, however, I fell apart—the giddy high I'd been enveloped in during the time I'd spent with him suddenly disintegrated and I felt more alone than I ever had.

The braided woman and her perfect child are gone by the time I leave the park.

The Barnes & Noble at Union Square is less a bookstore and more a monolith devoted to distraction: a multifloored Taj Mahal of books and magazines and anything else that could temporarily distract a girl who's determined to stay out of her apartment but doesn't want to have to interact with people. And unlike, say, an arcade or a library or a movie theater or any other place that could offer such all-encompassing diversions, this one is enormous enough that if that girl felt overwhelmed and had the desire to recurl her body back into the fetal position, she could potentially do so and not be disturbed, or possibly even noticed.

But the magazine racks all seem to feature one Kardashian

or another and even the tables of new releases and paperback favorites can't seem to excite me. I get on an escalator, wander around, and ponder a latte from the café before finding myself in front of a shelf devoted to relationships. *Last One Down the Aisle Wins: 10 Keys to a Fabulous Single Life Now and an Even Better Marriage Later* screams one title. *Single-Minded Devotion: Reflections for the Single Journey* calls another. *For Better: The Science of a Good Marriage* offers a third. Rejecting the first as too optimistic and the second as too dreary, I pick up *For Better* and read that it's by a *New York Times* health writer who always believed in the institution of marriage until her recent divorce. Maybe, I think, this is what I need: a smart person's assessment of why marriage doesn't work. I was already mentally aligning myself with the writer, deciding that she and I, as savvy, urban writers, were smart enough to realize that happily-ever-after doesn't actually exist. But then I remember that she managed to get married and I can't even picture myself in a serious relationship with someone who's available. I put that book back on the shelf and pick up another one, which informs me via an alarming paragraph on its back cover that I'm never going to be able to have a happy relationship unless I can go back and heal whatever went wrong in my first relationships—that is, with the members of my family. Christ. I sit down on the floor and rest my head in my hands.

While I was incredibly lucky in terms of most of the outward circumstances of my life, my early bonds were also fraught with complications. Part of this is because I was a colicky baby who supposedly cried so much that it forced my mom to go back to graduate school just to get away. When I was growing up,

I heard a lot about how much I cried and how crazy it drove everyone and I would feel guilty for these hysterical fits I didn't remember, wondering why I had to be such an imposition from right out of the gate. I begrudgingly came to accept my role as "the difficult one" while my older brother, who was a genius from day one, relished his part as "the smart one." As I got older, my tantrums continued, causing my parents to regularly declare me a monster and the whole thing to escalate more. But at some point, my dad decided that my outbursts were actually hysterical: he began to taunt me whenever I got upset by calling me petulant and jutting his lower lip out in what I would assume was an imitation of me. "My poor little actress," he'd say in mock pity and then begin cackling. My mom, who suffered through more than her fair share of his typical depression and anger, would also start laughing, and my brother, surprised to witness his usually disconnected parents so entertained, would join the fray. This would only make me cry harder.

My parents weren't sadists, and I've always been incredibly close to my mom. And they're actually quite loving and were just doing the best they could in a situation they didn't know how to handle. They also showered me with affection in other ways—especially my dad, who all but clobbered me with it in the form of worshipful declarations that I was more beautiful than my mother and that he loved me more than her, whispered confessions which always made me feel incredibly guilty and like I was an unwitting participant in something inappropriate. And the shame I felt over always hearing this, combined with his insistence that I was a monster, only made me start to live up to the label as I grew up. I'd learned rage from my dad—though he never hit us, he'd lose it on appliances and other random objects semiregularly—but my fury wasn't physical. Instead I'd take people hostage with my words. Heaven help you if you were one of my high school or college boyfriends and said or did something that I felt was remotely critical or dismissive: I relentlessly tortured these guys, coldly and repeatedly insisting that they explain their words or actions until they regretted them with everything they had in them and were in as much as pain as I was. I didn't want to do this—in fact, the whole thing was probably more upsetting for me than it was for them—but it often felt as if there was a furious second self that lived inside of me and couldn't *not* lash out at the vaguest sign of disrespect. I knew, even then, that this was misdirected anger—that I was really furious at my dad for making me feel both humiliated and complicit in some sort of secret and just taking it out on the closest male in the vicinity—but no amount of self-knowledge quelled the behavior.

When I pulled this kind of thing with my parents, they called it, rather accurately, "abusive." But that also became a convenient way to describe anything I did that they weren't in the mood to deal with. "I won't take your abuse" my dad would say if I calmly but directly explained that I didn't want to be sent to visit his dad and stepmom because they were cruel (my grandfather having been the one who taught my dad rage). Or later, if we were on the phone and I asked him why he didn't read a book I wrote or watch me on a TV show I'd told him I was going to be on, I'd hear, "I'm hanging up if you continue to abuse me." If he was in a yoga phase and responding through e-mail, he'd simply write, *I can't be abused by you—Namaste, Dad.* I understood that because of my eruptions earlier in life,

I'd lost the right to have my feelings heard. But even if I'd been warned of this later repercussion, I wouldn't have been able to do anything to control my flare-ups: once triggered, I seemed unable to stop until we were both emotionally bloody. The monster was relentless.

Drugs and alcohol initially helped me control my emotions: first by quelling my insecurities, thus tempering my fear and anger before it could take hold of me, and then by helping me to check out. Drugs—especially cocaine—allowed me to float above my pain and sadness, elevating my mood to a manic joy I'd never thought possible; I went from doing it when people offered it to me at parties to seeking out those I knew had it at parties to buying and doing it with friends to buying and doing it on my own in roughly 18 months; by the time Brandon moved to New York, about a year after we'd broken up, I had a full-blown habit. When I was high, I felt like I was finally experiencing life how it was supposed to be: a stretch of time and space that crackled with excitement and giddiness, where mundane worries and familial obligations were afterthoughts, where all that mattered was continuing to stay as happy as I was. But existing in this state had some serious drawbacks and eventually my life became a succession of jittery nights when I was so wired that I couldn't do anything but hole up in my apartment alone, feeling like I couldn't move, nearly jumping out of my skin whenever the phone rang, peering into the apartment of the neighbors I was convinced were watching me through a telescope, thinking I was having a heart attack and welcoming the thought. Nights where I'd drive to meet a cocaine dealer at 2 a.m. in South Central or suddenly find myself at Home Depot at four in the morning because I'd been shaking so much at home that I'd become suddenly convinced I needed to buy a new heater. At a certain point, I stopped calling my family and began ducking most of their attempts to reach me, but an offer to spend the Christmas holiday with my mom and stepdad in Paris one year proved too much for me to resist; I spent my two weeks there uncovering the seedy underbelly of French nightlife—discovering, to my utter joy, that Parisian cocaine was far stronger than anything I'd tried in the States. I'd return every morning to wish my mom, stepdad, and brother a happy day of sightseeing before taking to my bed for the following eight hours, only rising to go out that night to meet my new, drug-addled French friends. One morning when my mom watched me return from one of my nights out and pop a handful of Ambien, she tried to talk to me about what I was doing, but hearing her say, "I'm worried" caused simultaneous rage and defensiveness to sweep through me; I coldly assured her she had nothing to worry about before closing the door in her face.

I was the last girl who looked like she was going to embrace a life without drinking and drugs but I eventually got so miserable that I was willing to try it and then I shocked myself and everyone else by taking to it immediately. Even more surprising, underneath my party persona lurked a sort of inner obsessive workaholic who crossed every T, balanced every checkbook, and was determined to have everything under control.

But, I suddenly realize as I sit on the floor of Barnes & Noble, in getting my life together, it's like I went too far; I'm so terrified of regressing back into the colicky baby, monstrous child, and wild drug addict I used to be, of becoming the angry and hysterical girlfriend that eventually drove Brandon away, that I've instead transformed into a sort of automaton who won't ever allow herself to be with someone who's available and looks like he'll stick around. In my nearly nine years of sobriety, my romantic relationships have consisted of a series of month- to six-month-long unions with either charming and unstable dreamers or avowed womanizers I've been determined to change. I meet nice ones, ones who look like they could actually make good long-term partners, but I never seem to end up feeling too attracted to them.

Exasperated, I stand up and scan the bookshelves. Why can't there be an answer to my particular problem—a tome called *How to Make Yourself Open When You Felt Humiliated by Your Emotions as a Child and Also Always Got a Creepy Vibe from Your Dad Even Though You Know You Weren't Sexually Abused*? I wipe away tears that I hadn't even felt accumulating and am about to leave the aisle and bookstore when I glance at a pink-covered book someone left on top of the shelf: *Sex and the Single Girl* by Helen Gurley Brown. I pick it up.

While I know Helen Gurley Brown was the editor-in-chief of *Cosmo* for what seemed like a hundred years, I hadn't realized she wrote a book. I guess it makes sense, though: magazine editors probably all get book deals. I turn to the first page and see that this one originally came out in 1962; the back cover reveals that it was on the best-seller list for a full year and was published in 16 different languages. Those aren't exactly vanity book deal statistics. Since I don't want to leave this store thinking about how a relationship will always be out of reach because of various family dysfunctions I didn't cause and couldn't help, I crack open the cover and start reading. And I'm so surprised by the first line that I almost drop the book on the floor.

"I married for the first time at 37. I got the man I wanted."

Helen Gurley had married that late and was *proud* enough of this fact to open her book with it? If 37 is considered an old maid today, in 1962 it had to have meant senior citizen. I sit back down on the floor and start reading. An hour later, I'm still there—shockingly, almost embarrassingly, riveted. It offers advice on every aspect of a single woman's life—chapter titles range from "The Apartment" and "The Care and Feeding of Everybody" to "The Wardrobe" and "How to Be Sexy." And while it's filled with some crazy statements—like that you shouldn't make a man dinner until he's taken you out 20 times and that you ought to welcome your period as "abiding proof of your fertility"—it also makes a lot of sense. It brims with optimism, offering beauty, health, cooking, and decorating tips to make you more sought-after, suggestions for "conversation piece" accessories to attract interest when you're out (a colorful beach towel, clothes that fit well, a conversation piece pin!) and places to meet new men (planes, beaches, your friend's address books!). But there's a contradiction in the book's surprising and uplifting message that somehow meshes perfectly with my own contradictory desire for independence and partnership. Because Helen, it seems, wasn't just out to convince women that they needed a guy to complete them; she also wanted them to see that a single woman in her 30s wasn't a pariah or someone to be pitied but "the newest glamour girl of our times." As I smile at a bookstore employee walking by, I marvel at the fact that Helen felt this way in 1962—long before marriage rates dropped, divorce numbers rose, and fertility treatments began helping women deliver babies throughout their 40s. And if she could preach such a theme a good 36 years before an HBO TV series brought the concept to life, then maybe she just knows a lot that the rest of us don't. Her book essentially says, "Hey, single woman, you're fantastic—you provide for yourself, have enough free time to read Proust, and know how to survive in a competitive world. But maybe you ought to open your mind a little about the men you'd consider and, while you're at it, here are some things you can do to land them."

Somehow this attitude makes all those suggestions about attracting men, which otherwise might trigger my cynical defensiveness seem reasonable, if not appealing. The book is so nonjudgmental that it even casually condones getting involved with married men! "It seems to me that the solution isn't to rule out married men but to keep them as pets," Helen wrote. Then later, more ominously: "To take a married man seriously and fall in love is like dope addiction—dangerous and degrading." Oh, Helen, if you didn't have me before, you do now! Her overall message seemed to be that all single women need to do is see what a glorious position they're in and then, if they want the next stage—the ring and ceremony, the mother-in-law and nursing children—do everything in their power to reach it.

I take the book downstairs to the cash register, faith building in me for the first time in weeks. I'm not the sort of person who transitions from a state of hopeless despair to one of zany optimism just because of a book—let alone some guide to living as a single girl in the '60s—so part of me wonders if I'm in a delusional state where I only *think* I feel better. But I also know that I'm not really in a position to care. This is the first time I've felt something other than miserable since my birthday, and these days, I'll take whatever I can get.

Later, at home, I find myself looking up everything I can find out about Helen Gurley Brown. And I discover that although she perpetuated some less than liberated ideas about how women needed to cater to men and shouldn't have an ounce of body fat, she's also long been considered a true feminist icon. She was one of the first women, I learn, to hammer home how important it was for us to work hard and provide for ourselves, and she regularly insisted that sex wasn't a sign that you were slutty but an expression of natural, God-given desires.

While other feminists were spouting off about how we had to burn our bras and not wear makeup if we wanted to make any sort of progress, Helen, in other words, was telling us to doll ourselves up so that we could use our sexuality, along with our brains and wit, to have the fullest life possible. Betty Friedan's *The Feminine Mystique*, which argued that women were marginalized by a culture that believed their sole purpose was to make themselves appealing to men so that they could become housewives, was released a year after *Sex and the Single Girl*, and while what she wrote was reflective of society as a whole at the time, it's worth noting that Helen was already one of America's highest-paid advertising copywriters by then. Besides, I've never understood why women often feel like they have to choose between being smart or being sexy—in my mind, the two have never been mutually exclusive—so I immediately gravitate toward Helen's point of view; the woman was essentially putting out ideas more in sync with third-wave feminism back when the second wave was just gaining speed. Plus, if Betty Friedan was a 1 on the fun scale, I rate Helen an 11.

Sure, some of what she wrote in *S&SG* is dated—few today would say that gay men aren't "really" men—and she doesn't even try to feign an interest in parenting (she never had children herself and the only mention she makes of them in the book is that you should "borrow" some from friends if you want). But the more I find out, the more convinced I become that Helen Gurley Brown is a brave, original, slightly off her rocker, and altogether appealing role model for me.

And looking at my life now, it occurs to me that things aren't so bad. Of course, I know I'm blessed in that I'm not one of the three million homeless people in America, that I have freedom and the use of all my limbs and that I'm not shackled by an oppressive, sexist society. But considering these things when I'm depressed tends to just depress me more. I'd never thought, until I read Helen's words, that it was actually possible to feel *grateful* about being single. With sudden enthusiasm pouring through my veins, I decide to make a list of the reasons I'm happy not to have a husband and child:

1. I get to sleep whenever I want (and with whomever I want).
2. I don't have to worry that my husband wants to trade me in for a bright, shiny, body fat–free girl he spied at the gym.
3. I won't wake up in middle of the night, ponder the

snoring hairy creature next to me, wonder what's become of my life, and go research Neti Pots and powerful earplugs online while the creature sleeps soundly.

4. I needn't wrestle with whether to buy myself a new computer or use that money to enroll my child in a summer school program that I'm desperate for her to be in so I can actually type on said computer.

5. I don't have a mother-in-law.

6. I can take any assignment, accept an invitation on any trip, and stay out as late as I want without upsetting a soul.

7. I'm not discovering that a husband who thought he'd cleared his caches has viewed porn so twisted that it makes me question his mental health.

8. I'm not screwing someone up during her formative years, all but guaranteeing that she'll spend hundreds of future hours working out her precise feelings of rage for me.

Looking at the list, I feel, for the first time in my life, inspired to confront the shame I've felt about my single status and do something about it. Yes, Helen Gurley Brown—the woman who, I just learned, thinks "you may have to have a tiny touch of anorexia nervosa to maintain an ideal weight"—was giving me something that no parent, therapist, sponsor, or friend ever had: a hopeful message combined with a realistic plan.

Then a new idea occurs to me: if just reading her book once transformed me from pessimistic to positive, what would

happen if I devoted myself *entirely* to living the Helen Gurley
Brown way? What if I tried every last suggestion she gave for
becoming more feminine and meeting men? I stand up and
start pacing around my apartment as I begin to weigh the possibility of completely Gurley-afying myself. Why shouldn't I?
I've tried therapy, recovery work, and endless analysis of every
last date with friends. Why not consider a more old-fashioned
approach?

This project, I decide, will give me a chance to examine my
choices: to see, once and for all, whether I want the husband, the
baby, the sagging boobs and joy over first words, the mortgage
and the normalcy—or not. I can use every last one of Helen's
tools to break down the walls I've erected to keep myself from
having to really answer this—my busy work life, large group of
single friends, defensive refusal to get out of my comfort zone,
and attraction to unavailable men among them. And if I do everything possible to embrace wife and mommyhood and discover that I'm still not any closer to it, I can then commit to
accepting myself as single, childless, aging, and fabulous without reservations, shame, defensiveness, or excuses.

The more I read through *S&SG*, the more I realize that relationships were probably much simpler back when it was written,
both because we all knew our roles and because our expectations were lower. People didn't hope to find their equal, their
best friend, their lover, their cushion against the harshness of the
world, their counselor, their everything. Men needed wives and
women needed husbands and so they mated. Romantic love—
marrying for reasons other than acquiring property and land
or political or social connections—was still a relatively new no-

tion. While I'm grateful for the advances that have been made since then, I can't help but wonder if our collective thinking about marriage has only grown more unrealistic. Maybe there are some things we've lost that it would be nice to gain back. I can't tell you the number of people who have suggested, when I've told them I'm single, that I make a list of all the qualities I want my future mate to have. I've even listened a few times, and scratched out lists that I've then carried around with me. But what if it's the opposite that would really help? What if the answer is lowering our expectations and letting go of modern-day ideas that our partner should fill our every last fantasy?

The women of Helen's time certainly didn't have it all figured out, something that's brought home every week in *Mad Men*. We're all regularly privy to the notion that we were either resigned to the Christina Hendricks sexpot role or the Elisabeth Moss plain-Jane careerist one, and we're constantly reminded that wives had to look perfect, place perfect meals on the table, and raise perfect progeny. This is all meant to look oppressive, and it does, but what if some of what the women were doing—activities like making stews from scratch or creating beautiful homes—was actually, dare I say, beneficial? I'm certainly not arguing that we should go back to only being allowed to cook, raise kids, and clean our houses, but, looking at my life now, I realize how much I feel like I've been pushed too far in the other direction—led to believe that I should focus *solely* on developing the cutthroat skills necessary to compete in a man's world. Something about *Sex and the Single Girl* helps me to see just how much I've forgotten that I'm a woman—if, in fact, I ever really knew it at all.

Helen's suggestions for becoming more feminine actually appeal to a long-dormant part of me. I've long speculated that I shouldn't walk around makeup-less and in the same sweats and T-shirt I slept in but I somehow internalized the idea that, as a woman in pursuit of a serious career, primping was just a waste of time. And I've always wanted to be a better cook and decorator, longed to let delicious-smelling dinners simmer in a cozy home replete with comfortable cushions, flowers, and candlelight. But it's just never seemed all that *important*, and a firm refusal to do anything that I'm not already good at has prevented me from even trying. It's also kept me from becoming that intellectually curious single woman she writes of, the one who spends her free time learning new things and challenging herself by trying what scares her. I've quietly yearned to travel to places where I don't speak the language and to find new creative outlets to nurture the parts of me that have somehow gotten neglected as I've focused on my career and whatever activities are easy or familiar. Now I have a chance to change. And if embracing these things doesn't make me more attractive to men—well, at least it could make me more attractive to me.

So I map out a plan. First, I'll follow her recommendations for meeting men. Next, I'll try everything she suggested to become both more appealing to them and better prepared for partnership—I'll learn to cook, put myself together better, and decorate my apartment. I will, essentially, accept the fact that I don't have the answers for everything by finding experts—a cooking teacher, a decorator, a stylist, whomever I need to help craft me into the most appealing woman I can be. Then I'll work on improving the less-than-ideal parts of myself—whether it's the way I think, talk, or flirt—while still trying to "furnish my mind" in order to develop a richer inner life. Along the way, I'll challenge myself to do the things that have always scared me. At the same time, I'll take advantage of—and appreciate—all that I wouldn't be able to do if I had a husband and child, whether that means taking off on an international jaunt or saying yes to an attractive stranger. The whole time, I'll chat up new men on every plane, street corner, and beach I can—not just the ones I respond to at first sight with the sort of gut-to-groin instant passion I felt for Will but the ones that I may well discover I like if I only give them a chance. Ideally, this process will either help me to attract new men or change me enough that I'll be attracted *to* new men. Maybe both. And possibly, forcing myself to attempt whatever has always terrified me, whether it's online dating or traveling alone, will help me to face the aspects of intimacy that also scare me.

Helen says that to be a secure single woman who can "lay a trap for the glittering life," you need to "develop style, leaving no facet unpolished," "have a job that interests you," "cook well," live in a "chic, beautiful, elegant" apartment, "go to everything from company picnics to embassy balls," and "take long, gossamer, attenuated, pulsating trips before finally arriving in bed." While I have the job part down, my style is definitely unpolished, knowing how to poach an egg doesn't qualify as cooking well, my apartment looks like the dwelling of your average college student, I can go months without stumbling across a new man, and I don't think I've taken a long, gossamer, attenuated, pulsating trip anywhere, let alone to bed. Oh, Helen, how on earth do we start?

CHAPTER TWO

Coming Together

If you're partially dead, it takes a little doing to begin to venture again.

—*Sex and the Single Girl*

Roger gazes at me somewhat skeptically. We've been down a long road together, Roger and I, and over the previous month—when I've used up almost his entire Kleenex supply weeping about a married man I only knew for two weeks—I've received more than my fair share of skeptical gazes.

With Roger—and the shrinks who have preceded him—I've reached the same conclusions most people do in therapy: that all I need to do is get over what Mom and Dad did and didn't do. Why on earth did my parents—who have been divorced for almost 20 years but are literally best friends now—allow me to sit on a couch and pay someone to analyze my life with me? My particular brand of blame involves going over all the colicky, monster child memories ad infinitum as well as analyzing why I always feel judged by them and like I don't measure up. We also examine why I think it's somehow my duty to save or take care of them if they're the slightest bit uncomfortable or sad, and how that's left me believing that relationships are oppressive. But we talk as well about how tiresome it is when adults try to blame their every last issue on their parents rather than take responsibility for their own lives.

Roger's primary theory about me is that despite what I say about how ready I am to move to the next stage, there's a large part of me that doesn't want to be in a serious relationship. Thus, this new me—this together but slightly manic girl who's optimistic about her future love life and has a plan—is confusing to him. "Despite all the time and energy I spend struggling to find and maintain a healthy relationship," I explain, "I've never stopped to appreciate the life I have right now and to try to prepare for the next stage."

Roger cocks his head. "Meaning?"

"Meaning I've never had a strategy. I go out with one guy or another one and then come here and try to figure out why things didn't work out with him." I sit up straighter. "But I never look at the big picture."

"Well, you—"

"And I have this sort of fear-based mentality—with Will, part of what felt so horrible afterward was that it made me think I'll never be able to feel with another man what I felt with him. But why not stop mourning what I think I won't have and relish where I am now?"

Roger looks like he has no idea what to say. Finally he offers, "I would agree that your fear impacts your perspective."

"So I think the best way to examine how my fear impacts my perspective is to really try to get myself ready for a relationship by embracing new ways of finding one."

Now he nods. Therapists do love it when you sign off on their theories and then start throwing them around in sentences. "I think it's worthwhile for you to consider new methods if you feel like the old methods aren't working," he says. The skeptical look is now long gone but a more concerned one has taken its place. "I'm just not sure if the best way to do that is to follow an advice book from the '60s."

I nod, understanding why Roger's saying what he is—it must be in the shrink handbook to poke at least a few holes in any plan a client comes up with, particularly if said plan follows a month of weeping—but I'm uncharacteristically convinced that I've stumbled onto the right path. "I hear you," I respond. "But this isn't some crazy way I've found to distract myself from what I'm trying to accomplish in therapy. It's a new way to address the same old problem."

Then he asks me about Will. I tell him the truth—that since I've chosen to embrace this project, my feelings about him have diminished a little and that I'm not a hysterical wreck who sobs at burger stands anymore. But I don't admit that I'm still thinking about him all the time, that I cry when I do, and that he has a starring role in most of my dreams. A part of me thinks that convincing my therapist I've moved on will also convince me.

Roger's concerned look remains so I start talking about one specific line in *S&SG* that I keep thinking of—"I've never met a completely happy single girl or a completely happy married one"—and how it's helped me to see that I'm somehow convinced that getting to the next stage will make me instantly joyous and that one of the reasons I may seek out situations that will leave me feeling alone and unsatisfied is that it gives me an excuse not to be now. "I'm beginning to understand," I say passionately, "that if I can't be happy with what I have now, I probably won't be when I find the relationship I want."

I wait for him to tell me I've just uncovered the secret to life or to praise me for my revelations. Instead he nods and announces, in that slightly apologetic tone that always reminds me I'm just another client, "Time's up."

Everyone knows the rule of the rebound—that trying to get over someone by finding someone else doesn't work—but I want to get started right away, and getting started involves meeting new men. The fact is, I now see, I've only dated two types: the tortured artist or the womanizer (sometimes, God help me, both wrapped up in one shiny package). Usually writers, actors, or artists of some kind, these men tend not to make terrific partners since they're narcissistic and prone to panic. It's time to find a new playing field.

Though part of me would rather gnaw off my left arm than try online dating, I have to admit that it is perhaps the most significant advancement for single women wanting to meet men since Helen's time. Knocking into a man bringing drinks to a woman in a bar or going to a racetrack and placing bets— recommendations she gives in *S&SG*—simply aren't necessary in the era of a thousand dating Web sites. While the thought of being on one horrifies me, I reason that in the '50s, men and women met at sock hops and drive-ins; in the '60s, at church, temple, and bars when they knocked into someone bringing another person drinks; in the '70s, at rallies; in the '80s, at discos; and in the '90s, at work. Now we meet online. And where else could I encounter non-tortured artistic womanizing men who have normal jobs, 401(k) plans, and minimal shrink bills? Speculating that JDate is too limiting, Nerve too sexual, and eHarmony too Christian, I opt for Match.com's six-month special. Barreling through my discomfort, I remind myself that if I keep doing what I've always done, I'm only going to get what I've always gotten.

I fill out my profile as quickly as possible, thinking that this will make me stick with my first instinct, the way those SAT tutors my dad always sent me to told me I should. Otherwise, if I weigh the answers too much, I'll just try to make myself look the way I think I should instead of simply explaining who I am. I provide information about my gender, hair, eyes, and body type before listing the age range I'm interested in (I type in 35 to 45, knowing I'm willing to go lower and higher) and explaining what I like to do in my free time. When it asks me my favorite places, I put down Seville, Spain, a city I visited when I was in college where the streets smelled like perfume; the people were beautiful and friendly; and the buildings, bridges, and river were the most stunning I'd ever seen. For the inevitable "What do you like to do in your free time?" question, I go for a combination of honest and wry, listing "Coming up with clever activities to list in the 'What I Like to Do in My Free Time' section of my Match profile" along with a few things I actually like to do. I breeze through the sections on books and movies and don't hesitate on the "Do you want children?" query, clicking on "Definitely" rather than the far less committal "Someday." I come clean about not drinking, being Jewish, and having cats. The "Describe Yourself and Your Ideal Match" section is where

I ease up on the sardonic tone and get a bit more real. I write that I feel slightly uncomfortable being on a dating site and that I'm not looking for a meal ticket or to be someone's meal ticket. Then I upload pictures and hope for the best.

Almost as soon as I'm done, I begin receiving e-mails that send me running from the computer in horror: missives from unattractive, much older men who love car racing, Pabst Blue Ribbon, gambling, or something else just as unappealing to me and who think that we're perfect for each other, a sentiment they express with numerous grammatical errors and even more emoticons. This, I think, is what my lifelong pickiness had gotten me: a future with a man twice my age who writes in the space that asks him to list his favorite books, "Who has time to read when they're are wrestling matches to watch?" But Helen would never let herself be defined by the men who were asking her out. So I ignore the ones that scare or depress me and begin responding to some of the men who are at least close to my age and live in Manhattan.

The most appealing of that group is a guy named Bill. Bill is a doctor, a fact that thrills me because it means he's not a writer or an actor. While those men are contemplating their navels or staring into mirrors, I reason, Bill is saving lives. I imagine that Helen would be very proud of me.

His response to my e-mail, however, is full of unfunny jokes and questions about what I meant when I wrote this and that in my profile. Since nothing I wrote on the site was particularly cryptic, his questions suggest that we may not be on the same wavelength, and his jokes imply that we don't have a similar sense of humor. I don't write back. But he sends another e-mail

a few days later saying that he hoped his "silliness" in the previous note hadn't scared me off. I make the mistake of sharing this
information in therapy and Roger seizes on it, telling me that he
thought such a follow-up e-mail showed that the guy was self-
aware and thoughtful, and reminding me that I often rejected
what would be good for me while embracing what would be
bad.

I thus e-mail Bill again and we make a plan to have coffee
that Saturday afternoon. I feel reasonably optimistic about this.
But a few hours before we're supposed to meet, my phone rings.
Unknown caller. "Hi," the voice says when I answer.

"I'm sorry, who is this?" I say, trying to quell how much I
hate it when a voice I don't recognize doesn't identify itself.

"It's Bill," the voice responds, sounding miffed. "I was wondering what time you wanted to meet today."

"We're meeting at four—that's what we agreed on," I remind him.

"We did? No we didn't."

I glance at the e-mail from him confirming the four o'clock
meeting. "Well, could that time work for you?" I ask.

"I guess." He sounds distressed. "Actually, let me call you
back."

Minutes later, the phone rings again. He wants to know if
we could change the meeting time. I explain that I can't because
I have to be somewhere else afterward.

"Let me guess . . . do you need to go to a recovery meeting?"
he asks.

"Excuse me?"

"Well, I saw on your profile that you don't drink, so I figured you had to go to a meeting. I know all about things like that."

Under most circumstances, I'm thrilled to talk about being sober—how I got there, what I do to maintain it, any aspect people are willing to hear about. But I've never had a stranger confront me on the topic. And I'd resolved when I first signed up for Match to keep the experience as anonymous as possible: I didn't want to be the girl who gives sex advice on television or the writer who uses her own life as material or the sober chick who never shuts up about it. "No, I don't need to go to a meeting," I say. We confirm our initial plan, after which he calls back to find out the address of the coffee shop again. I'm thoroughly annoyed by Bill before we've even met.

There aren't any men sitting by themselves at Café Grumpy, my local coffee spot, when I arrive so I just go up to the counter and order a latte; when it's ready, I find a table by the door and wonder where Bill is. I don't want to admit that I'm nervous, mostly because I don't like to think of myself as someone who gets nervous before dates but also because being nervous about meeting a guy who's already driven me crazy during the pre-date planning seems especially pathetic. And yet I am. Putting out the message "I'm so interested in meeting someone that I'm willing to go out with a complete stranger" feels terrifying, almost humiliating on a certain level. I take a deep breath, trying to breathe in through my heart the way an acupuncturist once told me I should whenever I'm stressed, even though I'm not really sure what that means. I feel slightly calmer but then I start to wonder if Bill is potentially standing me up. You hear about things like this happening to people. Maybe he's watching from outside the café, trying to decide if he thinks I'm worthy of even meeting. Maybe he and his friends are all pointing and laughing. Maybe he—

"Hi." A man is suddenly standing in front of me. I can't imagine that it's Bill—five feet plus eight inches couldn't possibly be this tiny—but when he starts apologizing for being late, I understand that it has to be. I can hear myself talk to him, am aware of the fact that I'm suggesting that he go get his coffee, but my mind is actually stuck on the thought that *there's no way* I'm supposed to be on a date with this thin, gray-haired, avuncular man. How had I found him attractive in his pictures? Did he actually look this *old* in those pictures—or were they from a decade ago? But then I remind myself that everything happens for a reason. Maybe he has the kindest soul imaginable, is some sort of a modern-day Gandhi who operates on those people other doctors won't or devotes all his free time to burn victims pro bono—or at least has a best friend I'll like. He excuses himself to go order his drink and I watch him all but force the barista into a rather lengthy conversation about the song that's playing. The barista's responses are all one syllable—"Yes," "No," and "Hmm"—but Bill doesn't seem to be taking the hint. I try to dig deep inside for empathy: he may be scared, just like I am, and engaging in a one-sided musical conversation with an indifferent barista instead of coming over and talking to me now that he has his drink could be his way of expressing it. At the same time, I reason that I may not have to give this the one-hour try I'd heard was the online dating standard.

There's nothing wrong with Bill once he sits down and starts talking, especially if you're someone who's into hearing about organic eating. I happen not to be but that doesn't stop him from rattling off all sorts of recommendations for the best kale and broccoli and telling me which juices and fruits have the most antioxidants. He keeps talking about Michael Pollan's food book and insisting that I read it, finally stopping when I firmly tell him that I'm not interested in it and probably never will be.

Somewhere between 45 minutes and an hour after meeting, I explain to Bill that I have to go but that it was nice meeting him. I ask him which direction he's walking and when he tells me, I pretend I'm going the other. But he stays with me until I eventually lie and claim I have to make a phone call. I all but run home and, once there, stare at my computer and contemplate deleting my Match profile. This wasn't how dating was supposed to be—spending several hours making a plan so that you could sit down with a stranger you know within a minute you never want to see again. I'm not asking for interactions like I had with Will, not expecting an instant connection and deep attraction, but I also hadn't anticipated 49 horrible minutes in a coffee shop awkwardly blurting out likes and dislikes. Sure, you could show up, sit down, and really connect with the person, but how often does that happen when you only have pictures, a few hundred words, and some conversation to go on? One in 100 times? One in eight million—the number of people allegedly on Match? I call my friend Elizabeth, a willowy marketing executive I met through friends when I moved to New York almost two years ago. Elizabeth is far more together and practical than any of my other friends.

She hasn't, she tells me, tried Internet dating. "But someone once told me," she says in her throaty, Demi Moore voice, "that you shouldn't think of what you're doing as dating. You should think of it as a screening process—you're sitting down with a guy to try to figure out if you *want* to go on a date with him."

This makes me feel better: I'd had a terrible pre-date, not a terrible date. "Why don't you do it then?" I ask her.

"I don't know," she says. "Maybe I will." But I know she won't. Elizabeth's main focus these days is on having a baby and, unlike everyone else I know who thinks about these things, she's actually committed to conceiving on her own through artificial insemination. "You should try to have fun with it," she tells me before we hang up. "Don't feel bad if you don't like the guy. Remember: the worst dates make the best stories."

After that, I call my friend Nicole in L.A. A hip-hop publicist I've known since high school, Nicole's planting in her garden when I reach her. "You did online dating, right?" I ask. I have a vague memory of her telling me about filling out an eHarmony profile.

"Yeah, and it was terrible," she says. "There's nothing like having the worst time of your life while wondering if the people sitting at the next table can tell you're on a horrific Internet date."

I laugh; I'd practically felt like I was wearing a "We Met on Match" sign on my forehead at the coffee shop. "Remind me why I'm putting myself through this again?"

"Because you read that Helen Shirley Brown woman's book and are changing your life because of it."

"Gurley Brown."

"Whatever. And you're also doing it because those people

who go on and on about how you can find the love of your life on a dating Web site get us all at some point."

I sigh. "Have you ever noticed how it's always 'My friend met this great guy' or 'My sister's roommate found her husband that way'? You never run across people who have actually had the experience *themselves*."

"Exactly," she says. "I think they're all urban legends perpetuated by Match." Then she starts telling me about the guy she's started dating—an aspiring movie director named Tim that she met through her cousin. "Setups are much better," she says. "You need a screening process done by a person, not a computer."

Later that night, I get a text from Bill that says he's sorry he was a little out of it today and I'll see how different he is the next time we go out. I'm not sure what online dating etiquette is but I'd sort of assumed it was like nonvirtual etiquette—that is, that during the course of the experience, you made it clear if you wanted to see the person again and possibly even made another plan. I'd never received a text from someone I didn't want to see again that presumed we would, of course, have another date. The text is very long and I'm a little concerned there may be more if I don't respond so I write back that it was nice meeting him but I don't think we're much of a match. His response is immediate: *I agree. Best of luck in your search*.

The experience is discouraging enough for me to decide to put dating aside for a moment and consider some of Helen's suggestions for improving my life.

• • •

Even though I'm not afraid of hard work, I go into a mini panic when I look through Helen's ideas for the exciting, adventurous, intellectual activities I could take on and slowly realize that I've only been willing to do so much. Meaning: if something's within my comfort zone and I can work hard to have it, I'm all in. If it's not—and this goes for people as well as activities—then my attitude is one of indifference bordering on disdain. And my comfort zone, truth be told, is quite small. Essentially, I like writing and reading and talking and exercising indoors to choreographed routines. Not exactly a wide net.

Sure, I'll try something or someone new—once or maybe twice. But as soon as I discover that this strange and uncomfortable new activity is far more challenging than those things I'm already familiar with, I quit so fast that I can forget I even made an attempt. My list of aborted attempts is endless: I gave up on water skiing after not being able to stand up the first time I tried; I lasted about a week on the cross-country high school running team; my brief foray into stand-up comedy was so brief that it really doesn't even count as a foray.

The twice-used Rollerblades gathering dust in my closet are a perfect example. I bought them when I was newly sober with all the enthusiasm in the world. I was with a friend from rehab who Rollerbladed all the time and I figured that since I was no longer going to be donating my free time to alcohol and drugs, this would be the sort of exciting new activity I'd be embracing. That day, I skated with my friend along the bike path off the Pacific Coast Highway, reveling in the fresh ocean air and the fact that I was now someone who *did things*. Until, that is, about 20 minutes into it when my ankles started to ache. My friend told me that once I'd used the skates two or three times and my feet were acclimated, my ankles wouldn't bother me at all.

I wasn't able to put that theory to the test, however, since I only went Rollerblading once more over the next six years. The rest of the time, the skates sat in my car trunk, stored for the day when I would feel like using them—a day that I always sort of knew would never come. They traveled with me when I moved to New York two years ago, and since I no longer had a trunk, they went in the closet, where they stayed.

On the surface, this doesn't sound like a big deal; surely lots of closets are filled with Rollerblades, badminton rackets, swimming goggles, and all sorts of other relics of abandoned activities. But my relationship with fear has always been out of whack: I'm not scared to, say, go on live television, fly in or jump out of a small plane, or speak in front of hundreds of people. And yet those things that everyone else seems able to handle with ease—say, sharks, bees, and trying new things—fill me with terror.

The fear of sharks and bees at least makes sense; I occasionally encounter others who share my anxiety. But I've never really understood why the concept of attempting something out of my comfort zone and not being able to immediately excel gets me so riled up—or why asking for help in these situations and hearing people say things like "We've all been there" or "You'll get better" only makes me feel worse. It's like I internalized long ago that to struggle—and most of all to be witnessed struggling—was shameful and something to avoid at all costs. That, I decide as I pull the Rollerblades from my closet, is going to change. The point of what I'm doing, after all, is to challenge everything I think I know about myself.

I don't exactly whistle as I walk over to the West Side Highway with my Rollerblades in my backpack—I don't know how to whistle, and besides, I find whistling to be one of the most annoying sounds in the world—but I'm undeniably calm. The reason? I've decided that I'm not going to like Rollerblading. Part of what's so disappointing about new activities, I now realize, is that I imagine they're going to be a delight from the get-go. My goal for the day isn't, then, to enjoy myself, but simply to survive.

Arriving at the path entrance, I pull my skates and various skating accoutrements from my backpack and start putting them on, a process that moves rather slowly since I do everything in the wrong order—put the wrist guards on before the skates (wrist guards off, blades on), the skates on before the kneepads (skates off, kneepads on, skates on again), and the headphones on too soon (headphones off when the cord is yanked out, headphones back on once everything else is dealt with).

When I have everything in place, I look both ways to make sure a collision isn't imminent and push myself onto the path. Then I skate. My ankles hurt but it's okay. A guy skates past me, then another guy—this one moving at such a hasty pace that he looks like he's potentially being chased by secret demons. I cringe: I'm that slow, lame person with her ankles caved in. Then I tell that part of my mind to shut up. I'm not lame. I'm just learning. I skate a little more.

After a while, I get into something of a groove. I begin noticing handsome men whizzing by on skates, bikes, and their feet. But I'm not really thinking about them; I'm not even thinking about Will. I'm thinking instead about how good I feel as my legs propel me forward and sweat starts lining my face and body. I'm listening to an audio version of *The Brief Wondrous Life of Oscar Wao* on my iPhone, a novel that had long intimidated me because it sounded like it was about political unrest in some foreign country and had been awarded about a thousand literary prizes. But out there on the West Side Highway bike path, I discover that I love this book I spent so long avoiding— the lush language, the Spanish phrases I can't understand but can nevertheless tell from the context are filthy, and the ability it has to transport me from the side of a New York City highway to the marketplaces and cafés of the Dominican Republic.

Before I realize it, I've arrived at a field—Hudson Park, the sign says. People are lying down and picnicking and kissing and playing. It reminds me of McKegney Green, a slab of grass in my Northern California hometown where my friends and I would gather on weekends. It reminds me of the quad at my college, where I spent glorious falls and bright springs pretending to do homework but really just flirting and laughing. This place I've discovered because I'd forced myself to do something I'd long wanted to do, in other words, reminds me of some of the happiest times of my life. I remove my skates and pads and fling myself to the grass, a grin building from inside as I soak up the sun.

Rollerblading becomes a part of my regular life over the next few months, and I marvel at how long it took me to embrace it. That isn't to say the process is easy. The fear of doing something I'm not good at doesn't vanish after that first solo attempt; a discomfort and near-terror actually looms large the next five to 10 times I go out there. Once I'm skating, I'm always happy I made the effort, but I still have to keep pep-talking myself into it. I start to think of myself as the disciplinarian to a petulant but ultimately good child—one who doesn't always know what's best for her but, with a bit of guidance, can be led down the right path. And then slowly—very slowly—I start to like it. I begin packing books and snacks in my backpack and lolling about for hours on the grass at Hudson Park.

Even better, wrestling that wild boar of fear that lives inside of me to the ground—quieting that voice that says I can't do something—makes me see that I can, indeed, be the single woman Helen writes of, the passionate adventurer who takes advantage of her own income and free time. Yet rather than simply copying the possible activities Helen suggests in *S&SG*—reading Proust, whipping up a "silly, wonderful cotton brocade tea coat," and taking up oil painting, for example—I decide to make a list of everything I've said I want to do but either gave up on long ago or have found excuses to avoid. I decide to call it my fear-conquering list.

MY FEAR-CONQUERING LIST

1. Start riding a bike again. Get over the fact that I never really rode one as a kid so I felt stupid when I decided to try it in L.A. and a) a cop on a bike informed me that I had my helmet on backwards and b) I was almost killed by several Los Angeles drivers after I

snapped at the cop that I liked my helmet that way and scooted off into traffic.

2. Learn ceramics. I always say I want to take an art class and every time I pass the ceramics studio down the street, I tell whomever I'm walking with that I long to be able to make pottery. Stop talking about it and start spinning the wheel.

3. Study French. Forgive myself for having gotten stoned every day before French class my senior year in high school, in turn receiving the lowest possible score on the Advanced Placement test. Could there be a better time to refamiliarize myself with the language of love?

4. Take a lesson that involves the water. It can be surfing, water-skiing, or windsurfing—it doesn't matter, just find something that will help me finally let go of having seen *Jaws* at the age of five. For years I couldn't go anywhere near water of any kind but first I got over my fear of swimming pools, then my fear of lakes, and now I can actually swim in the shallow part of the ocean without panicking that a great white is going to swallow me up. The final frontier: making myself learn a sport that requires having to be on or in the water.

5. Travel. I say to people, "The great thing about being a writer is that you can do it from anywhere," but I do it from inside my apartment. And I haven't taken a vacation in years. The excuse I always make for this is that, as a freelancer, I could plan an elaborate trip

only to have the TV show or book opportunity of a lifetime come up. But it suddenly occurs to me that perhaps the deeper reason I avoid taking time off is that working all the time has become what cocaine used to be: a method for keeping my mind busy while I check out. And while I'm not necessarily the wan-derlust type, I had some amazing travel experiences before I became so career-obsessed—like when I went to Seville, Spain, my junior year in college. Perhaps I can get back in touch with the 20-year-old me, who could just close the computer (who didn't, in fact, even have a computer), fling herself onto a new city, and fall in love with it.

Although no item on my list seems too terrifying once they're written out on a piece of paper, I also know I can't tackle all of them at once. So I commit to trying one more now and then doing the others later, once I've already begun incorporat-ing some of Helen's fashion, beauty, decorating, and cooking ideas into my life.

So I take the subway over to 42nd Street and rent a bicycle. Nothing about this feels scary once I'm doing it and I easily put the helmet on correctly. I head uptown—through parks and past people on benches. I feel incredible whipping by a part of New York I've never seen. Who are all these people that are lounging and talking and reading papers, I wonder and how long have they been soaking in the glorious river view while I've been looking at the four walls of my apartment? I stop for a steak lunch at a café by the river and, rather than trying to find a paper to read, focus on tasting every delicious bite. I'm suddenly filled with gratitude over the fact that I can be out here, in the sun, sweaty and spent, in the middle of a weekday, and ask myself why I'm not in a permanent state of giddiness over the life of ease and comfort I lead. The last time I worked in an office was nearly a decade ago, when I was a staff writer at *Premiere* magazine. One day my position was eliminated, and I assumed I'd freelance until I got a new job. But some combination of a newly discovered work ethic and the sheer determination I had to earn a living made me an ideal candidate for self-employment. Magazine assignments led to book writing and TV jobs, and now I can barely imagine a life that involves a human resources department and coworkers and office coffee. Yet most of the time, I lament the frustrations of this sort of arrangement while wholly ignoring the benefits. I almost never, in other words, go sit in the sun by the Hudson River on a shockingly beautiful day while all the people who work full-time are inside.

I vow to remember this feeling the next time I'm immersed in self-pity.

On my way back to the subway after returning the bike, I pass a bakery. I go inside, asking first for a cookie and then if they offer baking classes or if I can apprentice there. Apprentice? I barely know what I'm talking about, but my anything's possible state has left me nearly unhinged with possibilities. The wizened female baker looks at me like I might not be well before shaking her head and handing me my chocolate chip cookie. For me, even gratitude can be a semidangerous drug.

While I don't end up biking as often as I Rollerblade, my day by the water motivates me to order a Razor kick scooter from Amazon. Who knows what I could get into next? For the moment, it remains in the box it came in, waiting for the day I get sick of Rollerblading. Until then, the prospect that it could bring on previously unimagined feelings of joy remains.

Part Two

CHAPTER THREE

Feathering the Nest

A chic apartment can tell the world that you, for one, are
not one of those miserable, pitiful single creatures.

—*Sex and the Single Girl*

"You've got to stop looking at your apartment as *you*," Chris
says. "You have to look at it through the eyes of someone who
might think, *She could be my wife. Would I want our future house
to be decorated like this?*"

I'd met Chris Stevens, a gorgeous, gay interior designer, at
a mutual friend's birthday dinner and immediately began telling him what I was doing—how I was embarking on a project
that would make me start appreciating where I was in life and
also help prepare me for the next stage, and how part of that
involved fixing up my apartment. I'd imagined him giving me a
questioning glance and then doling out a few tips—suggestions
for plants that even a person with a brown thumb couldn't kill
or the best solution for a room that has no overhead lighting.
Instead he'd nodded crisply and said, "I'll come over tomorrow"
before asking me to pass the pepper.

And now my apartment is withering under his discerning

eye. I feel self-conscious and am immediately reminded of the many times I've been embarrassed by something about me—my clothes or words or eagerness or lack of a boyfriend. In adulthood, I've learned to cover this up with bravado but for whatever reason, the look in Chris's eyes brings me right back to the time in first grade when Katy McLaughlin and I wore the same dress but I had mine on backwards. Causing a sea of fellow six-year-olds to break into mirthful laughter can stay with you a long time. But, I remind myself, I'm an adult now and don't need to feel ashamed in front of someone who's here to help me.

He's looking at my antique carved wooden mirror—a piece I picked up at a Los Angeles garage sale for $20, a price so low and agreeable to the seller that I had no doubt when passing him the bill that I was purchasing something stolen, probably recently. Chris nods with semiapproval before his eyes flit over my Staples-purchased lamp resting on top of a cheap, off-white nightstand. Then he moves on to my shapeless curtains hanging from flimsy rods that barely cover my windows, and my two prints hanging on the wall next to them—both selected solely because they seemed to be the right size for the allotted space. He examines my enormous wooden bookshelf and the red aluminum table and chair set I bought because it was both inexpensive and small enough to fit in a studio. Finally he focuses on my big, brown, hopelessly ugly couch. "There's potential," he finally says.

Before I got sober, "potential" was a word people often used to describe me—though my Chelsea studio probably sparkles with far more possibility than I did back when I was a chain-smoking cokehead. "It's so big!" friends often exclaim when they walk through my roughly 500-square-foot apartment, a space that manages to seem about twice the size it actually is because of a creative layout that includes an alcove I use as an office, a hallway that connects the alcove to the entryway, and a main room that's two steps below all of that. I moved into this third-floor abode of a quaint 1930s Art Deco building almost two years ago, after a brief experimentation with the Upper West Side, and many have marveled at the adorableness of the space and structure. Occasionally they'll praise the chair from Goodwill that I had upholstered at my friend Nicole's insistence or say something nice about the distressed white coffee table my mom took me to get at the San Francisco Shabby Chic store over 15 years ago. Every now and then I'll hear an "I love this" about the antique sleigh bed also picked out by my mom, or a positive comment about my surely stolen mirror. But no one has ever complimented the overall look and, gazing at the space now, I see why: it's a collection of items cobbled together haphazardly—usually at the insistence of other people. The indifference of the person who lives here is evident in every lamp purchased more for function than form and each item selected simply to fill up what would otherwise have been blank space.

"I like my place," I say to Chris. I go on to explain that I think people's homes should be comfortable and not overly done up so that everyone who walks in can feel as relaxed as possible but the real reason I'm yammering on like this is that I want to avoid admitting that I don't care that much about decorating and that if I could get away with the tapestries, posters, and eggshell crates I had in my college dorm rooms, I would. But then I surprise myself by suddenly saying, "I think the real reason I haven't invested any time or energy in decorating is that in the back of my mind, I think I'll do it later, when my life starts—in other words, when I have a man to help me pick out china patterns and measure the space for the couch."

While I'm surprised to hear myself being so vulnerable and honest, Chris nods like this is what he'd been expecting me to confess. We start talking about how almost all of my friends are more into putting their places together than I am—except for Shari, my fellow big-breasted Jewish brunette writer pal, who told me that the first thing the hedge fund guy she recently started dating said about her apartment is that it looks like it belongs to a man. "I really have no excuse for being this way," I tell Chris, explaining that my mom has the best eye for decor I've ever seen and that I spent my first 18 years in a beautiful home with Spanish-tiled bathroom, French provincial bedrooms, and an English-style garden. "But it's not only that I seem to be waiting for someone to help me with all of this," I say. "I also panic if I have to spend a lot of money at once, so I'm always trying to find the least expensive item. Which all but guarantees that I'll fill my living space with nothing I really love." Again, I'm shocked by how he's gotten me to reveal something I hadn't even realized until the moment it came out of my mouth.

"Maybe," Chris says, "you need someone to help you by explaining that there are certain items you just have to spend money on."

Helen makes the same claim. And while I'm not sure I agree with her that a sumptuous living space is a "sure man-magnet," her assertion that men are "pleased and soothed by a beautiful apartment" sounds accurate. I mean, aren't we all pleased and soothed by beautiful things? And since this is the place where I spend the majority of my time, it begins to occur to me, shouldn't it also please and soothe me?

Chris glances around the room. "Your first problem is that you have too much," he explains, pointing at my six-rowed wooden bookshelf that houses over 300 books. "Just look at that shelf! It's bowing and groaning like a pregnant hippo because of the amount of accumulated knowledge crowding its shelves."

I nod; when I'd run out of room on the shelf, I'd started pushing books into a makeshift new row and stacking others on top of and in front of them. "Having a lot of books is important," I say, somewhat weakly.

"True," Chris says. "But this many?"

That hadn't even occurred to me. "My mom's an English professor," I offer defensively. "Every room in the house I grew up in has a bookshelf filled with books."

Chris puts a hand on his hip. "Are *you* an English professor?"

"Of course not."

He points to a shelf that only holds copies of books I've written. "And who knows, maybe it's time to rethink having stacks and stacks of your own books displayed so prominently?"

I'm instantly embarrassed. "But I'm not displaying those! They're just there for easy access—if I need to send someone a copy or bring one to . . ." My voice trails off as I face the fact that I do probably have them there in order to impress people, even though I know that there's nothing less impressive than someone who's trying to be impressive. I clear my throat. "I guess I could keep those somewhere else."

He nods and gestures toward the shelf. "Now, how many

of these do you think you'll read again?" he asks. He runs his fingers over the D's , E's, and F's of the fiction section.

Out of the dozen books my eyes take in, I see only one—*The Great Gatsby*—which I know I'll reread. "This one," I say, grabbing it.

"And have you even read all of them once?"

I don't even bother to feign offense. The fact is, I have plenty of books I've never cracked open as well as a number that I started and didn't like enough to finish. I trail my fingers over to where the D's transition into the F's. Dostoevsky's *Notes from the Underground* (which I'd grabbed off my mom's aforementioned bookshelf at one point and never considered reading, since I was far too intimidated to even try to say Dostoevsky's name, let alone read his work) and Nell Freudenberger's *Lucky Girls* (which I bought after hearing that she was a literary sensation and never read, for pretty much the same reason). "You never know when—"

"You're going to be in the mood to pick up"—Chris bends down and pulls out *You Mean I'm Not Lazy, Stupid or Crazy?! The Classic Self-Help Book for Adults with Attention Deficit Disorder*—"something with the word 'crazy' in its title that implies you have a disorder?"

Embarrassed, I grab the book from him. "A friend who thought I had ADD gave me that."

"And do you?"

"I'm not sure." I look at him and smile weakly. "I never actually read the book."

Chris bends down again—alas, he's in the self-help section— and I brace myself for what's coming. "*Toxic Parents*? *Affirma-*

tions for the Inner Child? Treatment of Sexual Dysfunction? Jesus, are you trying to reel men in or keep them away?"

I take the sexual dysfunction book from him and place it on my bedside table. "This one's for a class I'm taking."

"Well, a man glancing at your bookshelf doesn't know that! The point is: you need to get rid of at least half of what you have here." My eyes graze quickly over the shelves and while I see many books I passionately love, I notice a number of others that I don't want: freebies sent by publishers looking for press, tomes I'd needed for magazine stories but never looked at again, odd publications I'd accumulated without even realizing it. I nod.

Then I watch Chris look at my armoire, coffee table, and dresser, all of which seem to be drowning under a sea of magazines and tchotchkes and other useless crap I hadn't noticed until now. He points to a blue ceramic bowl on top of the armoire. "Why, for instance, do you need that bowl? What purpose does it serve?"

"My mom gave it to me."

"And the purpose it serves is what? Reminding you that your mom gives you presents?"

He does have a point. And my mom's gifts tend to break my heart a little: they're always things that would be perfect for the daughter who *would* enjoy picking out antiques for the French provincial bedrooms or might want to create her *own* Spanish-tiled bathroom. Not that I'm willing to admit this. "There's nothing more important than holding on to the things that have sentimental value," I say to Chris. "I mean, when people's buildings catch on fire, they don't—"

"Oh, God," Chris interrupts me as he lifts up my bed skirt,

and I cringe, knowing he's discovering that I've made the under-bed area into a place to keep everything I don't want to see: boxes and boxes of things I never seem to need, gloves that have lost their mates but I still somehow haven't given up on, and a sea of suitcases, all linked together through an unhappy combination of pet hair and dust. "You need a storage space," he says as he stands up.

"But I've never understood the point of a storage space," I say. "If you don't need the stuff now, then why would you need it later?"

"Oh, you won't," he says cheerfully. "It's so that we can avoid my having to ask you why"—he smiles and picks up a small square pillow that's sitting on top of my white wicker chest— "you need this in your life?"

"My mom did the needlepoint on that! It's a picture of her dog . . . which she made me because . . ." My voice starts to trail off. "Well, she made one for my brother of the dog he gave her and then she wanted me to have one, too." Chris doesn't say anything. "Both dogs are dead," I finish feebly. A pause. "I see what you mean. And actually I think we have storage in the building."

"Perfect." Then he motions to the couch and says, "This has to go—and not to storage. To a place where we never need to look at it again."

"Agreed." I had this hideous brown couch because, on my way to Pottery Barn one day to buy a good couch, I'd wandered into the Housing Works thrift shop and seen what looked like a nice one on display. The sign next to it said "Bauhaus," and while I didn't know exactly what that meant, I was pretty sure it was a style that was considered elegant. Only when I got the thing inside my apartment did I come to understand why someone had donated it to Housing Works: it was potentially the ugliest thing on earth. I opt not to tell Chris that tale.

He's examining the bookshelf again. "I'd say, donate at least a hundred." I nod; purging myself of that many sounds like a relief. "And we need to get you a new bookshelf," he adds.

I'd been quite proud of my dark wooden bookshelf, or more about how I'd gotten it by befriending an aspiring comedian selling furniture at an L.A. flea market and talking him into custom-building it for me at a very low price just before he was cast on a reality show where he redesigned people's living spaces. I explain all of this to Chris.

"Meaning it was custom-built for your apartment in L.A.?" he asks. I nod. "Where you no longer live?" I nod again. "As soon as we get rid of it, we can put two smaller bookshelves in its place," he says as he takes out measuring tape and holds it against the wall. Then he glances at the red aluminum table and chairs and smiles. "And who knows, maybe we can get rid of the patio furniture?" I nod yet again, not bothering to tell him that the red chairs leave indentations on my butt every time I sit in them.

Chris then moves into my entryway and begins to examine the cat litter box. He turns to face me. "Now I have a question."

"I think I know what it is." I glance at my gray-haired cat, now sniffing her ass, and brace myself to defend her.

"So you're attached to them?"

"Very."

"Had to ask."

"Look, I get it," I say. "Living with two furballs in a place this small sometimes makes me feel like I'm a few bad days away from *Grey Gardens* territory. And I know that cat hair, cat food, and cat litter are about the least alluring things on earth. But what am I supposed to do—give my cats away so that I can be sexier?"

Although this speech may make me sound like PETA's proudest member, the truth is that I fantasize about a life without my cats on a semiregular basis. I'd acquired them before I got sober, back when I thought nothing of making a spontaneous decision that would impact the rest of my life. But no matter how crazy they drive me and how sick I am of cleaning up after them and arranging pet sitters and opening cans of wet food, I'm equally terrified of the day when I no longer have fluffy little beasts burrowing against me. I don't say any of this to Chris, nor do I share with him the kitty voice I only use for talking to them.

"I understand," he says. Then he looks from me to my ass-sniffing cat. "Still, the goal of this project of yours is to find a man?"

"No," I say. "The goal is to prepare me for the next stage in life but also help me to appreciate where I am now."

"The next stage being a serious relationship with a man?" he asks.

I nod. He looks at the litter box and then at my orange cat, who's emerged from her perch under the bed to throw up a hairball and is now hissing at Chris with the fervor of a Bengal tiger. "I admire your determination," he says quietly.

• • •

meet Derek online.

As a woman, a right brain, and a Jew, I'm not remotely handy around the house and I have a lengthy history of finding incompetent scammers who charge me exorbitant fees to, say, install shelves that tumble to the ground once they're gone and their number's been changed. Never do I feel more single than when those shelves fall or I'm attempting to hang curtains or put together an IKEA table; I'm actually semiconvinced I kept dating someone who was wrong for me my first summer in New York because he knew how to operate a drill and equally convinced I broke things off with him when I discovered that he didn't know how to operate the drill very well. Helen knows my pain. As she writes, "One of a single woman's biggest problems are the pippy-poo, day-to-day annoyances that plague her."

Derek, a carpenter and all-around fix-it guy with an ad on Craig's List, is excellent at handling the pippy-poo. Dark-haired, with tattoos snaking around his bulging biceps, he's completely different from the handymen of my past. For one, he's a professional carpenter—does it as a full-time job and is merely picking up work on the side—which means that, unlike everyone else I've ever hired, he doesn't take each request and try to handle it as quickly and cheaply as possible. Instead he analyzes, assesses, and takes his time. And, for reasons I can't understand but am nonetheless incredibly grateful for, his prices are the most reasonable I've come across. This allows me the luxury of looking around my place and really seeing the way I've been living, which is when I notice a sea of horrors I'd been managing to mostly tune out: how my plasma TV is attached to a piece of wood on the wall of the main room because one of the previous carpenter scammers had drilled the wood up there when pieces of the wall kept falling off. And how my plastic Wal-Mart desk, purchased solely because it was the smallest one I could find and the alcove is tiny, is falling apart and sliding slowly to the ground. When Derek walks in, laughs at the random piece of TV-holding wood on my wall, and then says he can buy and install a linoleum block exactly the size of the space between the alcove walls for me to use as a desk, I feel certain he's my karmic payback for my having endured all those handyman shysters over the years.

While he paints my apartment walls the sky blue color that Chris and I believe will be cheerier and cleaner-looking than the pale yellow I inherited from the previous tenant, I begin going through my bookshelf and pulling out every book I know I'll never read, stacking as many as I can into my portable shopping cart that makes me feel like I'm a little old lady. I wheel them over to Housing Works and return for more, making six trips in all. Then I box up and bring down to my newly rented basement storage space everything I've determined I don't need right away—work and tax files from the past decade, cords that have long since lost the devices they're meant to power, lamps, suitcases, copies of my books, and everything else that was creating clutter. Despite my intention to make the storage space organized and well marked, it quickly becomes a horror show—brimming with objects stacked on top of other objects in a way that ensures it will all tumble to the ground at some point. I close the door behind me, hoping I never need anything from the middle of the pile and knowing full well that I will.

Next, as Derek continues to paint, Chris and I examine my

curtains: four cheap-looking green panels from Pottery Barn that hang over two windows with bars on them—the whole look suggesting either tenement or state-subsidized mental institution. I can't do anything about the bars—there's a fire escape right outside my window and even though I'm willing to have the bars removed and take my chances with would-be thieves, my landlord isn't. While I've known for some time how terrible the windows look, nothing I've tried seems to help: the green panels were preceded by even uglier shades, which were preceded by even worse blinds.

"What, exactly, is the problem with my curtains?" I ask Chris.

"Everything," he answers without hesitation. "The color, the fabric, the length, the rods, and the fact that the rods look like they're falling off the walls."

"Yikes." I think back to the day in college when, hungover and irritated by the bright sun poking through the flimsy dorm shade, I nailed my comforter to the wall in front of the window and allowed it to serve as my curtain for the rest of the year. I opt not to tell Chris about that.

"Why don't we go deal with it now, while the horror of what's wrong is still fresh?" he asks.

At Restoration Hardware, we figure out that four panels of light silver sage, casual twill, grommet-top, floor-length drapes that we both like, along with the required rods, will cost close to a thousand dollars. I feel dizzy but Chris reminds me of our conversation about how there are certain things you have to spend on and explains that curtains is one of them. While a part of me pines for the days a comforter nailed to the wall seemed like a perfectly adequate window covering, I also know that having to dip into my savings account in order to shield my domicile from the outside world is something of a rite of passage—a thought I have to repeat to myself again when Chris reminds me that we need the curtains to be 94 inches and since they only come in lengths that are shorter or longer than that, I'm going to have to get the 96-inch panels and then pay more to have them shortened. He tells me to go home and measure the distance between the wall and the shelf below the window so I can make sure the curtains will hang out far enough. The list of things I never knew about grows longer.

I end up doing everything he suggests—measuring the space, returning to the store to buy the curtains, having them shortened, and bringing Derek back to do the hanging. And although I can't believe I could have bought a round-trip ticket to Paris for the amount I spent, I have to admit that they're gorgeous and hang perfectly. Helen says that "an elegant apartment has unmistakable traces of grandeur around it," and while some may not consider my wall of curtains the embodiment of Versailles, for the first time since I moved in, the window area looks so good that I stop even noticing the bars. A man spending the night could open his eyes, glance at the thick panels, and feel basked in luxury.

Before I even have time to relish this new addition, however, Chris announces that we're taking a trip to the Brooklyn IKEA.

Once there, we make our way to the couch section, where Chris points to a simple, modern piece called a Karlstad; we both like the cream color. We then examine bookshelves and kitchen tables but Chris explains that they don't have what we're looking for. Thinking of Helen's line about how if you work with a decorator, you should "put yourself in his or her hands" and not "interfere too much," I simply nod. Then I watch Chris select a white file cabinet on wheels, an oval full-length mirror, and an enormous white lamp for me.

When we get back to my place, Chris helps me bring my new mirror, file cabinet, and lamp inside and, just for a second, it feels like we're a couple putting our place together. But then he remembers that he has another appointment and the door shuts behind him before I've even had a chance to really let myself feel how nice it was, for once, to not be in it alone.

May I please speak to someone in customer service?" I inquire. I've learned to start off these regular calls to IKEA pleasantly, carried along by the delusional belief that this time, I'll manage to unearth some information as to the whereabouts of my couch.

The initial round of calls was confusing more than anything. I'd phone the number listed on my receipt and speak to someone in a warehouse who had no knowledge of my couch, my order number, or me. Then I'd call IKEA directly and be transferred around for a few hours, after which I would either be hung up on or hear a person I knew I'd never hear from again promise that he or she would find out what was going on and call me right back.

Sometimes I'm told that my couch is on its way to the warehouse and that the people from the warehouse will be calling me any day to let me know when I can expect my delivery, but usually I encounter a person who expresses sheer confusion over my situation—who doesn't know why my couch hasn't arrived yet or what I can do to figure out any more information. Depending on my mood—often determined by how much better or worse the "IKEA delivery nightmare" stories I've found online and spent my hold time reading are making me feel—my tone is usually somewhere between irritable and abusive.

Chris isn't the bastion of reassurance I want him to be— "Par for the course," he trills when I relay what's happening, though he does add, "unfortunately"—and I hate how much I wish I had a man to help me. Will, I just know, would be able to call IKEA, calmly relay the necessary information, and get the couch to show up the next day. He had that clear, calm focus that all but forced people to respond.

One of the days that I'm on hold, I break down and Google him. I had promised myself I wouldn't and had resisted the urge so far but a combination of frustration and self-pity suddenly supersede my desire to move on. And I find an ungodly number of photos, as well as article after article praising his talent, courage, and individuality. For some reason, looking at all of this forces me to face something I hadn't wanted to before: that who he was and what he'd achieved impressed the hell out of me. When we were out in public and people recognized him, I'd smile at the eager-to-please faces, the faces that couldn't believe the good fortune they had to have stumbled across someone they admired so much, the faces that respected me because of my proximity to such greatness. My ego would alight at the notion that he could be around anyone he wanted, and had picked me.

Before long, my Internet search becomes obsessive. I can't stop—I let one link lead to the next. Eventually I Google his name with the word "wife" next to it, looking for clues, wanting to see and read about the woman who got to sleep next to him at night and share his life. But there wasn't really anything— no photos and just one interview he gave where he mentioned how much he loved her. I feel stupid, like I've been misled. But I know that's silly. Of course he loved her. What did I think I was going to find—quotes about how he actually didn't? She's the mother of his children, the woman he'd chosen to spend his life with.

Then I start deriding myself. I'm an idiot. Everyone knows not to believe a married man. How could I have thought that this guy—this guy whose talent and courage was widely praised— actually loved me? I think about Helen's line, "Heaven knows a married man on an all-out I Love You campaign can be one of God's most persuasive creatures," and curse my naïveté. At the same time, as I let my keyboard lead me to increasingly ir- relevant information about him, I know that what we shared was real. In a way, it still is. A strong part of me is certain he's thinking about me, too. But, now that the pain of finding and then losing that passionate connection has abated, I'm grateful that I can somehow stop myself from reaching out to him. I let my fingers lead me back to the IKEA delivery stories.

A week or so later, I'm talking to Shari on the phone. Ever since the trip to IKEA, I've left the new light, file cabinet, and oval mirror propped in the entryway, waiting for the day the couch comes and I can have Derek help me put it all together. Shari's telling me about the hedge fund guy's apartment— how it's massive but doesn't really have anything in it except for a couch and enormous TV and how this makes her worry that he's a spy. As she talks, I move my purse from the floor to my bench, where it knocks up against a broom that starts to teeter back and forth. She's saying, "Plus, every time we watch a thriller, he seems to know everything that's going to happen before it does. I mean, is it normal for a Wall Street guy to be an expert on murder and espionage?"

I tell her that she's being paranoid, but at the same time, I understand her thinking: when you run across as many disappointing men as we do, finding one you like who shows up and acts sweet causes you to seek out the inevitable shoe drop, the explanation for how, exactly, he's too good to be true—the quest for evidence that he's crazy or secretly married or hiding all of his ex's underwear in his freezer. While I'm saying as much to her, I watch the broom make its final descent, and I'm somehow not surprised when it ends up crashing into the mirror, which then smashes on the ground and shatters into what looks like several million pieces. "Let me call you back," I say.

I know I have two choices: I can declare that woe is me, resign myself to seven terrible years, and fall apart. Or I can reason that superstitions are for those who can afford to be superstitious, remind myself that I need to call IKEA again later today so I'll be having a breakdown soon enough anyway, and start sweeping. I pick up the broom.

Once I've disposed of the pieces, I decide that since I've lost the mirror I've been using, it's a good time to try to attach the extra one I have to the inside of my closet door. A part of me knows that this is not a good time for such an activity—that this is the opposite of a good time because I'm rattled and feeling sorry for myself—but a stronger part is convinced that this will prove I'm self-reliant and is thus exactly what I need right now.

I grab a nail and hammer from my tool chest and start trying to hammer the plastic edge of the mirror to the closet door. "You're going to go up, damn you," I declare. Somewhere inside, I know I'm attempting the impossible—that nails aren't meant to go through plastic mirror edges and that even if they were, I'm surely not strong enough to make it happen. But I want to prove to the world, to myself, to all those women who have husbands to help them with this sort of thing, that I can do it.

"This is going to work," I say out loud as I hammer and hammer and hammer. The nails go all the way through the door, boring holes I'll never be able to fix, but the mirror doesn't stay up. Sweating, hysterical, tears now streaming down my face, certain I'm driving my neighbors crazy with my continuous hammering, I keep at it, hitting and hitting and hitting the nails until what I'd always somehow known was going to happen finally happens and the mirror fractures into tiny shards.

Having accrued 14 years of bad luck in under an hour and made certain that not a single reflective surface in my house remains except for the one above my bathroom sink, I commit right then to stop trying to control everything—to just wait and see if my couch does indeed arrive one day. As I sweep up the mirror, I realize that I might want to turn over my love life in the same way. The time has come to put the hammer down.

One day, as if I've imagined the wait and all those phone calls, the couch arrives. I feel somehow certain that this is when it would have gotten here had I never made a single phone call, that they say a few weeks but what they mean is that you're getting a great deal so it will just be there whenever they get around to it. The delivery guys are happy to bring my atrocious brown sofa down to the basement, where my super disposes of it. And once I move a few things around, Derek and I rehang the stolen mirror a bit lower and it works perfectly as a full-length one, which means that I hadn't needed to buy and destroy one of those other mirrors, let alone two. Had I just taken a step back from the beginning and considered the big picture, the hammer could have stayed in the tool chest.

Chris and I accrue a few more items, like a perfect little white table and chairs to replace the patio furniture, two half-steel, half-glass bookshelves so I can throw out the wooden one that was custom-made for my place in L.A., blue pillows with Moroccan prints for the couch, and a bright new bedspread. Still, I'm not prepared for how glorious the place looks once everything's put together.

I suddenly have a real New York apartment, the kind a chic woman you could picture serving a man crudités would live in while going about her shiny, put-together life. And I start to enjoy it—lighting candles and cozying up under a blanket watching movies or cooking something simple and eating it at my cute little table-and-chair set, activities that once would have made me feel like the quintessential pathetic old maid. I even begin putting my clothes away or in the hamper instead of throwing them on the floor. The anxious, must-only-be-home-to-sleep-or-work mode I've been in for years softens as I begin to appreciate my living space as a peaceful oasis away from the fast pace of Manhattan. It's so lovely that even my inadvertent circuitous survey of the customer service representatives for a Swedish furniture superstore feels like a small price to have paid.

Shortly after that, my upstairs neighbor Molly—a British jet-setting business consultant—knocks on my door holding a vase of lilies. "Do you want these?" she asks, explaining that the real estate mogul she's seeing sent them to her but that she's running off to catch a plane and would rather give them to me than let them wilt and die while she's gone.

Now, as a woman, I've obviously received flowers before. As an ever-practical person, however, I've never really seen the appeal of spending money on something that withers in a few days. But these lilies smell amazing—they seem to transform my Manhattan studio with bars on its windows into a Hawaiian beach bungalow, and just being around the scent makes me instantly peaceful. When they wilt, I replace them and continue to do so. Since lilies are expensive and Helen and I are both pragmatic ladies, though, I look up information on making flowers last longer and read that keeping them in water that's mixed with bleach, sugar, and lemon juice can help. Even more surprising than the fact that I've become someone who looks up life-extending flower tips is that the method works: I'm used to flowers drooping in a few days but now they start staying in full bloom for over a week. Even better, I understand that I'm not doing this because I think a guy might come over, see them, and marvel at what a feminine and together being I am. It's so that I can.

CHAPTER FOUR

The Cook Out

You must cook well. It will serve you faithfully.

—Sex and the Single Girl

There's a semiapocryphal tale my mom and brother like to tell about me making a sandwich for Eric, a boy I dated my freshman and sophomore years in college. Here's the part that we all agree on: Eric and I were at my parents' house and he was hungry. I made him a cheddar cheese sandwich.

And here's where the story gets somewhat controversial. I think the sandwich was fine. But my mom and brother felt that it was—well, kind of disgusting. The disgustingness had something to do with, I believe, the freshness of the cheese, or maybe it was the brand of cheese, or it might have been the bread choice, or it could have been the lack of condiments. I'll confess that a lot of thought and care did not go into the making of this sandwich. A kitchen, you see, isn't the kind of place where I naturally belong. I don't know where to prop myself, don't marvel at the KitchenAid appliances, and don't offer to help when I'm invited to dinner parties (or, if I do, I pray the person doesn't take me up on it).

Some of this I come by honestly. The kitchen when I was growing up wasn't a spot where we lingered. My mom was teaching at a college 90 miles away, suffering from multihour commutes and relentless stacks of papers to grade, and my dad often came home after we were asleep. There was a lot of fast food, pork chops–and–applesauce combos, and Toad in the Hole, a pancake and sausage conglomeration most commonly eaten by British people for breakfast but which my brother and I often had for dinner.

Despite coming from this environment, my brother some-how evolved into a cooking connoisseur—flying to Europe for pastry classes by the time he was in college and whip-ping up chocolate molten lava cake and crème brûlée at every opportunity—while I struggled with cracking an egg without getting any of the shell in it. And my mom, once she was out of the commuting and teaching mode, took a latent interest in cooking and began turning mealtime into a gourmet experi-ence.

The "orange sandwich incident" was sometime during those transition years—when my mom was in between the Toad in the Hole phase and the one that involved grilled radicchio and eggplant pizza from the wooden pizza oven she had installed in the kitchen. The sandwich that, I should add, this old boyfriend of mine *very happily ate*.

By my account, all was fine. In my mom and brother's ver-sion, however, Eric was repulsed but liked me too much to ad-mit it. So, they claim, at the bottom of our driveway (and we had a very long, twisty driveway), he had to pull over to throw up. Several times.

It's all very funny when my mom and brother get going on

their routine about Eric and the rancid cheddar and the up-chucking, and while it's true that the sandwich was never going to win any Best Sandwich in America awards, their teasing also had a way of chipping away at whatever confidence I had in my culinary skills, which was practically none at all. I mean, how hard is it to screw up a sandwich?

For a long time, this wasn't a problem. No one expects a college student to be able to make a flan or roast a turkey. But once I was out in the real world, it was quite a wake-up call to discover that I was meant to feed myself. Since my salary was right above the poverty line for my first few years of employment, you'd think I'd have learned a few things out of bare necessity. And I did learn a few things, but only a few things, and I didn't practice them all too often.

There were some chicken recipes I picked up along the way, an elaborate pasta sauce my mom taught me to make, and some low-carb recipes I learned at a spa my dad took me to. But I never felt all that motivated to make the Green Valley Spa twice-baked potatoes or tofu scramble, not to mention the chicken or pasta sauce. I was just someone who didn't cook. The pattern I developed was, essentially, to pick up a muffin and cup of coffee from the café downstairs from my office in the morning, eat a salad or sandwich from a nearby deli for lunch, and have either whatever the chicken dish was at whatever restaurant I happened to be in for dinner or, if I was home for the night, making do with a Balance Bar, popcorn, or some other snack food that could occasionally pass for a meal.

Every now and then I did spend some time in the kitchen—at some point I've cooked for or with every boyfriend I've ever had, probably with more success, or at least less criticism, than I experienced with Eric. And I even went through some specific but ephemeral phases (one for making mashed potatoes, after my dad gave me a KitchenAid mixer; another for baking muffin tops before, I swear, bakeries sold them). But for the most part, I ignored cooking and it ignored me.

Yet since reading *S&SG*, I've been thinking for the first time about cooking as a wooing technique and wondering why I've chosen to dismiss the notion that I could get to a man's heart through his stomach.

In the '60s women did all the cooking, but this wasn't a popular notion when I was growing up. We may have had Easy-Bake Ovens, but for a lot of us, that's pretty much where the culinary experience ended. "Shop" classes were a thing of the past by the time I got to high school, and though our mothers didn't all spell out the fact that they thought cooking was an oppressive task we no longer had to partake in because society had evolved so much over the years, the sentiment was always there. And yet, cruelly, in the past decade, it's as if cooking has became the most important talent a woman—a person—could possess: chefs and people who pretend to be chefs are now celebrities with their own talk shows and magazines to prove it, the Food Network is in hundreds of millions of homes, and it's not uncommon to hear people at parties engaged in lively debates about whether the person who made the vegetable puree on the most recent season of *Top Chef* was eliminated unfairly.

Still, I wonder how many of us are actually cooking. People watching the Food Network aren't necessarily slicing, dicing, and pureeing themselves. Considering the fact that a new study is released almost every year about how many more hours Americans are working than they were before, considering the accessibility of premade foods in our Whole Foods era, and considering how the microwave—which didn't become a kitchen staple until the '70s—is always taunting us with the notion that we don't have to waste time on all that preparation, I don't think as many women are cooking as those shows would have us believe. Out of my friends, only two spend any time in the kitchen at all: Nicole, my friend from high school, who is a nester extraordinaire and also decorates and gardens, and Molly, who grew up in England back when you took home economics in prep school. Shari is the quintessential "good orderer," while Elizabeth swears she makes a mean corn bread, but I have to take her word on this because I've never seen or tasted it.

"Most people don't make time for cooking," Nicole says when I call her to discuss the idea. "For me, it's part of being creative and it's self-soothing, but I think the women's movement made us feel like we weren't evolved or smart if we liked it." She's been making elaborate roasts and chicken dishes for Tim, the aspiring movie director, almost every night.

Whenever, in the past, a guy has asked me if I cook, I haven't made an effort to act like I do or want to; I probably offered up the anecdote about Eric and the sandwich, not even considering the fact that the man could very well be thinking, *Dear God, if I marry this woman, is she going to fix me rancid cheese sandwiches that will make me vomit?* Helen, who writes that when I have a man over for dinner, "it should be one of the most exquisite little meals he has ever eaten," would be horrified. According to her, anyone can learn. And, she notes, "cooking gourmetishly is a particularly impressive skill for a career woman."

Now let's be perfectly clear. *Gourmetishly* is probably out of the question. But *exquisite*—well, perhaps with some training and a few hat tricks, I could pull off exquisite. The truth of the matter is that I'm not certain I *don't* like cooking because I haven't given it much of a try. I made only one real attempt on my own: last year, in a burst of I'm-new-to-New-York-so-why-not-try-out-some-of-what-the-city-has-to-offer enthusiasm, I signed up for a chicken cooking class at a place called the Institute for Culinary Education. It ended up being delightful and I went home that night with leftovers, the e-mail addresses of my fellow classmates, and printed-out recipes, swearing that I would practice at home and then e-mail everyone so we could all get together for some chicken potluck class reunion. But while I did exchange a few friendly e-mails with my fellow fowl cookers, no mention was ever made of getting together for a potluck of what we'd learned. I cooked the roasted chicken once, the chicken burgers two times, and then reasoned that all of that sure was a whole lot of effort when I could just grab a piece of grilled chicken from the Korean deli down the street.

I decide that I'll start small by cooking simple dishes for friends. Then, over time, I'll work my way up to preparing that "exquisite little meal" for whatever man—men—I have over. Considering Helen's 20-meals-out-before-one-meal-in ratio, I have plenty of time to whip my culinary muscles into shape but I also know myself: finding a guy I'd even want to go on 20 dates with, not to mention going on the 20 dates, could take a very long time, so I'm going to have to play around with her numbers a bit if I want to give this a real try. Perhaps 10 dinners out—er, five—could justify a home-cooked meal?

The first thing I do is study the recipes in *S&SG* and search for one that looks unintimidating. And I find it: Caesar salad! Not only is this something I eat at least a few times a week, but it doesn't even require an oven. I rush over to the supermarket to buy romaine lettuce, Parmesan cheese, garlic, lemon, and Worcestershire sauce. (As a lifelong fish hater, I skip the anchovies.) Once home, I move my iPod into the kitchen—it feels like a commitment to making the cooking process something I'm going to enjoy and not just something I'm going to *do*—turn on music, and chop up bread for croutons. I lament the fact that I forgot to get French bread at the store and figure that the Ezekiel bread from Whole Foods that I have in my freezer is going to turn out some pretty nasty croutons. But that's, I figure, why I'm practicing this recipe now and not trying it for the first time when I have guests over.

I rub a garlic clove on the skillet, add olive oil, put the burner on a low heat, and let the bread chunks simmer. Then I mix together olive oil, salt, pepper, Worcestershire sauce, lemon juice, and mustard to make the dressing. I slice the lettuce into chunks and toss the dressing over, add an egg, Parmesan cheese, and my croutons, still hot.

Sitting down to eat my Caesar salad, I feel unmistakably proud of myself, not to mention relieved to discover that Ezekiel bread doesn't make disgusting croutons at all—that, in fact, the croutons it creates are so delicious that I may well have just found Ezekiel bread's raison d'être. Before I even stop to consider that this is a salad that's meant to serve four to six as a first course, or two for an entire meal, I demolish the entire thing. Caesar salad, I'm happy to report, tastes even better when you've made it yourself. The roughage overdose doesn't hit until much later, and it's well worth it.

Having mastered the art of preparing something that isn't only edible but actually tasty, I figure it's time for me to begin trying out my new skill set on others. The first recipient of my newfound knowledge will, I decide, be Michael, a friend of a friend who's agreed to help me make my DVD player work with my DVR. Just before he's due over, I put on a recently acquired apron and start making the Caesar salad. I will, I imagine, appear to be an authentically domesticated person when I casually say, "I put together a salad for lunch. Would you like some?"

All goes as planned and Michael has no idea that I'm beaming with pleasure as I watch him eat. Of course, I want him to praise the food, to tell me it's without a doubt the best Caesar salad in the history of Caesar salads, but instead he just asks for more dressing.

"More dressing?" I ask, stalling. A more seasoned chef would surely be able to mix together a small new batch easily, but trying to calculate how I'd do that right now feels overwhelming.

"Yeah—it's a little dry," he says, smiling.

"Well, there's no more." I can hear the defensiveness in my voice. The poor man has no idea that my cooking ego is as fragile as it is. "And I happen to think it's more than enough."

"Oh, okay," he says, and finishes the rest. I vow to double the oil next time I make it.

A few days after that, I start to feel like an actual cook and, when I'm struck by the urge to roast a chicken, I discover that roasting is far easier than frying or baking: all you do is buy a chicken, stuff it with garlic and lemon, tie the legs together, douse it in butter, and slide it in the oven for 90 minutes. I struggle a bit with tying the legs—the string I find in my kitchen drawer isn't very strong and I can't figure out if I need to keep the legs upright or just together—but the rest of the preparation is simple. While the delicious aroma fills my apartment, I go onto message boards to ask people why tying the chicken legs together is so important, and learn that it's so that the bottom half of the bird can cook evenly. *I'm someone who poses cooking questions online*, I think, feeling like a bastion of domesticity.

And the result is even better than it was with my Caesar salad. The chicken is moist and yet crispy and flavorful without being too garlicky. This time, pride in my accomplishment doesn't give me a superhuman hunger so I eat about half and put the rest away. Over the next few days, I use the leftovers for everything: a chicken omelet in the morning, a chicken sandwich for lunch, and chicken with broccoli that I sauté for dinner, meals that I otherwise would have eaten out. I am, I think, not only becoming a genuine chef but also saving money. Helen, who recommends cutting corners by negotiating with doctor's offices over your bills and borrowing someone else's newspaper instead of paying for your own, would certainly applaud.

In October, when it's my turn to host my monthly book club, I commit to making food that will put the chips and dips the other girls have offered as sustenance to shame. And one day at the gym, when I pick up a discarded magazine off a treadmill rack and see a page dedicated to the favorite hors d'oeuvres of a Food Network show host, I decide to make everything she lists: bruschetta topped with Parmesan cheese and sun-dried tomatoes, toasted baguette slices with crumbled goat cheese and sautéed mushrooms, and maple-coated bacon with mustard. At home, I slice off pieces of French bread to make the bruschetta, douse them in oil, sprinkle on Parmesan, add the sun-dried tomatoes, and grill the entire concoction in the oven. Then I sauté the mushrooms with garlic and let both simmer until they're crisp and brown and my kitchen smells like an Italian restaurant. I feel, if not quite like Carmela Soprano or the Food Network host whose recipes I'm bogarting, at least like a girl who knows her way around a cutting board and oven. When the girls walk in and I offer them the delicacies on a special hors d'oeuvres plate, my image of myself as an actual person who entertains is complete. And when I take a step back and see all of them sitting on my new couch beneath my half-steel, half-glass bookshelves, I feel confident that my orange cheese sandwich days are behind me for good.

A week later, I'm invited to a cookie party where prizes are going to be awarded for most creative. In the past, I would have picked up Oreos and mumbled something about how I thought they would be considered creative in this environment since everyone else had brought homemade. But now I decide to make something special. After discarding several options, I settle on homemade fortune cookies; I type up a silly ditty about the cookie party 20 times on a page, print copies, and cut each one into a fortune-size shape. Then I mix together egg whites, vanilla, vegetable oil, flour, cornstarch, salt, sugar, and water;

drop spoonfuls of the mix onto a baking sheet; and bake it for 15 minutes. After they cool, I discover the difficult part of the operation: bending the cookie around the fortune before it hardens, which burns your fingers even if you're covering it with a paper towel. The cookies taste delicious—like sugar cookies—but folding hardened batter into a fortune cookie shape is more difficult than I thought it would be and they end up not looking so much like fortune cookies as mini spaceships folded in half. I lose to a girl who made ice cream cookies designed to look like hamburgers, but I'm in too much of a sugar coma by then to care.

The time has come for me to prepare a meal for a man.

Jack usually eats aruvedically and although I don't really know what that means, it may be a prerequisite for every actor/choreographer/modern dancer living on the Isle of Manhattan. Because he's gay and my good friend, I don't need to wait for him to take me out for 20 meals or to pull any gastronomic wool over his eyes. Instead I tell him the truth: that this will be the first full meal I'll be making on my own.

I look through *S&SG* for some more recipes. Because I don't like fish, crabmeat puffs, stuffed lobster tails, and lobster en brochette are out of the question. So I settle on escalopes of veal, broccoli almondine, stuffed mushrooms, and chocolate angel pie for dessert. Helen's recipes are sparse (some are only three or four lines) and she doesn't specify what type of veal to get so I return from the store with the only kind my local supermarket sells: veal chops. But they look weird and I know in my soul that they couldn't be right so I head over to the Chelsea Marketplace, a food mecca that contains the sort of stalls found in European supermarkets: meat from one store, cheese from another, fresh fruit and vegetables from another still. At the butcher, I buy fillets of veal as well as chopped veal because the stuffed mushroom recipe calls for cooked meat and since Helen didn't specify what meat that should be, I figured I should stick with a veal theme for consistency's sake.

The broccoli and stuffed mushroom preparation goes well but I grill the veal longer than I should and before I even try it, I can tell it's going to have the consistency of a sneaker. And the pie looks good but I don't realize until right before Jack arrives that it's supposed to be chilled for two hours. I can't very well make him wait until one in the morning for dessert so I shove it in the freezer and hope for the best.

"This is amazing," Jack says as he scoops bites of the stuffed mushrooms into his mouth. "Amazing" is a word he uses somewhat liberally but not liberally enough, I discover seconds later, to describe my veal. "It's good," he offers unconvincingly, despite the fact that he's earned a large part of his living as an actor. Even if he could fake it, the fact that it's taking both of us a good five minutes to chew each bite tells me everything I need to know.

When we're done with dinner, I remove the pie from the freezer but it's still not quite solid enough to cut into slices so I forget about the presentation and scoop spoonfuls of it onto plates. "Yummy!" Jack declares, but his acting skills still aren't at their best. And I have to concede that even though I find such a massive infusion of sugar delightful, someone who was taking a break from any sort of a regular healthy eating plan might choke on its richness. After his third bite, Jack puts his fork down and I retrieve a 100-calorie chocolate-covered pretzel pack from the kitchen and toss it to him. He takes a bite of a pretzel and his already enormous blue eyes double in size. "Amazing!" he declares with more enthusiasm than he's displayed all night.

Rather than allowing myself to be discouraged, I force myself to adopt my Rollerblading attitude when it comes to cooking by accepting the fact that I'm not going to excel at it from the beginning. At the very least, I reason, cooking doesn't make my ankles hurt.

Soon after, I get an e-mail from David, a sexy if slightly odd acquaintance from college, telling me that he's taking a break from L.A. and is going to be in New York all summer. I'd always been attracted to him so the message is a welcome respite from the dismal black hole Match has turned out to be. But I'd never been able to tell how David felt about me since the one time we went out for dinner in L.A., he ended up spending most of the time talking about the importance of flossing your teeth if you wanted to prevent gum disease—a lecture which managed to kill every romantic vibe that may have been in the ether.

We agree to meet at one of David's favorite Manhattan restaurants, a West Village place that specializes in tofu, and, over food that's far healthier than anything I've eaten in years, I find myself opening up to him about the ways I'm trying to change my life. He's enthusiastic and encouraging and I feel more comfortable around him than I ever have before. He walks me home afterward and, just as I'm reflecting on what a nice evening it was, he leans in and kisses me—so passionately that it renders all previous unsexy conversations about gingivitis completely obsolete.

The next morning, he calls to ask me out for dinner again, and before I know it, he and I are dating. I'm still thinking rather obsessively about Will but David is a nice distraction and I'm elated to be following Helen's advice that I consider all the "eligibles"—the men that I already know—without even having to try.

But while the kissing remains somewhat intoxicating, it quickly becomes evident that David is too critical for me. He's someone who clearly feels there are right and wrong ways to do things and who furthermore doesn't have any problem informing me when he thinks I'm verging into the territory of wrong. Why are these qualities never noticeable until we're locking lips with someone? I begin making excuses when he asks me to dinner until our dates peter out to near nonexistence.

Then, one late fall afternoon a few weeks after our most recent date, I become obsessed with putting my hard-learned cooking skills to the test for a straight man—my desire to practice making the exquisite little meal suddenly outweighing my desire to avoid criticism. "Would you like to come over for dinner tonight at eight?" I ask David over the phone, the words flowing from my mouth with the sort of ease I just know Helen would appreciate. He accepts.

At seven, I start stirring and roasting and removing and cooling. When there's still no sign of him by 8:20, I keep reheating and cooling. By this time, I'm sweating and marveling at women who can put steaming plates on a table and also smell good and not have grease stains on their arms and clothes. I don't want to shower again for fear of not hearing the doorbell so when he doesn't show up for the next half hour, I stay at my post by the oven, stressing and reheating and cooling while texting to find out where he is and not hearing back.

David shows up about 45 minutes later, apologizing and explaining that he had been in the midst of a serious misunderstanding with his writing partner and that he hopes I won't mind him continuing to work it out now. I act like this isn't a problem since Helen says that when you're cooking for a man, you should be creating "the most serene atmosphere" imaginable. Even though she probably wasn't talking about a man you don't want to date but who was available when your domestic urge hit, I also know that telling him I'd prefer he not take care of this now will only make the situation worse. I've created just the sort of environment Helen told me to—my apartment is "spic-and-span," I have fresh flowers "about," candles are lit, music is playing, the glasses have been chilled in the freezer, cloth napkins are being used, and I smell "fragrant" and not like I've been trying to will various goods into submission for the past few hours. And yet all of this is lost on David, who has a heated phone conversation while I start in on my Caesar salad and the now-cold chicken and broccoli.

Eventually David sits down, telling me how sorry he is. I smile the way I imagine Helen might have for her own David—her husband, movie producer David Brown—when he was working on *Jaws* and Spielberg had called during dinner. We eat in uncharacteristic silence for a minute before David examines a piece of broccoli and asks me how I prepared it.

"I sautéed it." I somehow know this is the incorrect answer.

"Did you ever consider steaming?" he asks, and then launches into a lecture about why steaming keeps all the most important nutrients while sautéing is so bad that you might as well be eating potato chips. After a while, I tune him out. Then I start yawning, and explain that a sudden fatigue is overtaking me. He offers to help with the dishes but scrubbing a pan is a small price to pay for the freedom I feel once he leaves.

Of the 15 people gathered for the Thanksgiving cooking class, 13 are women, one is a gay guy, and one is an older man named Jerry who manages to tell us in a way that doesn't make us feel sorry for him that he's here because his recently deceased wife was such an amazing cook that he never learned to make anything. He's accompanied by his daughter, who has frizzy brown hair, two kids, and a friendly smile. I immediately want the two of them on my cooking team, but I don't know if that's because they seem so kind or because they're each one step removed from a woman they both declare had serious culinary skills.

I'm here because, while it's all fine and good to be able to cook oily salads and weird bacon hors d'oeuvres and fortune cookies resembling NASA vehicles, what good is that going to do me once I've succeeded in landing my mate? I need to know how to make the necessary basics of a household. And what, I think, could be more basic than a holiday meal? So I'd found a class that prepared people for Thanksgiving. In a fit of temporary insanity a few days before, the class suggested during a phone conversation with my mom that she come to New York from the Bay Area for the holiday and let me cook Thanksgiving for the two of us. My intentions were good: since my stepdad is older now and needs taking care of, I'd been thinking that he could spend the holiday with his son and his family and she could get a nice break from the stress of her everyday life. She accepted my invitation before I had the time to really consider what I'd done.

And now here I am in class with 13 fellow women, all of whom seem to be wearing glittering wedding rings. I feel like the resident loser—a girl who not only can't get a husband but also can't find anyone to come eat her Thanksgiving meal besides her mother. Their seeming confidence in their cooking ability only adds to my inferiority complex—two mention "fine dining" classes they took, one is in "the program" at the school, and none asks if "bread dressing" is code for stuffing, so I end up having to do it and then feel silly when the teacher confirms that it is and the others smile at me like I'm the half-wit they're allowing to take the class but nobody expected to actually ask questions.

After a while, I'm too busy trying to write down everything the teacher is saying to even care if anyone's judging me for being a neophyte. *If you brine the turkey, you don't have to worry about the dark meat catching up to the light meat whereas if you don't, the dark meat takes longer* I write on the back of the recipe booklet. *Kosher turkeys are more flavorful and moist than non-kosher,* I write below that. *The thermometers that come in turkeys suck!* I scribble at the bottom of the page. *Get an instant read thermometer instead.* By the time we divide into three groups so we can start the actual cooking, my entire recipe booklet is filled with notations.

I find myself, through a combination of design and destiny, working with the widower Jerry and his daughter, as well as a put-together blonde and one of the brunettes who'd mentioned the fine dining cooking class. While the teacher chops up vegetables which he then stuffs into two different turkeys, we divide our group in half—two will work on stuffing (still being called bread dressing) and three on apple pie. Jerry's daughter, the blonde, and I all say that we want to be in the pie group, so Jerry and the fine cooking woman get started on the stuffing while we embark on crust making.

So focused are we on the exciting new things we're learning as a result of our pie quest—there's a special kind of flour called cake flour! All you have to do is slice apples into pieces and put them in the pie tin without mixing them with anything! Nutmeg is an actual nut and you scrape the spice off!—we forget to pay attention to the stuffing and turkey preparation. It doesn't occur to me until it's too late that those are the two most crucial Thanksgiving dishes of all and that my future family surely wouldn't want a turkey and stuffing–less Thanksgiving meal. Just then, an image of Will as my future husband pops into my head. I see him smiling at me, blue eyes ablaze, over our non-turkey Thanksgiving dinner. Before I start imagining our future children and the tears that accompany most every thought I have about him begin to gather in my eyes, Jerry's daughter whispers that another group making apple pie had to start again because they screwed theirs up. "Ours is going to be so much better," she says. My competitive spirit rises to the surface as my tears disappear.

"Damn straight." I smile.

"Oh, but look," our third teammate says. She gestures to third pie team, who are now creating a pretty dough leaf for the top of theirs. "Should we do that?" she asks.

The teacher interrupts our conversation to ask us where we stand with the mashed potatoes and gravy and, because he scares us, we pretend we have everything covered and I claim to be on top of the potatoes while they say they're handling the gravy. We break up and I peel and boil and rice while the rest of my group makes the gravy, cranberries, and eggnog.

Finally the teacher pulls the turkeys from the oven. We whip our aprons off, rush toward the table, grab plates, and pile them with breast meat and drumsticks and gravy and mashed potatoes and cranberries and stuffing that only I keep calling stuffing.

Our pie turns out gorgeous—more gorgeous, we whisper, than the one with the leaf on top—and I feel the need to eat every last morsel of my piece, along with the scoop of vanilla ice cream, while Jerry's daughter stops halfway through because she's full. Knowing that I was stuffed long before the pies were even brought out, I wonder if you simply start making healthier choices when you have kids. While we eat, she and I chat about what picky eaters her children are and, just like in most of the child-rearing conversations I have, I relate more to the children being described than to the adults doing the describing. At the same time, the night makes me feel distinctly grown up. Though Betty Draper might not agree and Betty Friedan would surely be aghast, baking a pie fuels me with a sense of empowerment by showing me that I'm a lot more capable than I give myself credit for.

. . .

Making the pie and mashed potatoes in a class with some cheerful, like-minded people is one thing. Preparing an entire Thanksgiving feast for the most discriminating person I know—my mother—is another. And, the week before her visit, I'm struck with dread. I tell myself that everything's going to be great, that I'm only being oversensitive when I think she's criticizing me and that spending this holiday with her will be fun. I try to think of us as two Manhattan escape artists, avoiding the typical familial obligations and interactions with obscure relatives by having a Thanksgiving à deux that we can finish off with a walk through Central Park. But I'm unmistakably nervous. I know that everyone has issues with their family, but I'm convinced that being single exacerbates mine: not only do I feel inadequate because I haven't managed to partner up yet, but ever since my brother got married and had a child, it's like he's relinquished a responsibility that I often now feel like I'm carrying for the both of us. Of course I don't share any of these thoughts with my mom. While we're direct with each other about many things, we also talk in and around subjects, reading each other's voices for nuances and secrets, reacting to what we believe the other is thinking while working overtime to play the part of devoted daughter and devoted mother. The umbilical cord may have been cut decades ago, but in many ways, I still feel like it's tethered around my neck.

In therapy, Roger and I discuss some of the things my mom says that make me feel insecure and possible ways I can avoid being triggered, but this does nothing to assuage my anxiety about her visit. So I force myself to obsess over preparing for the meal. The Sunday before her Wednesday arrival, I roll out the two piecrusts I've made and stick them in Ziploc bags in the freezer. Two days before Thanksgiving, one day before my mom descends, I make the cranberries and go to Citarella, one of the city's hip gourmet markets, to pick up a turkey breast (which I've decided to roast instead of making a whole turkey).

When my mom shows up, everything seems fine at first. The new bookshelves, couch, and curtains look chic, the lilies in the vase on the table smell glorious, and the candles provide ideal lighting. We have a quiet dinner and catch each other up on our lives. On Thanksgiving Day, she teaches me how to do things that I didn't learn in class, explaining that brining just means dunking the turkey in salt water and showing me how to baste the turkey skin in a butter paprika concoction to make it brown. But for some reason, being in the kitchen with her feels stressful, almost hostile. She chides me for not including a salad or green vegetable or soup in my meal plan, and I feel ashamed. How had that not occurred to me? Why didn't my cooking teacher mention it? Then I realize that he surely thought every-one knew something so obvious and I begin to beat myself up. If I lacked such common sense, how was I ever going to cook for my own family one day? I ask my mom if she wants to go to the store to get everything she thinks I've forgotten and when she's gone, I feel guilty and commit to being nicer and more loving and less defensive. But when she returns and says that it sure seemed like I had wanted her to leave, my best intentions evaporate. I take my frustration out on the potato I'm peeling as she unpacks green beans and a premade pumpkin soup.

"You're making mashed potatoes?" she asks. I nod. She says nothing.

"Why?" I ask. "Do you not want me to make mashed potatoes?" I enunciate each word slowly.

She wrinkles her nose. "I think sweet potatoes are better."

"Since when?" I feel irrationally ashamed and sad, back to being the little girl who couldn't do anything right—the little girl who didn't even know how to express her feelings without being laughed at. Within seconds, before I'm even aware of it, the sadness morphs into anger and I'm simmering along with the gravy on the stovetop. "You always made both," I snap.

"But I prefer sweet potatoes." Her tone is aggravatingly cheery. "Or baked potatoes."

I start slicing my potatoes into pieces far too tiny to be baked. Neither of us says anything. "Why don't you go read, Mom?" I finally ask.

"Okay," she says, and leaves the room.

I continue slicing the potatoes and find a modicum of peace amid the peeling and stirring. I sing along to what's blasting out of my iPod, and check on the turkey when suddenly—

Bleep! Bleep! Bleep! Bleep!

The fire alarm is blaring. This never happened during my previous cooking adventures: it must be because I have so many pots going at once. It keeps blaring. The gravy is boiling. Is gravy supposed to boil?

Bleep! Bleep! Bleep! Bleep!

"Mom, can you do something?"

She runs into the kitchen, looking annoyed. "What am I supposed to do?"

I could tell her—grab the ladder, climb up it, and deactivate the alarm—but I'm in martyr mode now so I do it myself. I return to the kitchen, my mom to her book. Peace again. Until—

Bleep! Bleep! Bleep! Bleep!

This happens about six more times throughout the meal preparation and each alarm turn-off (my mom takes over the duty after the second time) is punctuated by my mom telling me that she needs to make the green beans and me explaining that I'm using every burner and inch of counter space. By the fourth time, I abandon all hope of timing the dishes right, accept the fact that the potatoes will have to be cold, and let her move past me to make green beans that I know I won't eat. I wonder if this is what cooking Thanksgiving will be like with my future partner: the two of us competing for burners and believing that whatever we're making is the most important. Maybe it would be better if I find a man who can't cook at all.

Against all odds, the meal turns out delicious. It's hard to say which of us is more surprised by this. We end up eating so much that neither of us can do anything for the next few hours but watch a succession of bad romantic comedies that are either starring Kate Hudson or seem like they should be starring Kate Hudson. I find it quite adorable that my intellectual mother, who wrote her dissertation on English heroism in pastoral literature, has a secret soft spot for silly romantic comedies, and the hours we pass watching Kate and other Kate-like actors quip and kiss and fall in love on my TV screen are the most pleasant I have with her for the entire trip. There are no silent recriminations, no clever jokes masking hostile criticism, no devastating indifference, no battles for control or the spotlight—there's just me, my mom, the tryptophan we're under the influence of, and the apple pie we keep eating.

The next day, I make turkey sandwiches on rye with Russian dressing and tomatoes, just the way we used to the day after Thanksgiving when I was growing up. But these tomatoes are from the Union Square Farmers' Market, the rye is from Amy's Bread at the Chelsea marketplace, and the Russian dressing is homemade. "How divine," my mom says as she takes an enormous bite, the orange cheese sandwiches of my past clearly a distant memory.

CHAPTER FIVE

Fashion Focus

You must develop style. Every girl has one . . . it's just a
case of getting it out in the open.

—*Sex and the Single Girl*

I've never been what anyone might call a fashion maven.

Whether this is because I grew up in a Northern California suburb where Jerry Garcia was the main cultural icon or
because I'm just not that aesthetically inclined, I simply wasn't
the girl who gazed at *Seventeen* magazine to come up with ideas
for outfits or got rapturous over whatever model was most in
vogue. While I always had a strong sense of what I liked—I still
remember a bitter battle I had with my mom when I was seven
over these overalls with buffaloes on them (she insisted I wear
them; I refused; she insisted again; she, ultimately, won)—my
taste has always been simple: jeans and T-shirts, sundresses and
flip-flops.

Helen, in other words, would probably not sign off on my
wardrobe. She believes that I should "count the fashion magazines as friends" and that "markdowns are usually things people
didn't like well enough to buy at the original price," while I'm

apathetic to *Vogue* and *Harper's Bazaar* but have intimate relationships with Loehmann's and Filene's Basement.

I've definitely known girls over the years who gleefully save for a pair of Louboutins, who wait in line for Rick Owens sample sales and are thrilled when they score something there that they "only" had to pay a thousand dollars for, and who dog-ear fashion magazines, but my good friends have usually tended to be too practical or focused on their careers or lives to be willing to invest the kind of time and money a true dedication to fashion requires. "Why would I spend $800 on a pair of shoes," Nicole asks me one day, "when I could get a cool piece of art or couch or table for that same amount?" Shari mostly dresses to showcase her figure (she's said to have the best rack in Manhattan), while Elizabeth focuses on playing down her nearly six feet in height. Molly is my only friend who really turns it on, fashion-wise: she has a closet full of designer dresses and, on any given workday, is decked out in sexy skirts, flattering blouses, and knee-high boots. And her style doesn't only apply to what's on the outside. Once, when she mentions casually that she always wears matching bra and underwear sets, I tell her I've never done that in my life. Her mouth drops open. "Even when you know you're having sex that night?" she asks. I nod and she doesn't seem to know what to do with her shock.

As a society, we've unquestionably grown sexier, as well as more casual and far more individualistic, since Helen's time. In the '60s, women dressed uniformly, whether it was in cable-knit sweaters, miniskirts, and Jackie O pillbox hats, or the full skirts and cleavage-boosting tops of *Mad Men*, but it seems like fashion fell out as politics became a focus in the '70s. Then came the '80s, our era of excess, when everything was overly ornamented—shoulder pads, parachute pants, everything Madonna did. But in the '90s and up through today, fashion really feels like it's come to reflect the multicultural, eclectic world we increasingly inhabit. Now a woman in a kilt and kimono can look great, so long as she's pulled it all together right. And we wear jeans on airplanes and at the theater, something that would have shocked the '60s women right out of their kitten-heeled pumps.

My goal is not to try to convert myself into some sort of a fashion plate—that would defy who I naturally am—but just to follow Helen's suggestion that I become more fashion-conscious. To get started, I focus on one particular line in *S&SG*—"Copycat a mentor with better taste than yours"—and decide that mine will be Dana Reynolds, a girl who works at a designer consignment boutique near my apartment and is far sassier and friendlier than anyone who knows the important distinctions between Christian Dior and Christian Lacroix probably should be. I don't go in the store all that often but whenever I do, she's always wearing, say, a ruffled sheath skirt with motorcycle boots or a pair of cargo pants with a lacy cardigan—eclectic items I would never have thought to unite but which look perfect on her.

So one day near the beginning of December when I'm there because I have to find something for a formal event that week, I confide in Dana that because I'm relatively small and look younger than I am, I've been able to get away with throwing on the first few items I spy in my closet, but now I'm beginning to wonder if having a wardrobe more appropriate for a teenager than a grown woman is a sign of my inability to accept my age and where I am in life. Also, I explain, because I have big boobs and a short torso, a simple sundress can end up looking positively pornographic on me. Dana nods sympathetically, her dark eyes earnest as I tell her that I'm both inherently cheap and have something of a shopping addiction, which means that I usually don't make major fashion purchases but have a whole bunch of temporarily trendy skirts, dresses, and tops from places like H&M and Zara. But, I add, stinginess has its benefits—it's what drew me to her shop and secondhand stores in general. Helen, I tell her, says I should wear everything I buy and not have too many clothes, and I don't obey either of these things. Dana continues to nod, acting like these are perfectly normal confessions for a consignment store customer to be making to an employee, and promises she can help me. "Let's start by seeing what you need to get rid of," she says gently.

Cleaning out my closet is a task I'm all too familiar with—those H&M and Zara items that I accumulate without even seeming to realize it tend to weigh down a closet, especially a New York closet. So I know how to put old or unworn clothing in garbage bags and drag them over to Housing Works. But what good is an excavation when I end up filling the space with minor variations of what I've gotten rid of? The truth is that I'm a bit addicted to the process of procuring, throwing away, and then procuring more: in L.A., I lived next door to a vintage store called Crossroads and I would take the clothes I didn't want anymore there and then use whatever credit I accrued to buy other items from their racks. More than once, I'm pretty certain I bought back pieces I'd sold them a few weeks or months before. But, as Helen writes, "a closet jammed with half-decent and half-indecent stuff can make you feel you haven't got a thing to wear," and that is certainly true in my case. Besides, if I'm to one day share a closet—or at least a living space—with a man, do I want to go into that with 30 variations of the same black T-shirt, half with stains, the other half coated in cat hair?

With an eagle-eyed Dana sitting on my floor supervising, I pull out a black sundress from BCBG. "Cute!" Dana observes. Encouraged, I unearth my entire black sundress collection: one from H&M, one from Zara, one from an obscure L.A. designer, one from Forever 21, and another from H&M. Dana looks from my right hand, which holds the dresses, to my face. "They're all the same," she says.

"No, they're not." The dress on top has spaghetti straps, the next is made of an unusual, stretchy material, and the third is knee-length. There's silence, which I fill with a confession that I know I wear a lot of black. "But they really *are* different," I add. My voice sounds higher than usual, like I know I'm lying.

"Pick one of the black sundresses," Dana says gently. "The rest have to go." I consider the fact that my goal is to create my own sense of style, not Dana's. Then I come to terms with the possibility that this closet could qualify for an episode of *Hoarders*. Five dresses go in the throwaway pile.

Before long, we hit a stride. The rule she gives me is that I haven't worn something in a year—"all four seasons"—it has to go. And even if I have, we should assess whether I need it. Because she's the tactful type, I ascertain that I'm going to have to read between some of her lines. "It would be great for painting your apartment," loosely translated, means "Get rid of it now."

"Cute if you need to go out and get coffee" is another way of saying, "Don't even think about putting that on unless you're trying to keep people away from you." "Good for working out" signifies an item that I shouldn't wear again—probably not even to the gym.

I fight her on some of her declarations, but when she has a solid argument, I acquiesce. In the process, I discover some odd justifications I make in my head for hanging on to things: when I find myself saying "But it would be great for a Christmas party" about a succession of formal black dresses and she starts asking me how many Christmas parties I go to, I realize that I've been using some fake devotion to the Yuletide season as an excuse to hold on to things I haven't looked at, let alone worn, in years.

At a certain point, we move on to shoes. My black Justin cowboy boots—a Housing Works find—get high marks, as do the patent leather knee-high boots that I'd been questioning since a French guy I dated last year told me he didn't "understand" them. And she loves a pair of black-and-tan-checkered fleece-lined Vans. Flats, Chuck Taylor sneakers, sandals, and heels all pass muster as well. My Hunter rain boots—purchased last year after I learned the hard way that Uggs aren't meant to withstand the snow and rain—also get a thumbs-up. She actually declares them—and believe me, this is exciting—a "must-have."

She then shares with me what else is on her fashion necessities list: an Alexander McQueen skull scarf, a pair of Jackie O sunglasses, a gray cardigan, a black blazer, a printed coat, Sass & Bide black "Rats" leggings that are like normal leggings but have fabric gathered together on the thigh area in what I learn is called a "ruche," mesh footless tights, a vest, heels that aren't black, and skinny black jeans.

We unearth a pair of skinny black jeans I hadn't even known I owned and since she's wearing the Sass & Bide leggings and I can thus see that they're both edgy and basic, she doesn't have to talk me into getting them. (Finding a pair is another matter—she tells me they're hard to get outside Australia—but eBay delivers.) The Theory blazer I have and never wear meets her approval, and even better yet, at the end of the day, she gives me an Alexander McQueen scarf—black with bright pink skulls—that she swears she's sick of, a gift I would giddily accept even if Helen hadn't told me to welcome hand-me-downs.

When it's all over, we go to the Barneys Warehouse sale—an event that has, in the past, left me miserable, clutching something I don't want but nevertheless felt the need to buy to justify having stripped down in public and been shoved around by overzealous shoppers.

But the sale's been going on for over a week and so it isn't very crowded when Dana and I go. Once inside, we immediately find a long-sleeved Dries Van Noten knit dress that looks a bit like everything I own so I like it and yet is different enough for her. We both also love a black sleeveless silk knit tank with a collection of fabric woven into a flower in the front and a green and blue jersey shirt. Then Dana spies a tweed vest that she says I need to have. Since I balk at the $400 price tag, she suggests that we look for one in the men's section—and that's where we find almost the exact same one for $80.

The total is just over $300, about what I spent when I went

to the Barneys sale in L.A. and came away with black heels bedecked in fake flowers that I never wore and ended up throwing out a year later. On the way home, we stop by Loehmann's —it is, apparently, my day to defy Helen's anti-markdown stance—where I pick out a pair of Jackie O–type Chloé sunglasses, navy heels, and a gray cardigan.

Later, sliding my new clothes into my closet, I marvel at the fact that I can now see everything in there. I have about a half of what I did before but it somehow feels like it's twice as much.

Over time, I start to notice that putting on clothes is more fun than before. Getting dressed used to be an oftentimes frustrating experience that tended to culminate in my coming to the conclusion that everything I owned was horrible or that I probably needed to lose weight in order to look good before ultimately throwing on the same sundress or jeans and shirt I'd worn the day or week before.

But incorporating Dana's castoffs—which now also include a multicolored knit Missoni hat and a bright striped scarf—with the good pieces I either already had or have recently acquired helps me to start thinking of getting dressed not just as something I have to do so that I won't get arrested for indecent exposure but as an actual enjoyable activity. When the weather grows cooler, I tend to find the fact that I have to wear a scarf, hat, and coat a major inconvenience. But now it starts to feel like a puzzle, a riddle that can be figured out if I focus hard enough. Putting on my faded jeans with a new white tank that has asymmetrical pieces of fabric hanging from it and adding a black military half coat we found hanging in the back of my closet with the multicolored scarf and a pair of Chanel knockoff flats I got at Top Shop feels like an accomplishment of some kind. And I love that while Dana has influenced me, what I end up wearing is altogether me.

Yet one does not become Diane von Furstenberg or an Olsen twin overnight. Some days I still struggle to make all the disparate pieces come together as a cohesive whole. But I also manage to pull off some impressive feats, like deciding one day while looking at a pair of silver suede boots with leather flaps that I want to cut the leather flaps off. Not only does this transform silver suede boots with leather flaps that were always kind of ugly into a pair of adorable silver suede boots that are now flapless, but I've also unwittingly followed Helen's advice that I take what I have and make it more "up to date."

The more I accumulate—a leopard-print winter coat from Top Shop here, a long black top with an off-center neck there—the more I can see that my work in this area isn't done. Dana is a perfect fashion mentor, someone to point me in a sharp and original direction, but I still feel like I could be mistaken for a college kid. I need to find someone who can help me dress my age.

Research leads me to a NYC-based stylist Kendall Farr—a chic, tall blonde who's styled Angelina Jolie, Diane Sawyer, Halle Berry, and many others, as well as written two books on fashion. Her focus is on helping women dress for where they are in life, not for where they want to be. When I call her, I confess that I'm loath to give up my youthful dressing habits; she assures me that I don't need to, but that she'll help me find a style identity that suits both my age and my body type.

In person, Kendall does not disappoint. She starts by telling me what she feels are the pieces every modern woman in her 30s should have, a list that's quite different from Dana's: a pair of black slim pants, a pencil skirt, black or nude pumps, white jeans, and curator pants from J. Crew. Then she suggests that I look at photos of the stylist L'Wren Scott as well as of Ellen Barkin and Victoria Beckham because they all manage to look sexy and feminine without ever wearing clothing that's too young. She also talks about how Angelina Jolie dresses against type—meaning that even though she's always been devastatingly sexy, she plays that down more than up. I can't say the same for myself—shorts and cleavage-revealing tops are wardrobe staples of mine—and I confess as much to Kendall.

"Women who have always dressed to be sexy have the hardest time realigning themselves as they age," she offers sagely.

Her words sound like something of a death knell but one I need to hear. I think of the women I've seen wearing the same miniskirts as their teenage daughters and then of the tiny jean miniskirt hanging in my closet. Have I been dressing like a mother determined to look like her teenager, only without the teenager? Before I can worry too much about this, Kendall distracts me by explaining that I'm what she calls a Body Type C since my shoulders are wider than my hips and my waist is short, and how my goal should be to wear clothes that "elongate and skim over the middle." Since I'm on the short side and often lament the size of my stomach, these words make perfect sense. We begin going through my closet the way I did with Dana, and when we stumble on some long dresses and skirts that made it through the Dana editing process but I nevertheless don't wear, Kendall suggests that I get all of them shortened to right below my knee. It seems that while some of my wardrobe has been too young, other parts of it have been too old.

"Incremental is key," she says. "If you move along subtly, you avoid getting to 45 and asking yourself, 'How am I supposed to look now?'"

I write down everything Kendall says—about how I should avoid turtlenecks since the mantra for my upper body should be to "simplify and elongate," about how cargo pants make legs look shorter, about how it's better if I wear patterned clothing on the bottom rather than on top, and about how Marni dresses are slimming. I then decide to implement two of her suggestions right away by shortening the dresses and skirts and using the steamer she recommended to get rid of every last wrinkle in a white, long-sleeved button-down shirt. Pairing the wrinkle-free shirt with a newly shortened skirt, I feel sophisticated and feminine—as well as entirely confident that no one could mistake me for a college student anymore.

By the beginning of December, it seems like the right time to test drive my new look, which means paying attention to Match again. It's not that Match has been ignoring me—I'd just been ignoring it. The "winks" I'd been receiving from men who frightened and depressed me had essentially stopped me from even going onto the site. Worse than the profiles included in those e-mails were the notes explaining that out of "millions of members," this man had picked me. "He picked you" was bolded, in case I didn't quite understand the significance of this honor. Apparently I was supposed to be dancing a jig because a man who looked like he should be hanging from a tree branch while clutching a pair of binoculars had gifted me with a virtual wink.

Equally dismal were the "You've sparked someone's interest" e-mails—e-mails, I learn, that are coming to me because Match had determined that this man and I would be good for each other and had sent him my profile along with the profiles of four other women as part of his "Daily 5" and he'd clicked on some sort of a button under me. In order to incentivize the situation, Match would then inform me of all the things that he and I had in common: *Like you, he's not a smoker*, it might say. Or: *You both enjoy nightclubs and dancing*. What criteria were they using? And what on earth had motivated me to check a box that said I liked nightclubs and dancing? What's more, why didn't any of the appealing men on Match—please, dear God, tell me there *were* appealing men on Match—click on me?

But, I think, with my improved fashion-savvy, I can make Match work. I add pictures to my profile of me in the Dries Von Noten dress and Dana's skull scarf and another in my leopard coat. But appealing men do not immediately start contacting me as a result. Determined to make the most of my Match experience, I decide to get proactive and scan the site for alluring men; when I find two that seem worth pursuing, I send them each e-mails.

I also begin e-mailing with a guy named Jonathan whose notes are a bit bland but whose pictures reveal a potentially hot guy in various fabulous-looking situations—on ski slopes, on tennis courts, in formal wear. I also respond to a guy whose sole photo shows him in a tux making a *Zoolander*-esque model face.

After Zoolander—who turns out to be named Zach—and I exchange a few e-mails, he asks if we can Instant Message. I respond that I don't IM, which means that I IM all day long with friends but am hesitant to give out my IM name to someone I don't know and may end up not ever wanting to hear from again. He writes back, *Too bad. Well, if you change your mind, let me know.* He includes three different IM addresses.

So I send him an IM and our exchange is surprisingly lively and funny. But I've known people who can be great in e-mails and IMs but are duds in person, so I IM Zach that I'd like to meet up. Nothing comes through on his end of the conversation. Finally a message appears: *Oh, no. That would be too soon. But let's chat a few more times on here and see how it goes.* I'm annoyed: e-mail and Instant Messaging give people a cushion, a way to craft how they want to be perceived, and are, in my opinion, a waste of time unless you've met the person. I decide to ignore him and instead focus on the two men I've targeted and contacted.

Intense focus, however, doesn't get either of them to respond. At first I assume that they're just not logging into their Match accounts but the site doesn't let you get away with such delusional thinking because it places notices like "Active within 2 days" below the picture of the guy you've been telling yourself has been too busy to read your e-mail from last week. I wonder, briefly, if I would have heard back from them if I hadn't changed my photos—maybe I now look overly fashion-conscious, which translates into shallow or silly—or if they think I'm too old, even though both are older than me.

But I'm distracted from this thought process by a message

from Zach. *Yes, I AM thinking about you, too*, it reads. Later, I get another from him that says, *Wondering what's going on with you.* I don't respond to either but the next time I see him on IM, I type that I'd realized that sending virtual messages to strangers wasn't my thing. His response is thoughtful and charming and I tell him that I'm still up for meeting if he wants to but I can't IM back and forth anymore with someone I don't know. He says that while this is much faster than he normally likes these things to go, he can make an exception.

Remembering some piece I saw in the *Times* about a guy so determined to find love that he scheduled a succession of Internet dates back to back, I plan to meet Jonathan and Zach on the same day. It turns out to be the coldest I've experienced—one of those days where weather Web sites claim it's around 10 degrees but you swear it's much colder, when your skin is red and frigid underneath three pairs of pants, where blustery winds leave you whimpering and smart people have the good sense to stay inside. Abandoning my plans to wear some fantastic new outfit, I settle for multiple layers of whatever I can find and add the McQueen skull scarf as I'm walking out the door.

I keep my expectations low.

I'm thus shocked when a tall guy who looks like he could be cast as, say, a handsome ranch hand in a movie walks into the Roasting Plant on Greenwich and introduces himself as Jonathan. A toothy smile reveals bright teeth, and his jeans, button-down shirt, and red jacket indicate that there's an impressive but not steroidal physique underneath. Even the footwear—that element so many men can screw up despite their best intentions—is a pair of snow boots that manage to be sexy. And the situation gets even better when he opens his mouth: he's funny and quick and can banter. As we talk, I imagine myself encouraging other women to try online dating by confessing that one of the very first guys I'd gone out with had been the one; I even picture us starring in some sort of a Match commercial together.

My feelings about Jonathan start to flag, however, when we're reaching the one-hour mark of our date and I'm still hearing about his job in software sales. I'd asked him about it a few minutes after we'd sat down and he's showing no signs of being ready to abandon the topic anytime soon. Now, I'm open to believing that any job can be interesting if the person who has it finds it interesting but Jonathan appears to be as bored by software sales as I am hearing about it—most of his monologue seems to actually be focused on how horrible his job is. And that banter I'd found so impressive at first begins to grate when I realize it just means he's mocking everything I say before returning to his soliloquy on the day-to-day travails of life in the software sales lane. When he starts talking about a sales conference in Indiana, my mind wanders; I reflect on Helen's comment that "finishing a good book or polishing the silver may enrich your life more in the long run than a free dinner with a drag." When he pauses for a breath, I ask him if he'd like to know anything about me.

His forehead wrinkles. "What do you mean?"

"I mean that we've been here for over an hour and you haven't asked me anything." I'm half saying this because I want to see what he'll do and half because I believe making him aware of this fact is the least I can do for the other women on Match that will go out with him.

He looks confused, blinks. Then he says, "So what do you do?"

I tell him that I'm a writer and he nods but doesn't ask any follow-up questions. Instead he offers, "You sound like you're really bummed about that."

"Not at all." We sit in silence for a moment and then I tell him that I have to go. As we walk outside, I screech when I feel the cold. "I can't believe how freezing it is," I say.

"Are you always this glass-half-empty?" he asks. His smile is self-satisfied.

"I'm sorry?"

"Well, you sounded bummed about being a writer. And now you're like"—he raises his voice an octave to imitate me—"'I can't believe how freezing it is.'"

This is when I understand that there's nothing more I can do for Jonathan's future dates, not only because I can't feel my limbs anymore but also because I'm not certain he would be able take my advice on why you shouldn't mock a freezing woman or tell her she's a pessimist for commenting on the weather on what might be the coldest day of the year. "Good-bye, Jonathan," is all I say as I shiver and walk away from him. Helen advises us to remain "frappe cool" when turning someone down, and while I don't know if I'm turning him down, "cool" certainly does describe the situation. I walk down the street to Stand, a burger café in the West Village, where I'm meeting Zach.

I'm still attempting to defrost from both the temperature and my experience with Jonathan when Zach walks in. He's late but, he explains, it's because he was running an errand for his little sister, who's staying with him. The sweet older brother thing, along with his shy smile and dimples, warm me right up.

"That's a great scarf," he says, pointing to one of the skulls. I'm ecstatic—finally my fashion knowledge has received some recognition!—until I think back to his *Zoolander* photo and wonder if he's gay. But Jonathan's nonstop chatter about software sales and accusations of pessimism make Zach seem extra appealing so I end up not only forgetting about his potential gayness but also about the fact that I'm even on an Internet date. When he explains that the reason he wanted to exchange IMs for so long is that he's been stalked by a few of the women he's met on Match that he didn't suss out sufficiently ahead of time to make sure they were stable, it seems to make a lot of sense. He's handsome and employed, which I assume makes him highly stalkable in a city where, I'm always hearing, the women are all crazy.

He insists on picking up the bill, mumbling something about how I can get it next time (music to my ears if I want to go out with a guy again, a grating alarm if I don't), and then says he wants to put me in a cab since it's too cold for me to walk home. I leave excited—a feeling that only grows when I get an e-mail from him that night in which he says how much he loved meeting me. The concept that the still-very-active adoration I feel for Will could be transferred onto someone else, someone who doesn't already have a wife, is thrilling.

I find Zach on IM the next day. We go back and forth, the banter enlivened, for me anyway, by the knowledge that I'm now attracted to him. It dawns on me after about an hour of this kind of chatter, however, that he isn't initiating another plan.

So I think we should get together, I finally write.

Zach makes a smiley face. Everything in me abhors smiley faces in e-mails and IMs but everything in me also allows everything I abhor to cease to matter if a guy I'm attracted to does it.

When works for you? I continue.

Babe, I'm just in a serious work hole right now, he responds. He adds that he really has to churn things out if he wants to pay off his student loans.

My cursor sits untouched while I consider the fact that Zach must know that telling a woman you're wooing about your unpaid student loans isn't exactly a turn-on. If, biologically speaking, women are seeking out those men who will best be able to provide for our collective offspring, it feels almost instinctive to flinch at this. Then a more disturbing thought crosses my mind: Zach isn't trying to woo me. He's not even interested in seeing me again. Because I can be a slow learner, I reach out to him on IM the next day and ask again about getting together. He's sweet and seems to have all day long to chat back and forth this way but no time to go on a second date. I grasp around for reasons, desperately wanting to believe he's gay, married, or a workaholic—that there's some explanation aside from the fact that he's just not into me. But he seems straight, single, and pretty well adjusted. I wonder if he counts me as one of his stalkers now.

The "Custom Bra Makeover" sign seems to scream at me as I walk by. While I'm not certain what, exactly, a Custom Bra Makeover is, I feel sure I need one. The Zach and Jonathan experience had conspired to make me start ignoring Match e-mails again, and I needed a new project. Why not my breasts? Besides, the week before Christmas seems just as good a time as any to give myself this gift.

When I first moved to New York, I met a girl at a dinner party who had told me about "the bra man"—some guy who, with a tape measure, some boob knowledge, and a good dose of wizardry, would whip you up a brassiere that worked better than you ever imagined one could. She offered to take me to see him and I had wanted to go but we never exchanged information or ended up seeing each other again and Google searches for "the bra man" in New York resulted only in information about a band called the Chuck Braman Jazz Trio.

Yet now I've stumbled upon Ripplu, a sunny shop in the Flatiron district that promises something similar. I enter the store, announce my interest in a custom bra makeover, and am whisked into a dressing room where a sweet and efficient long-haired Asian woman wearing a sexy full-length girdle joins me.

"Size?" she asks as she twirls me around and measures my rib cage and breasts.

"34C." She looks at me skeptically and then leaves the dressing room. I stand there, still topless, wondering if I'm supposed to be following her. Suddenly she's back, holding several black bras labeled Chantelle. I don't bother to cover my chest; Ripplu is clearly no place for modesty.

"You're a D," she announces.

"Oh, no—I'm a C," I explain. "I've always been a C."

She shakes her head. "D."

"You mean I've been buying the wrong size bra for decades?"

She nods. "You will be much happier now."

"Happier?" How can I be happy after having found out that I've been trapping my most womanly assets in a contraption a full size too small? And why hasn't anyone confronted me on the matter before?

"Put this on now," she insists, handing me the first of the bras she's brought. It's tight and has a lot of lift and I notice an enormous difference from the one I'd walked in wearing. Then she says, "We have a system here," and before I have a chance to ask what she means, she reaches for my left boob and pulls it over and up into the cup and then does the same to my right one. I'm a bit shocked by her manhandling, especially when she keeps showing me the system until she's satisfied. When she's done, I put my shirt on and, looking in the mirror, notice that my breasts are incredibly high up—closer, it seems, to my chin than to my stomach. The saleswoman looks pleased. "Come out here now," she says, opening the dressing room curtain.

As I walk out, the two other saleswomen and another customer make a half circle in front of me, oohing and ahhing. "Beautiful," murmurs one while another beams with such pride that I wonder if she's Mrs. Chantelle, the bra designer. I feel like I'm participating in some sort of an ancient female ritual and half expect the group to burst into applause.

I return to my dressing room to try on the other bra and the saleswoman accompanies me. "Always fasten on the loosest hook," she instructs—something my mom told me when we bought my first bra. But this woman has a lot more to say on the matter. "After 10 times, you switch to the second hook," she says. "Ten more times, move to the final one." I nod as if I'm someone who really would keep track of the number of times I wore a bra. "Then you bring it in here for alterations."

"Alterations?" I ask, thinking I must have misheard her. "*Bra* alterations?"

"Oh, yes," she says. "Of course." We exit the dressing room together and my now uplifted breasts receive as much attention as they did before.

"How long should a bra last?" I ask the assembled group. This is something I've wondered about and inquired of many people over the years but I seem to always receive a different answer. If these ladies don't know, no one does.

"Two months," my saleswoman responds casually, as if there could be no other option. I reflect, with shame, on the bras I've kept around for years. Dear God, no wonder I'm single. She adds, "You need to wash the bra after every time you wear it." I nod but know I won't.

I end up buying both bras and Ripplu's special hand-washing detergent and as she rings me up, she says, "You know breasts are 80 percent fat." I give her a you-don't-say face and silently will her to not tell me any more disgusting breast facts I don't want to hear. On my way home, I think about how my friends will probably start rushing up to me and asking me if I've had a boob job, about how men may start gaping in the streets, about the number of times I'm going to have to write out and spell Ripplu for the hordes of women who will certainly want to follow in my stead. But no one gives me a second look as I make my way to my apartment, and at a party later that night, my breasts receive nary a mention. "How do my boobs look?" I finally ask Molly.

She gazes at me oddly. "Fine," she responds, glancing down. "Why? Is there something wrong with them?" Then, sympathetically: "Oh, do they hurt because you have your period?"

Lowering my voice, I say, "I got a custom bra makeover."

I don't explain that I'm not sure how customized it was, seeing as the saleswoman just brought out a few bras and then copped a feel, but she doesn't seem all that interested, anyway.

"Cool," she says. She looks at my chest again. "That's great."

"Well, don't you want to go get one, too?" I ask.

"Maybe," she says before changing the subject.

But I don't care that much that no one is marveling at my fabulous new breasts—I love the way the bras feel underneath my Kendall-approved tops and Dana-selected sweaters. And one morning when I'm adding jewelry to my outfit, I suddenly realize that the reason I'd always eschewed fashion is the same the reason I avoided my Rollerblades all those years: I didn't want anyone to see my trying. If people notice that I'm making an effort, then I'll feel vulnerable, and feeling vulnerable reminds me too much of being the little girl my family laughed at when she cried. Still, I realize that if you don't try, you don't ever end up finding the beautiful park by the Hudson River.

I look like I'm trying now. And you know what? It feels good.

CHAPTER SIX

The Outside Me

A beautiful outside has a way of making the most rational, charming and intellectual man go all apart.

— *Sex and the Single Girl*

Outside beauty is, of course, determined by the society that we inhabit. And because, alas, we don't live in Rubenesque times, today beautiful means thin. Despite the fact that this standard wasn't quite so established in Helen's time—Marilyn Monroe, after all, was hardly a waif—many women acted like it was. You don't see a lot of body fat on *Mad Men* and Helen certainly never bought into the notion that a few extra pounds were acceptable.

I'm not exactly unfamiliar with this mentality. Enough of my so-called high school friends starved themselves, swallowed laxatives by the handful, or puked up lunch in the school bathrooms that asking one of them if they had a tampon usually elicited an oh-I-haven't-gotten-my-period-in-years laugh. My family also verges on the obsessive—my dad spends several hours at the gym these days and, when I was growing up, my mom went on weeklong popcorn diets while my brother didn't feel right until he'd run at least 10 miles that day. We also endured regular comments from my grandmother on my dad's side, who liked to greet us with either an approving "You look thin" or a concerned "You've put on weight" whenever we visited her.

For some reason I can't explain—but it might have to do with the fact that fully anesthetizing myself with drugs and alcohol didn't leave a lot of room for extracurricular obsessiveness—I've never had an eating disorder. Starving myself has always felt simply out of the question, vomiting is about the most torturous experience I've ever endured, and my one experiment with laxatives left me in abject misery and unable to be anywhere but four steps from a toilet at all times.

That doesn't, of course, mean that my attitude about weight is normal. I occasionally find women who are verging on—or even suffering from—genuine eating disorders impressively skinny. A lot of the time, I consider bread to be the root of all evil. My mood can absolutely be determined by the number I read on the scale. And there's no denying the fact that I have an exercise addiction: I aim to work out seven days a week, usually make it about five, and beat myself up incessantly on the two ones I miss. I waste no time at the gym, forcing myself to go to the hardest classes, making sure to alternate—say, boxing one day and spinning the next and yoga the one after that—so that my body doesn't grow accustomed to the workout and is thus always being pushed to its limits. The truth is that I relate to Helen's attitude about exercise, and the woman was back to working out a week after getting a hysterectomy and once told the *New York Times* that her ideal weight was 95 pounds.

Because of my exercise devotion, people oftentimes mistake

me for someone who eats well. They see muscles and start talking about raw food this and tempeh that, not realizing that they're making my stomach turn. Helen, however, is a true health nut, convinced that eating specific high-protein low-fat foods not only keeps women attracting desirable men but also can make us "sexy, vibrant and unmorose about being single." Though the recipes she lists in *S&SG* contain oil, butter, and sugar, she makes it perfectly clear that those foods are for feeding dates but have nothing to do with how we should be eating on a day-to-day basis.

Helen's conversion to this way of thinking was, it sounds, sudden and extreme: one day, exhausted and feeling insecure after working at the Miss Universe Beauty Pageant for two weeks, she stumbled into a Southern California health food store called Lindberg Nutrition and had a revelatory experience with its owner, Gladys. Apparently, Gladys Lindberg took one look at the future editor of *Cosmo* and diagnosed her as vitamin deficient. Soon, Helen was drinking Lindberg's Serenity Cocktails, eating liver, and feeling transformed.

Something about Helen's description of Gladys Lindberg leads me to believe that this Lindberg woman wasn't young in the '60s so I don't expect to turn up much when I start researching her. To my surprise, however, I discover that Lindberg Nutrition is a still-thriving business with locations in both Manhattan Beach and Torrance. I call and ask about Gladys. While I'm informed that she's long gone, I'm cheerfully told that her daughter Judy runs the business now and offers free nutrition counseling on Thursday and Saturday mornings. This seems almost too good to be true: I can have a Lindberg experience just like Helen! Even better yet, I'm already planning to be in L.A. the following week.

When I first land, I expect to be overwhelmed with thoughts and feelings about Will since it's my first time in town since we met, but I'm relieved to note that I feel much the way I always do when I arrive: as if the two years I've been in New York haven't happened and I still live in L.A. the way I did for the decade before I came to Manhattan; in other words, Los Angeles is still Los Angeles, and not an ode to my experience with him.

That Saturday, I drive my rental out to Torrance, where I discover that Lindberg Nutrition isn't some quaint little boutique but a large vitamin emporium of sorts. It reminds me of an Auto Zone, but instead of aisles filled with tires and amplifiers, it's overflowing with vitamins and powders and energy bars. Overwhelmed, I ask a man with a ponytail where Judy's nutrition counseling is taking place. He introduces himself as Jeff, explains that he's the store's general manager, and says that unfortunately, Judy took an impromptu trip to Palm Springs so there won't be any nutrition counseling today. Disappointed, I explain to him that I'd still like to potentially go through the same transformation that Helen Gurley Brown did.

Jeff looks at me oddly. "Who?"

"Helen Gurley Brown," I answer, taken aback. I'd assumed that my guru had been the one that had put Lindberg Nutrition on the map—that she was at least in some way responsible for the size of the vitamin megastore we're now standing in. "She wrote *Sex and the Single Girl*? The book that every woman in the '60s read? Gladys Lindberg was mentioned in it?"

"I'm afraid that doesn't ring a bell," he says, somewhat

apologetically. Then he smiles brightly. "But Judy wrote a book. Do you want to see it?"

I nod and Jeff walks me over to a book section so that he can hand me *Aging Without Growing Old*, a tome—that looks like it's 600 pages—and has a photo of Judy on the cover. I know that six pages of information about aging without growing old might put me to sleep, let alone 600. "I'm probably not going to have time to get through that," I admit. "Could you possibly encapsulate what it says?"

He says he can try and starts telling me all about how important it is to be healthy, especially as we age. He breaks the Lindberg philosophy down into three main components: multivitamins, fish oil pills, and protein.

"Oh, that's great!" I exclaim, feeling like I've aced a test I didn't even have to study for. "I eat chicken pretty much every day so I already get lots of protein and I've been taking fish oil pills for years."

"A piece of chicken only contains 20 to 25 grams of protein," Jeff says gravely. "And we should all be having half a gram for every pound of body weight."

"That makes sense. Helen said 51 grams a day is a good goal."

"Who?" His ponytail swishes forward as he tilts his head.

"Helen—never mind. So how am I supposed to get the rest of the protein I need?"

"From whey protein shakes," he says, and then we're walking over to the whey protein shake part of the store. We go through the various kinds—he shows me regular, chocolate, and soy—and he explains how filling and not-fattening all of this is. "Each one only has four grams of carbs, two grams of fat and 130 calories," he relays enthusiastically. "And if you have two a day, you're almost at your protein requirement."

I try to picture myself drinking two protein shakes a day but can't; it's hard enough to imagine myself even owning a blender. "And what am I going to get out of all this protein?" I ask.

"It will help you to be leaner and stronger and more fit. Also less hungry."

All of those things sound good to me, so by the time we've walked back to the vitamins, I'm already fantasizing about the blender I'm going to buy and the shake drinker I'm going to become. Then Jeff starts telling me about the importance of taking vitamins in a pack—explaining that Lindberg is the company that invented the packet of vitamins and that all the other places offering them are copycats. I'd never given much thought to packets of vitamins except to see them in delis and wonder who would ever buy them besides people with hangovers looking for a miracle cure. "I don't even take a multivitamin," I confess.

Jeff looks a bit horrified. "I understand," he says somberly.

I don't explain to him that multivitamins sort of make me sick, that people always say they don't really do any good, and that whenever I've gone through multivitamin phases in the past, I haven't felt any different. But I somehow feel the need to explain that I appear to be doing all right despite my supposed nutritional deficiencies. "You know, I don't really get sick—I mean, maybe once a year," I tell him. "And I have an insane amount of energy. My problem is that I don't get tired." This is, for better or worse, my lot in life: I fantasize about being able to nap, sleep in, relax—all those things that most people want to do less of—but my system seems to be permanently set in Energizer Bunny mode. My pulses, according to every acupuncturist who's felt them, reflect this and often inspire these acupuncturists to urge me to start meditating. I then tell them that I already do meditate—that I learned transcendental meditation shortly after getting sober and, most days, do it for 20 minutes in the morning and 20 in the afternoon—and we're both silent while I consider what a mess I would be without meditation while the acupuncturist thinks about whatever it is acupuncturists think about before we typically conclude that, all things considered, I'm doing just fine.

"Oh, but you will as you get older," Jeff says, adding that, like my metabolism, my energy level is on a downward slope.

"My metabolism is much better than it used to be," I counter. This is, for reasons I don't understand, true.

Jeff looks skeptical. "Well," he says, "after 40, that will all change." It occurs to me that Jeff isn't so much a vitamin salesman as he is the voice of doom. "But everything we suggest will help your metabolism. Especially the protein."

"So am I going to feel different if I do all of this?" I ask. "Happier? I mean, am I going to notice a change?" I stare into his protein-nourished eyes.

"You'll just be more healthy," he answers.

I thank him and poke around the different aisles, wondering whether vitamin salespeople are completely full of it—swindlers trying to make money by convincing you that you won't be okay unless you buy what they tell you to. Ultimately, though, I realize that it doesn't matter. This project is about me following Helen's recommendations, and Helen found what

Lindberg had to offer crucial. Maybe it's like horoscopes or even spirituality—if you're a believer, it becomes true for you, and if you're not, it all seems like nonsense. And even if this isn't entirely, scientifically accurate, there's something to be said for trying to do everything you can to look and feel your best. Plus the mind is very powerful and, to a certain extent, determines our reality. So if I choose to believe that protein powder and vitamins are going to "chase away my single girl blues" the way they did for Helen, then who's to say they won't?

I leave with a Lindberg Nutrition catalog, the Lindberg newsletter ("Whey protein promotes greater satiety!") and the information that both Regis Philbin and Arnold Schwarzenegger are Lindberg customers. Back in my hotel room, I order a three-month supply of Pink Pack vitamins—an enormous bottle filled with sealed-off packets—and five pounds of unflavored whey protein powder. That's roughly three months of vitamins and five pounds of protein powder more than I want, but Helen never said transitioning into a health nut was easy.

Once I'm home and my order arrives, I'm determined to enthusiastically embrace Project Lindberg. Jeff had told me to use one cup of water for every scoop of protein powder, saying that if I wanted a "creamier" concoction, I could use milk instead. For some reason, the notion of milk and protein powder together sounds far more disgusting than the concept of water and protein powder together so I add a cup of water to my newly purchased blender, along with a package of fresh pineapple chunks. At the last second, however, I panic that a cup of water and some pineapple chunks won't be able to combat what could be a nasty taste of powder, and toss in another cup of water before adding the powder and hitting blend.

I realize my mistake when I pour the drink into a glass—um, glasses. Two cups of water plus pineapple plus protein powder makes an ungodly amount of protein shake, and the effort to down three large glasses of the stuff is more than I can handle. Also, it turns out that I didn't blend it enough because I stumble upon large clumps of the powder. So I put the task aside for the day and silently promise Jeff I'll get the proper amount of protein tomorrow.

One of my missions down, I take a vitamin packet out of the jar and stare at it, uninspired. My mom often talks about how my grandmother always gave her vitamins she hated so much that she fed them to their pet bird—who, she swears, ate them. I wonder if vitamin disgust is genetic as I wash the contents of the packet down with water.

For the next few weeks, I swallow the vitamins and drink the drinks, reminding myself how good they are for me to keep myself from gagging. Then one day when I'm on the phone with Elizabeth, the effort to force down a shake I detest feels like too much. "I just think protein is meant to be consumed in food," I say.

"I think you're right," she says. Then she tells me that she's pregnant.

"What?" I almost drop my glass of clumpy protein drink on the ground. "So it worked?" It seems like only last week she went in for the insemination, and now she's already growing a baby? A familiar ache rises in me—the feeling that someone close to me has something I'm scared I'm not ever going to get—but as she tells me that, yes, the process worked and no, she can't quite believe it herself, I instantly see how insane my thinking is. She's my friend and she wanted this and now it's happening and it has nothing to do with me. I don't know if it's that I just shoved my face in my own selfishness or if it's because Elizabeth is laughingly promising me that she's not going to become "one of those women you want to kill because she only talks about her pregnancy," but my own anguish disappears as quickly as it came on and I feel genuinely happy for her.

"Are you scared?" I ask.

"You know, for some reason I'm not," she says. A pause and then she asks, "So are you going to keep taking those packets of vitamins every day?"

"Wait, forget my vitamins," I respond. "Tell me more about being pregnant."

"Please. What else is there to say? I'm pregnant and I'm going to stay pregnant until I give birth. Your vitamins sound a lot more interesting."

We both laugh, but the truth is that my vitamins aren't interesting at all. Yet I keep taking them—until the January day that I come down with a vicious cold, feel betrayed by my massive vitamin medley, and make the conscious decision to rebel and stop. I know that my behavior isn't logical—that I'm not exacting any kind of revenge on Jeff from Lindberg Nutrition or the untaken vitamins by aborting the mission—but I simply can't motivate myself to unwrap those little packets anymore. As penance, I increase my fish oil pill consumption and also add echinacea to the mix.

Then I commit to trying the drink that changed it all for Helen and dart off to the vitamin store for calcium lactate and brewer's yeast so I can make a Gladys Lindberg Serenity Cocktail (Helen optimistically reprints the recipe in *S&SG*). Once I have everything gathered, I follow the recipe—placing chunks of pineapple, oil, the calcium lactate, vanilla, and milk in the blender and turning it on. I add powdered milk and the brewer's yeast and blend some more.

When I'm convinced that the concoction can't be mixed together any better than it is, I stop and pour. The result is foamy and looks like it might even be delicious—a beverage I could imagine putting in a thermos and taking to work, if I went anywhere outside of my home for work, like Helen recommends.

The first sip goes down all right and my initial impression is that the Serenity Cocktail isn't as disgusting as I'd feared it would be. But by the third gulp, all I can taste is the vanilla and oil—as if the more blending I did, the more I managed to weed the drink down to its most gag-worthy ingredients. But I keep forcing it down and the vanilla taste diminishes but the oil one remains. I think about how women used to give castor oil to babies who were constipated. Or did they give it to themselves to induce labor? Whatever it was, the goal, as far as I can recall, was to get the stomach to eject or release, which is what my stomach feels like it will do if I continue this process. I put the drink on my counter.

Determined to follow at least some of Helen's nutrition recommendations, I begin scanning through the diet books she recommends in *S&SG*—weird '60s artifacts like *Let's Eat Right to Keep Fit* by Adelle Davis, *Stop Dieting! Start Losing!* by Ruth

West, *Stay Young & Vital* by Bob Cummings, and *How to Keep Slender and Fit After Thirty* by Bonnie Prudden. But they recommend things like keeping a "daily eat sheet," substituting powdered milk for regular milk, adding wheat germ to various foods, and other ideas I know I won't try.

So I begin studying her specific food advice from her book, such as snacking on peanuts, celery, apples, oranges, and Romanoff soups, and using wheat flour instead of white and soy oil instead of olive. At the market, I begin buying carrots, celery, apples, and oranges. No one's heard of Romanoff soup and I have an equally difficult time finding soy oil—the closet thing I can find is one that's a mix of canola, olive, and soy. An Internet search when I'm home assures me that soy oil is the same thing as vegetable oil, information that seems unlikely (how could Helen be recommending Crisco?), but believing it is convenient, so I do.

I start chopping the carrots and celery into the sort of small pieces that might be packed in a child's lunchbox and stick them in a Ziploc in the fridge; by February, I'm pleased to note that I'm regularly reaching for them when my afternoon munchies cravings hit—either forgoing the 100-calorie pack of chocolate-covered pretzels that I really want or at least grabbing both on the same trip to the kitchen because, I believe, snacking on carrots and celery should earn me this as a reward.

Helen's other food advice isn't exactly unfamiliar to me— such as having large quantities of fruit and lightly cooked vegetables, and eating a big breakfast, smaller lunch, and even smaller dinner (she calls it eating "breakfast like a king, lunch like a prince and dinner like a pauper," a phrase that was actually coined by one of her food mentors, *Let's Eat Right to Keep Fit* author Adelle Davis). Though oatmeal, the breakfast that's become my standard over the past few years, isn't particularly sovereign, I begin adding frozen blueberries and raisins to it. I start regularly roasting chickens and making them into a variety of healthy breakfasts, lunches, and dinners, and either having a banana, cherries, or Granny Smith apples for dessert.

Although vegetables and I have long had an antagonistic relationship—my disdain for peppers of all colors, squash, cauliflower, and the like has always been strong—I reason that since I've failed at protein shakes and vitamin taking, I need to learn to like at least one vegetable. I settle on broccoli, which I initially get myself to eat by making sure it's doused in some sort of thick melted cheese but eventually manage to down on its own. While I'm not sure any of this healthy eating makes me look even the slightest bit different, it's nice to be fueling my system with more nutritious grub; I may not be the health nut Helen is, but, in a strange way, my improved eating habits make me feel closer to her.

Helen takes grooming very seriously—and by seriously I mean that she believes a manicure lasts only a week and that "the tiniest row of hair" should be cut every two to three weeks. I tend to be a bit more conservative on the grooming front: I'll get my hair cut just a few times a year and a manicure about once a month. I think that's because doing these sorts of activities makes me think of my grandmother, a woman who got every kind of treatment possible, had no less than 150 face creams—day creams, night creams, winter creams, summer creams, wrinkle creams, eye creams, any kind of cream you can imagine—and who thought plastic surgery was a necessity but open heart surgery an "indulgence" (a direct quote). I must inherently believe that I'm just a step away from extravagant self-indulgence and that if I spend too much time trimming and manicuring and cream applying, I'll suddenly find myself in the sort of vanity spiral that my mother so resented in her mother. But Helen's attitude helps me to see that regularly planting myself in a chair in some sort of a salon isn't a sign of wasteful excess but a way to drive home the idea that I'm worth spoiling.

So I focus on a paragraph in *S&SG* where Helen mentions how she and her friends Marguerite and Veronica had a "nice woman" come to their office every week to comb and brush their hair and massage their scalps. It sounds like this woman had her work cut out for her since, Helen explains, she used seven brushes and seven combs in order to distribute their hair oil and "give the scalp a real workout." How I want to call this nice woman—or any nice woman!—and have her come to my home with her 14 hair tools to work out *my* scalp. And luckily I find, once I look into the matter, that if I can let go of the idea of an at-home treatment, my city offers an array of options—hydrating scalp treatments, something called a NIOXIN Scalp Renew, and more. I settle on a shiatsu scalp massage at a place called Hisako Salon since I'm a sucker for anything that involves the word "shiatsu."

I'm not disappointed. The moment I hand myself over to Yuki and let her begin brushing clay into my follicles and pressing on various points on my head, I start relaxing to the point that it's almost difficult to stay upright and awake. I want to ask

Yuki if she has six other combs in addition to the one she's using on me but I'm not sure why more than one comb would be required for the job and besides, I'm too relaxed to even form such words. I do manage to ask her how often one should get a shiatsu scalp massage and want her to tell me every week so that I can justify spending money on this every seven days. Alas, she says that once a month should be enough. I float through the rest of the day, thinking that if what I've just experienced is ridiculous self-indulgence, I want to know where I can sign up for more.

Another Helen recommendation I'm able to implement quite easily is "gooping" on cream at bedtime. She believes that women should don soft white cotton gloves afterward and while I know I won't do that—would I even be able to sleep while wearing soft white cotton gloves?—I start putting lotion on both my hands and ever-dry feet. And I can't quite believe what a difference this makes: I'd essentially resigned myself to having rough, calloused feet, assuming it was the price one paid for the kind of foot abuse that comes from regular exercise. I'd make occasional rash and silly moves to combat the issue, buying egg-shaped products that promised to scrape away all dead skin but then only use them when I took baths, which was almost never. But I find a few weeks after dousing my feet with special foot lotion that this eradicates any need for spontaneously ordering absurd foot products that probably don't work. The ritual grows ever more elaborate until it eventually includes not only special foot creams but also hand creams, cuticle creams, dry lip creams, and after-sun creams for my always-burned upper chest. Apparently I am my grandmother's granddaughter after all.

Then there are suggestions of Helen's that fall into the "big change" department—those "expensive and think-twice-about-it investments," she writes, that could "push you over the edge into real beauty." One of the items on this list is using a "face saving" machine—something I fantasize about tracking down, even though I have no idea what it could possibly be. Her description—a "small electrotherapy machine" that "exercises facial muscles . . . so that they hold up your skin again"—doesn't help elucidate matters but she writes that she bought hers from someone named Venner Kelsen for $250. I have no idea who this Venner Kelsen person could be—I picture a Christopher Lloyd in *Back to the Future* type with wacky, unpatented inventions in his downstairs basement—but once I look into the matter, I learn that he was actually a female skin care legend in the '60s who worked with celebrities like Jack Benny. As I try to recall whether Jack Benny had great skin, I find a Web page that mentions a woman named Vera Brown who was a protégée of Kelsen's and also apparently coined the phrase "Until you're 30, you have the face you were born with and after 30 you have the face you deserve." Brown, it seems, owns a spa in Los Angeles, and while I have to imagine that all "face saving" machines have long since been retired, I figure I can maybe get a treatment or buy a product from Brown and thus still be at least in some way following Helen's advice. But while Vera's Retreat appears to have been in business until quite recently, I reach a dead end when the number I find for it is out of order. I ultimately conclude that since I wear sun block every day, I'm doing plenty of face saving already.

. . .

I have a very odd relationship with makeup. On the one hand, I'm like Narcissus: I've hardly ever met a reflection I haven't felt compelled to gaze at. On the other, I have a longtime dedication to not making any effort to look nice—or even to shower—unless I'm required to do so. Part of this is due to my obsession with working out—the fact that I tend to be planning to go to the gym later leads me to spend many days in sweats or their equivalent until I shower post-workout. If my exercise class is at 7:30 at night, then there goes an entire day where I could have been smelling and looking my best. The notion that I could put myself together once and then exercise, shower, and do it again feels indulgent, impractical, or both.

And then there's the simple fact that I somehow missed the makeup application phase of development. I can't blame my mother for this negligence—she's always had an excellent supply of shadows and powders for me to pilfer or at least practice on, and even a dressing table where I could have indulged. But the activity swept by me—I imagine I was learning to shotgun beers and blow smoke rings while other girls were discovering the finer points of eye and lip liner—so I found myself in my mid-20s with no makeup supplies and nary a clue.

I tried to catch up—earnestly. I'd do my best to put on bronzer and mascara but always ended up feeling like the little girl who'd raided her mother's makeup drawer right after giving herself that haircut that left the bald spot. I'd apply what felt like so much makeup only to have people commend me for not wearing any. And this wasn't because I was doing such a good job at it: I simply wasn't wearing enough for anyone to notice anything. Eventually I semiabandoned the project, concluding that I just wasn't good with my hands and that I'd be better off accepting the fact that makeup was something I would never really be able to do. I'd hear other women say that they felt naked without lipstick, while I found the notion of putting anything on my lips that would leave a lipstick ring on a glass repulsive.

Most of my friends have similarly barefaced tendencies. Shari is probably the most made up of the bunch because she wears lipstick on a daily basis, even if she doesn't apply it every day; she swears by a L'Oreal lipstick called Infallible that stays on so long "it's literally still there the morning after you spend the night."

I know that Helen, who included a 16-step makeup application list in her *S&SG* follow-up *Sex and the Office*, would call the way I put myself together when I do try—a method that involves a roughly 30-second application of under-eye concealer, bronzing powder, and eyeliner—lazy, if not a form of self-sabotage. In *S&SG*, she offers all sorts of recommendations—everything from adding silver, gold, or pink dust sparkles to the lids and making lipstick stay on by blotting over it with tissue and then powder before reapplying and blotting again—but I can't very well go from what I've been doing to a 16-step process: we need to learn to crawl, after all, before we can run marathons.

Baby steps, in this case, means starting to look at beauty magazines. While I'm bored by a lot of what I read—one says that you should always put mascara on your lower lashes while another says that you never should because it makes eyes look "saggy," a debate that intrigues me not at all—my interest is piqued when I stumble upon a page which says that using eyeliner inside your lower lid makes you look older but putting it on the outside of your lids makes you look younger. When I was 12, my best friend assured me that eyeliner needed to be worn on the inside, so I'd been doing it that way ever since. I decide that from now on, I'll apply eyeliner on both the inside *and* the outside, figuring that then I'll at least end up at my correct age.

Yet adding outside-the-lid eyeliner to my regimen wouldn't, I know, cut it with Helen. Indeed, when she writes, "Few women wrest from make-up half the magic it offers," I know she's talking about me. She says that Hal King, who ran Max Factor, believed a woman could do a professional makeup job on herself in 12 minutes, but since it only takes me 30 seconds, I'm not sure what I'm supposed to be doing with those extra 11 and a half minutes.

In late February, I call my makeup artist friend Bee Cohen and ask her to give me her version of the basics. The first step, she tells me, is lighting because women often put on makeup in places that aren't as bright as the places they're going. Since my bathroom light provides about as much luminosity as a flashlight that hasn't been used in a decade, I tell her that I'll start applying my face next to my bedroom window while knowing that the likelihood of my really doing that is about the same as my ever using the phrase "applying my face" in a sentence again. Then we discuss foundation, which Bee says can be mixed with moisturizer if it feels like it's too much. Concealer comes after foundation, she says, adding that the pinkish toned concealers are for under-eyes while the yellow toned ones are for pimples. The joy I feel over my newfound knowledge—I always wondered why concealer came in two colors!—is only slightly diminished when she "reminds" me that you should always apply under-eye concealer with your ring finger since that's where your skin is the thinnest. Before I consider what damage I may have caused my under-eyes, we move on to mascara ("Make a circle with the wand at the top of the tube," she says, "to get the excess mascara off before you put it on") and bronzer ("Smile," says Bee, "then you start the brush at the apples of your cheeks").

From that day forward, I relish my new knowledge—putting on concealer with the right finger, getting the excess mascara off the wand and not onto my eyelashes, and applying bronzer at my cheek apples and not covering over half my face in it. Then I incorporate Helen's elaborate and specific mascara recommendations that involve separating lashes, dusting them with powder, and applying more mascara before brushing, dusting, and brushing them again.

I eventually even transform myself into a lipstick wearer: one night, I'm admiring Molly's freshly lipsticked lips, thinking how polished it makes her look, and ask myself if it makes any sense to avoid this extremely easy method of making myself more attractive because of some vague sense of disgust I have about potentially leaving a ring on a glass. I answer by reaching into my purse, pulling out the tube that I always keep in there but never use, and applying it at the table—an act, I should note, that Helen says is perfectly acceptable. Within seconds, another friend leans over and says, "I love your makeup tonight. I never knew you wore any." This is all it takes to get me to commit.

I must admit that nothing about my life actually changes once I begin making this effort. I'm not suddenly drowning in compliments and the men on Match continue to be as unpalatable as ever. But I don't really care. I feel more attractive—to me. And I'm not impatiently waiting for—or desperately trying to find—the right man to appreciate my newly polished self. I seem to have dropped the hammer—or at least figured out that it's far easier to sit and calmly wait rather than make myself crazy trying to find out where something—or someone—is. When and if he does show up, I figure I'll be ready.

Or at least I'll look like I am.

CHAPTER SEVEN

The Inward Me

Your most prodigious work will be on you.

—*Sex and the Single Girl*

"I'm going to make a penis," a heavyset man declares in a strong European accent. He sits at a pottery wheel crafting a piece of clay into something that is, indeed, quite phallic-looking.

The woman next to him nods. "You should," she says.

I glance from one of them to the other. It's not that I think there's anything necessarily wrong with talking about penises, but I'm here because I finally feel ready to give another item on my fear-conquering list a try, and this simply isn't how I envisioned it going.

"A big, bulging penis!" the man screams. The woman laughs hysterically.

I stare at the man longer than is necessary, hoping to shame him with my gaze. I'm a new student, after all, and he doesn't know that I'm not going to be offended by this penis talk. I could be a total prude. I widen my eyes to further communicate my disapproval.

"A clay cock!" the man declares, and both he and the woman continue howling. They ignore me. Then again, so does everyone else.

It's not that I think the fact that I've finally gotten around to signing up for pottery class means I deserve some sort of parade. But the first day of anything always makes me feel vulnerable, like I'm back in grade school and wondering who will sit with me at lunch. And I'd imagined encountering a group of fellow ceramics neophytes who'd all have the same friendly I-can't-believe-I-signed-up-for-this-either attitude. It would be like camp with clay. We'd share secrets about our lives, gossip over our respective wheels, and giggle when we screwed up and our lumps of clay ended up resembling lumps of clay rather than beautiful pottery. Because Match has been such a black hole, I'd even allowed myself the luxury of envisioning a dashing male student—sweet, charming, single, possibly even literary, with an inexplicable desire to create pottery. But the penis maker, who has a protruding belly and beady eyes, is one of only two men here. The other's face is wrinkled everywhere that it's not pockmarked, as if the universe couldn't stand the idea of his facial skin not being decorated everywhere. They could, I remind myself, have beautiful souls.

"I'm Anna," I say after my initial queries—about how to get started and what to do—are ignored.

This appears to have been the right thing to say because it causes the penis maker to look right at me. "Oh, that's good!" he brays. Is he Israeli? Russian? He nods his head in the direction of the woman who'd laughed at his cock making. "She's Anna, too."

Anna, who has straight black hair and a willowy frame, doesn't look up from the perfect vase she's crafting, but this remark motivates the other man to come forward and identify himself as the night's teacher. "You're going to have to make it very clear which is your work so it doesn't get mixed up with Anna's," he says, uttering the name Anna with the same reverence the penis maker had. It's clear that my namesake is the star of the Chelsea Ceramic Guild. "I'll be with you soon," he adds.

Pleased to have been acknowledged, I sit at a wheel and watch the teacher and Anna and the penis maker and a few other silent but dedicated-looking students spin their wheels and then massage their clay with precise movements until they seem to have created order out of chaos.

Roughly a half hour later, the teacher sits at the wheel next to mine and says that I should watch him. I nod, as if I haven't been watching him for the past 30 minutes, and stay quiet as he balls up clay, tosses it onto his wheel, and then wets it. "The centering is the hardest part," he explains as his hands shape the clay vertically and then bring it down into something resembling the original lump. As the wheel keeps spinning, he holds his fingers on the inside of the clay, pulling the sides out and back in as he lists various tips and instructions I need to remember.

Of course, by the time I'm allowed to start my own project, I've forgotten everything. But I don't really care. Because setting the wheel in motion, wetting my hands, and then wrapping them around a piece of clay brings me back to some earlier, simultaneously disgusting and delightful mud-playing stage. The main way I use my fingers these days is to punch out letters on a keyboard, so to have them involved in some other purpose—a primal and squishy purpose—feels somehow restorative. And it reminds me of writing: the act of patiently smoothing out a mess. I'm a creative person, at peace, communing with my higher self.

But not for long. Because, it turns out, I'm doing everything wrong. What was once centered is now off-center. What had been perfect clay now contains air bubbles. And my positioning is apparently incorrect as well.

"You need to dig your elbows into your thighs and lean over like this," the teacher says. I try to copy what he's doing but my legs and torso must be too short because my body won't allow my elbows to stay embedded in my thighs unless I twist my neck into a painful position. I work that way despite how uncomfortable I am and think I'm making progress until my nearly beautiful creation suddenly has a massive hole in its side. The teacher shakes his head. "That's unsalvageable," he declares before he, Anna, Penis Man, and the other people make a dinner plan. "And," he says to me over his shoulder, "class is over."

The following Tuesday, I'm overwhelmed with dread for the four or so hours before class. I tell myself it's my same old fear I always feel and that soon enough I'll look back and laugh at this initial reticence. I'll be like the other Anna, who I overheard tell the Penis Man that she looks forward to being in the studio all week long. But the night doesn't go well: my biggest problem, aside from a basic inability to make my hands do what I want them to, is that I don't understand what centered means—when the clay looks perfectly fine to me, I'm informed that it's completely off, and on the rare occasions that I manage to luck into some centering, I assume it's wrong.

The next week, it becomes clear to me that what this place offers isn't so much classes as a room with pottery wheels where obsessed ceramicists who have been doing their thing for the past decade or so can be together. Beginners come along only sporadically, I'm told. By the end of class, I've managed to sort of make a bowl, but the frustration I felt getting there—annoying the teacher with my ineptness and watching my classmates craft gorgeous pieces while laughing with each other—leaves me more overwrought than proud.

About an hour before the following Tuesday's class, I have what feels like a profound epiphany. Roughly translated, it's that I hate, absolutely hate, ceramics. And more specifically, I really hate this class. It makes me feel alienated, irritated, and like there's something wrong with my ability to take in information and translate it to my hands.

Then I have a related epiphany: *I don't have to go.* Yes, I paid for the class up front and wasting money is never a good idea, but if I spend an entire day in a state of dread over what I have to do that night, then I'm not following what Helen recommends because I'm not celebrating my life in any way. Sure, I'll never have a Patrick Swayze type seduce me when I'm working on a ceramics wheel, but since I don't have my own pottery wheel, the only place that could happen would be at the Chelsea Ceramics Guild, and that's about the last place on earth I'd ever want to be seduced. Besides, I know that Helen would say that making an effort is good enough. She writes, after all, that you "can start lots of things you don't finish."

Going out to dinner with a now-showing Elizabeth that night instead of leaning over a ceramics wheel cursing my own incompetence feels incredibly liberating. And I don't even beat myself up for being a dropout because by now, I've already committed to crossing the next item off my fear-conquering list.

Je ne comprends pas," I say. It's a sentence I've grown quite accustomed to uttering lately.

The initial couple of weeks had been so easy! An online test had placed me into an accelerated class and my teacher and fellow classmates weren't anything like the incestuous group of ceramicists I'd abandoned. Although none was devastatingly sexy, none was shrieking about how they needed to learn the French word for "penis," either, so I'd figured I was making out well. My high school French came right back to me and I was delighted to be asking my fellow students their names, how they were, and where they lived.

By class number three, I began to understand why I might have felt so drawn to those midday bong hits back in high school: French was fucking impossible. At that point, we were on the various tenses—why, oh why, must we have to learn and understand *le futur proche?*—and I cursed myself for not having just signed up for the non-accelerated course.

We're now in the sixth week and I've grown accustomed to feeling stupid. Because my brother is a genius and his intelligence has always been so universally praised, I spent most of my childhood believing I must be a raving idiot. It wasn't until I got sober and found work I enjoyed that it began to occur to me that I might actually be smart, too. But the confidence I have in that arena is paper-thin; one or two incidents where I can't keep up and I'm back to thinking I have a learning disability. Still, following Helen's suggestions has imbued me with a new confidence and so I do something I've never done before and admit out loud in class that I'm confused. Even more surprisingly, this seems to take the shame out of the feeling.

At the same time, everything in me wants to drop out, just stop showing up the way some other people have. But I remind myself that one of the reasons I took on this project was to prove that change is possible. I don't have to always be the girl whose family laughed at her when she cried or the girl who can't be in a relationship. I can be whoever I want to be, provided I'm willing to not give up even when it's difficult. Besides, Helen writes that "you may have to 'discipline' yourself to care where a fire engine is going," and while I'm not altogether certain what that means, I feel like it has something to do with how I should stick it out and simply accept the fact that I won't understand everything. I'm not going to speak French perfectly—I'm really not even going to speak it well—but putting in an appearance and spending about half the time confused is far better for my future knowledge of French than not going at all.

When our teacher hands out the final exam, I come clean and explain that I probably won't be able to do it. Part of me feels like a complete and utter failure—I'm two for two in terms of trying new activities and failing at them—but I also know that I did my best in both cases, that I can't force myself to like and be good at things when I'm simply not, and that I met my goal, which was to put myself in challenging situations by trying new activities. "*Pas de problem*," the teacher says, giving me a cheerful smile and leaving me with a profound appreciation for grade-less adult education. But my appreciation that I get to lounge on a Caribbean island in order to conquer the final two activities on my list is even greater.

Kite surfing is very difficult," explains the tan, lean, shirtless British guy manning the desk at Vela Windsurfing, a combination windsurfing school and café on the beach of Cabarete in the Dominican Republic. "It takes weeks to learn. Most of us have devoted our lives to it."

"Devoted your lives?" I ask, staring into his eyes, trying to discover a clue to explain how someone could devote his life to this activity. But they're blank, albeit a bit red. John, a close friend of mine for the past 10 years is standing behind the kite-surfing devotee, raising an eyebrow.

We're here because when I told John that I'd vowed both to travel more and to conquer my fear of water-based activities, he'd jokingly said he'd be happy to help me by accompanying me to a Caribbean island; then he paused and said that he wasn't actually kidding. I picked the Dominican Republic, and he selected the beach city of Cabarete, but neither of us realized until we got here that we'd landed in one of the kite-surfing capitals of the world.

In the few days since we'd arrived, I'd resolved that I wasn't going to allow myself to be limited by a fear established three decades ago and had forced myself to swim in the ocean, though not too far out. I'd even liked it. But standing on something in the water—participating in a sport that requires not only letting go of my fear of shark teeth sinking into me but also having to learn an entirely new skill—still terrifies me.

The British guy is raving about how there's nothing like kite surfing and how it's the greatest high he's ever known and how he'll do it until the day he dies, but despite his enthusiasm, this "weeks to learn" news has me discouraged. I ask him if they teach regular surfing, and he says they don't but they do offer windsurfing. Then I hear myself say that I'd like to try that.

"You're going to love it," he declares, and I want to believe him but he doesn't know about my formative years' experience with *Jaws*, plus it's difficult to have much faith in someone who's abandoned whatever he had back in England to devote his life to a sport involving a kite. But I agree to come back in a few days for a one-on-one lesson with him. He then launches into a mini lecture about the basics of windsurfing that I have some trouble listening to because, I realize, I'm suddenly but unmistakably attracted to him.

"What's your name, by the way?" I ask coquettishly as soon as he finishes explaining something about upwind and down-wind.

"Martin," he answers, and goes back to what he was saying.

"I'm Anna," I say and give him my most winning smile. Now, I know that Helen probably wouldn't approve of Martin's long-term potential—the woman's advice in *S&SG* is nothing if not practical and though she never spelled out the fact that upwardly mobile men are the only ones worth focusing on, she surely wouldn't consider a kite-surfing instructor who appears to be in his 20s a solid choice. Still, she encourages us to surround ourselves with men in general in order to keep up morale, and Martin suddenly seems quite good for my morale, indeed.

As he continues his windsurfing lecture, I ask, "So what is it about kite surfing that you love? Why do you like it better than, say, surfing or windsurfing?"

He gazes out at the ocean and then looks back at me. "I can't quite explain it. It's just . . . when you're up there over the water, it's like . . . the best feeling in the world."

Discovering that my instructor isn't a wordsmith does nothing to diminish my crush on him. "Well, I'm really looking forward to my lesson," I say. I smile again, wishing that I'd thought to put on makeup before walking over to Vela.

Just then I hear "I feel the same way when I'm walking on water" from behind Martin, and I realize it's John, who I'd completely forgotten existed since I'd fallen for this kite-surfing-obsessed Englishman. The last thing I need right now is a gay guy—even a gay guy who happens to be one of my best friends—cramping my style as I try to Mrs. Robinson my so far unresponsive teacher. So I ignore John and hope Martin will do the same.

Instead Martin laughs and John adds, "I learned to walk on water a few years ago. There's nothing like it." Martin laughs again and I wonder if he's gay, if he thinks John is my boyfriend, or if he couldn't care less about these two grinning Americans standing in front of him. I give Martin a shrug that's meant to imply that I'm not even sure who this silly jokester is but he's looking back at the water again.

The morning of my windsurfing lesson, I feel a little depressed. I've come to understand that in situations like this, what I call depression is usually just unacknowledged feelings of terror. But in the same way that being aware of the fact that my monthly oversensitivity is caused by PMS doesn't do anything to diminish that oversensitivity, cognizance of my fear only makes me feel both depressed *and* scared. I remind myself that I'm here to celebrate my life as a powerful, independent, free woman: *I am woman, watch me windsurf.*

The instruction begins with Martin taking out a dry erase board and drawing arrows and stick figures on it so that he can go into a far more detailed version of the upwind and downwind lecture from the other day. I can tell that what he's saying is at about a third-grade level but I'm not as focused as I need to be since I'm now wondering how long it took him to get so tan. Aren't British people supposed to have a harder time tanning because their skin doesn't have enough melanin in it? And how is his color so evenly distributed? Suddenly, as if the volume's just been turned on, I hear Martin ask, "So which way is downwind then?"

I look at the dry erase board. Some arrows point in one direction and other arrows in the other. Fifty-fifty chances are more appealing than admitting I have no idea. "This?" I ask, pointing to one side of the board.

The way Martin smiles shows me that I'm wrong, and I feel humiliated. I'm the raving idiot again. But I'm also a little angry. I came here to confront my fear of water and revel in my independence, to align myself with nature and to feel the power of Mother Earth through the ocean waves. Or, at the very least, to flirt with a cute British boy. I hadn't expected to be tested on my ability to comprehend various concepts of aerodynamics on a dry erase board. "Why don't we move to the sand?" he suggests. I nod enthusiastically.

Much to my horror, the board-on-the-beach lesson taps into

that same uncomprehending part of my brain. Or perhaps I'm so blinded by fear of what I'm about to go do that I simply can't focus. Maybe I don't really even have a crush on him but just think I do because it's another way my subconscious has found for me to distract myself. As he shows me different foot positions and tells me what various parts of the board are called, I feel overwhelmed and finally say that maybe the best thing would be for him to stop giving me any new information and just tell me the crucial things I need to remember. I can see that I've disappointed him, but he smiles and says that I really only need to worry about putting my right foot back, keeping my right arm bent, placing my left foot forward, and straightening my left arm.

We go to the water and Martin says he'll stay at the shore and shout instructions. I paddle out without a lot of thought but once there, I think: *I'm in the water, about to try to stand on something*. I can feel my heart beating—a strong and steady sound that seems to be bouncing in the back of my ears. "There's nothing scary here," I say out loud. My legs are dangling in the water and I think about how there could be anything, not just a shark but . . . I don't know, a swordfish or a manta ray—not that I'm even sure what a manta ray is—could be swishing right below my feet. *Mind over matter*, I think. Or is it matter over mind? Either way, I manage to ignore the noise in my head long enough to pull myself onto the board.

But then, once I stand up—something which is much less difficult than I'd imagined it would be—I'm far more focused on making sure I'm sucking in my stomach for Martin than on remembering which foot and arm are supposed to bend. For the first time, I'm grateful for my crush because it's a nice distraction, but concentrating on my stomach and not on what I'm doing causes me to fall three times. By the fourth attempt, I remind myself that if my goal is to impress this guy, I'm far more likely to do that by following his directions than I am with my abs. The next time I stand up, I force myself to concentrate. Right arm bent, left arm straight. Right foot back, left foot forward. And then, amazingly, I'm windsurfing!

"Excellent!" I hear Martin yell from where he treads water. I feel a wave coming and order myself to focus. Some of what Martin had said when we were sitting in front of the dry erase board comes back to me. *A wave has two sides*, he'd told me. *Don't panic when the first one hits—breathe and it will pass.* As I breathe and let it pass, I realize how much I need to follow that direction in my day-to-day life. Then I remember that Martin's other main commandment had been to relax. Why is it that people only tell you to relax when you're lying on a chiropractic table, bracing yourself for a needle that's about to be inserted into your arm, or in some other situation that would make relaxation next to impossible? Standing on a board in the middle of the ocean with a gorgeous guy watching my every move isn't exactly a situation that imbues me with calmness.

I end up falling but then realizing, when I manage to stand again, that my attitude has everything to do with my success. If I decide I won't fall, that's pretty much what happens. But if I doubt my ability and start predicting that I'll probably lose my balance and go plunging into the ocean at any second—as I did during my first three attempts—then I do. This makes me wonder how much my being single is a result of my belief that I'll always be single. Standing in the middle of the Caribbean

Sea, I feel for the first time how it's my mind—not my age or what I do for a living or any of the other reasons I've invented—that's responsible for my not being in a relationship. I believe I can't be in one and so I'm not. I believe I can't stand up and so I fall. The day before, I'd been wading in the ocean during high tide when I suddenly became terrified that a wave would overtake me. Of course, my fears were realized—waves did, indeed, come crashing at my feet, legs, and waist, occasionally pulling me under with their force. But once I dove in and really submerged myself, the waves weren't only manageable—they were quite enjoyable. The key was to let them have control—to either jump up and be carried or dive under and avoid. I couldn't do that when I was still standing at the shore, contemplating how scary the waves looked. But if I surrendered to the experience and committed to going with their rhythm rather than attempting to make them go with mine, I could.

Despite these revelations, after a while I start to feel a little seasick. So I paddle over to Martin and tell him I need a break. I picture us lying on the beach, chatting the way people do once one of them has introduced the other to the activity he loves more than anything else, but he just nods and takes my board out to windsurf.

About 20 minutes later, he comes in and tells me that the waves are getting a bit choppy and I only have a few minutes of my lesson left anyway. He doesn't ask me what I'm doing the rest of my time in town and I don't offer up any information. And though I'm still dying to know what it would be like to touch his lips with my own, a part of me knows that what he's given me is far more important than any kiss.

CHAPTER EIGHT

Behavior Modification

There is a catch to achieving single bliss. You have to work like a son of a bitch.

—*Sex and the Single Girl*

Some of Helen's suggestions sound deceptively simple. Take, for instance, her straightforward three-word sentence, "Smiles are sexy."

You can't say it's not true. But who really works on something like this? One January day when I'm wondering if perhaps some people—say, Mother Teresa or Wayne Dyer or the woman who wrote *The Secret*—have beatific smiles on their faces all the time, a friend mentions that he'd started paying attention to the way people look on the streets of New York. "You wouldn't believe how dour everyone is," he'd said, showing me what he meant by grimacing and deadening his eyes.

"That's so depressing," I'd said.

"Depressing but true."

"Is that how *I* look walking down the street?"

"Probably. I've never seen someone who doesn't."

This motivates me to look up information about smiling,

which is how I learn that a Duchenne smile involves contraction of the zygomatic major muscle and the orbicularis oculi muscle; from what I understand, it just means smiling with your eyes as well as your mouth. The telltale sign that you're doing it is, alas, when your crow's feet show.

Since I've learned this year that no change is too small to end up making a major difference in how I feel, I commit to embarking on Project Duchenne Smile by grinning at everyone I pass while walking the four blocks from the gym to my apartment. I feel good about myself when I return after these jaunts, if not remarkably different. But then something odd happens. I start to notice, even when I'm just in my apartment alone, that my mouth usually tends to be clenched in a frown. I also see it whenever I pass a mirror. I try to figure out if this is the way my mouth is formed or if it's a reflection of my standard mood and think about how babies often have permanent grins on their faces. Even though a smiling baby can just mean that the baby is passing gas, I wonder why that has to change. Does growing up and becoming self-reliant shape all of our smiles into frowns? Do only foolish young people who don't know any better grin all the time?

I decide to amp up my efforts, smiling at everyone I can wherever I'm walking. And the more I do it, the better I understand that this practice is regarded with a great deal of suspicion in Manhattan. Most people passing me immediately look away, as if a brief but happy interaction with a stranger is too much for them to handle. Straight-looking men are the quickest to react this way, while pretty girls, interestingly enough, always gaze back. But their glance is usually followed by a distrustful look, as if I'm a lesbian trying to hit on them or am about to ask if they have a minute for the environment. The one exception: women walking with adorable children or wheeling them in strollers, who almost always return my grins; they, I figure, are used to smiles from strangers and know that the sole risk of returning the favor is potentially being subjected to a conversation about how precious their kid is.

After a week or so of smiling all the time, I start to feel a little creepy. At the same time, now that I've become aware of the typical downward slope of my lips, I can't become unaware. I decrease my street efforts somewhat but keep up the smiles when I'm in my apartment. I have no idea if this improves my mood at all; I actually wonder if it has a negative impact since I'm now spending all this time conscious of my intrinsic frown.

I can imagine what Helen would say: forget about what you're doing with your mouth when only your cats are around to see it! Just smile more around men. But I'm not encountering any men I'm interested in and besides, if I'm in the moment and having a nice time, I'm not thinking about what I should be doing to make myself sexier; if I'm not, I don't want to appear sexy to the person sitting across the table from me. I figure I'll let my mouth off the hook while I look for other ways to improve my behavior.

'm sitting rather happily in Hugo Cory's office on the Upper East Side of Manhattan when he tells me that a woman who cannot see herself married is "usually a very insecure woman." Hugo is a celebrated Israeli life coach and adviser to major corporations who I've come to see because a friend told me that a girl he knew went to him when she decided she wanted a husband and baby and didn't know how to get them.

But right now he's pissing me off. Because even though I'm highly aware of the fact that I'm insecure, I'm still horrified to hear that someone else thinks so. "I know many *married* women who are also very insecure," I counter, feeling ready to give him names if he wants them and also offer up some of Helen's words about how single women are really the strong and confident ones. But I keep that to myself because Hugo—bald, bushy-browed, with the energy of both a drill sergeant and a meditation teacher—intimidates me.

He seems wholly unruffled by my hostile tone. "Of course," he says. "All I'm saying is that if a person has issues and doubts about a particular thing, he or she has to go through a process to change and break the pattern."

This sounds more acceptable. "But how?"

"You have to find a particular way to evoke your fears and then gaze at them." I like the sound of this—it is, in many ways, the point of my project. "Just think," he adds. "If you're scared of dogs, the way to get over that is to get used to them."

I consider this. The other day, a friend had told me that she'd started spending more time around happy couples to better understand what she subconsciously feared. But I'm still feeling insecure for having potentially been called insecure, so I don't share this with Hugo, and even have an urge to tell him that I've never been afraid of dogs. I keep my mouth shut again, though.

Hugo then explains that our imagination is like a series of movies that play in our head which show the "tendencies, patterns, ideas, and habits" collected from our environment, and that these really have nothing to do with our current experience. "Your journey is the liberation from your imagination," he says.

"But imagination isn't always bad, is it?"

"Not once you've changed your attitude," he explains. "Our imagination is like a Hollywood studio—we can show comedy, horror, or drama movies. The problem is that you don't have the key to the studio."

"I don't?"

"No. Most of the time, you're putting energy out in the world on things that are totally useless."

"I am?"

He then talks about how we all get distracted by trying to create a name out in the world when all we need is to figure out our talent, and he manages to connect that concept to the idea that our supermarkets are filled with food but don't really contain anything that's of substance. "We're overwhelmed," he concludes. "Our solar plexuses are trembling."

I nod with the conviction of the newly converted. Everything he's saying is making a remarkable amount of sense and while I don't know where, exactly, my solar plexus is, I have no doubt that mine does, indeed, tremble and is in fact probably trembling right now. "So what should *I* do?" I ask.

I expect his brow to wrinkle as he tries to come up with an answer for such a grand question. Instead he unhesitatingly says, "I highly recommend that you never complain, gossip, curse, or judge people. If you stop doing those four things, you'll be a totally different person."

"Really?" I ask, surprisingly annoyed even though I know Helen would probably agree with him. "I mean, I get that judging and gossiping aren't great. But complaining? Don't we usually figure out our feelings by discussing them with another person?"

"Perhaps, but—"

"Well, sometimes my interpretations are going to be negative. Are you saying that I should only be able to have these conversations if my outlook is positive?" My voice is shrill; I sound incredibly defensive.

"I'm saying that complaining is a negative emotion that causes you to put scenarios out in the world that will later come and hunt you down."

"And not swearing is going to make me into a totally different person?" I huff, not exactly sure why I'm so angry. "That sounds like complete bullshit."

He gazes at me calmly. "Every time you curse, it's a symbol of your frustration."

I want to call bullshit again but instead find myself thinking that if he's right, I've spent hundreds of hours, days, and probably even weeks expressing symbols of my frustration. But he can't be right. Swearing is innocuous, acceptable, *standard*. "I'm sorry but I think that's a little overly idealistic," I finally say. "Not to mention prudish."

Hugo takes another approach. "You never know," he says, "when someone you want to be in a business or personal relationship with will be completely turned off by your cursing. It could be causing opportunities to disappear."

"Please!" I chortle. "I wouldn't want to be in business—or a relationship—with someone who would be that much of a stick-in-the-mud." I can't believe I've just used the phrase "stick-in-the-mud," but I can't quite believe I'm being advised not to swear, either.

"You may think so," Hugo says. Then he tells me about a client of his who lost out on an important business opportunity because of something minor he did that offended and horrified the decision maker. This gets my attention. What if the book or TV deal—or man—of a lifetime had been within my grasp but I'd pushed it away by saying "fuck" a few too many times?

I don't admit that I'm coming around. Instead, because I'm judging myself for not being more open to cutting down on complaining and swearing and also feeling like he may be judging me for the same reasons, I let him know that I meditate 20 minutes every morning and 20 minutes every afternoon. "I've been doing it for over six years," I say, and wait for him to be impressed and tell me that I'm far more like him than he previously realized.

Instead he says, "The path is self-awareness. It's not something we do in the morning before judging, gossiping, and cursing all day long. The path is 24–7 for years. If it's not used daily or hourly, nothing can change."

I nod and hear myself say that I could attempt to follow his suggestions. But at the same time, I can't imagine that I'll be able to make such major changes after only one meeting. I forgot to ask the friend who recommended Hugo how many sessions that other girl needed.

"The best thing you can do," Hugo says right before I leave, "is keep your mouth closed. You won't believe how much it will help."

. . .

I 'm amazed when I make an effort to try to live my life the Hugo Cory way—not at how difficult it is but at how easy. On my way home from meeting with him, I talk to my mom and explain that when I swear, I'm only expressing frustration. I expect her to tell me that I sound ridiculous but instead she exclaims, "My God, that's so true! I should stop, too."

Encouraged by her enthusiasm, I start my effort in earnest. And it actually works: I begin eradicating four-letter words from my sentences and, before long, literally feel myself wince when I hear one. Swearing begins to feel abrasive, hostile, and unnatural. When my book club invites a woman who wrote a spiritual guide to speak and she swears throughout the bulk of her lecture, I'm too distracted by these words to even hear her message. When I accidentally let a curse slip through my lips, I feel my mistake at once. I find myself using the word "eff" in place of the expletive it stands for when I'm talking and not only in jokey e-mails, and saying "God darn it" without worrying that I sound like a country bumpkin. I make certain exceptions—"Jesus" and "holy crap" seem okay since I am, after all, a Jew—but, amazingly, the major four-letter words simply flit away. I'd always heard that it takes 30 days to change a habit, but I swear my metamorphosis occurred within 30 minutes of my leaving Hugo.

If only my penchant for judging, gossiping, and complaining was as easy to relinquish. But these habits—ones I've been trying to break for the past decade or so—don't really dissipate at all. While I feel like I decrease the frequency of my ventures into un-Hugo territory, the struggle between improving myself and accepting who I intrinsically am grows increasingly oppressive.

Deciding that Helen would encourage me to try harder, I reason that the best way to really make progress on this is to track my movements more precisely. I commit to writing down my ventures into swearing, gossip and judgment. A sampling of my notes from one week in January:

Day 1

9:03 a.m.—Start gossiping about people I think are delusional with an acquaintance before remembering my commitment to myself.

9:04 a.m.—Resist gossiping further when the acquaintance mentions another delusional person we know.

11:09 a.m.—Stifle the urge to complain when I realize that I was told the West Coast time for a phone call so I moved around my entire day for no reason.

11:30 a.m.—Swallow the complaints I'm dying to make when a business acquaintance brings up a person I dislike. Instead I say, "I'm trying not to be negative these days so I'll keep quiet."

3 p.m.—Say the "s" word on the phone.

3:20 p.m.—Stop myself from complaining about how the NYC Finance Department cashed my check and then sent me a notice that they never received it.

9:30 p.m.—Hear the person I'm eating dinner with say, "Being around you makes me want to talk about other people because you're so fun to gossip with." Horrified by this revelation, I manage not to offer up any of the wry commentary I'm dying to make about the person we just ran into.

Day 2

2:10 p.m.—So far, so good. Then again, I haven't really talked to anyone yet.

2:16 p.m.—Erase an e-mail I've started writing to a friend in which I'm about to call someone crazy who we both already know is crazy.

This is where my notes stop—not because I give up on altering my behavior but because, I tell myself, I'm actually starting to get the hang of things. Yet I allow myself short vacations—times when I can say whatever I want about whomever or whatever I want with full awareness of the potential repercussions. I wish I could claim that these excursions into dysfunctional behavior feel regressive and terrible, but they don't. Maybe, I theorize, I'm so used to making myself feel bad by judging, gossiping, and complaining that the pain it causes feels good—the way hangovers used to. I commit to staying aware of everything Hugo taught me but not obsessing over it. Instead my focus will be on having some fun.

I've never been much of a party thrower, mostly because I haven't tended to live in places that were conducive to it. At times, I haven't let this stop me—I used to have keg parties in my single dorm room my freshman year in college and let the guests spill into the hallway. But as an adult, inviting everyone I know to huddle together in my tiny apartment—no matter how chic it now is—holds little appeal.

I've had parties at venues—mostly for book releases—but now I want to start throwing the sort of festive events Helen describes in *S&SG*: dinner parties, parties cohosted with friends, parties like the kind that Helen's friend Mark used to give where he'd "pack too many people into a small space."

The opportunity presents itself when I hear about a writer who's sending himself on a book tour by doing readings in people's apartments. I love the idea and want in on this grassroots effort so I e-mail him and offer to help arrange one of these events for him in New York. I enlist Molly, who lives two floors above me in a much larger apartment, and she agrees to host. She's not dating the real estate developer anymore and we commit to bringing together a group of sexy singles. "Helen says that everyone we invite should be charming and attractive," I tell her, and Molly smiles, nods, and gives me the same patient look I'm used to seeing whenever I reference Helen.

The day of the party, she picks up the ingredients for everything she's planning to make—an elderflower cordial mint cocktail, a yogurt onion dip, and figs stuffed with ricotta cheese and wrapped in prosciutto—while I get what I need for my Parmesan and sun-dried tomato bruschetta and crumbled goat cheese and sautéed mushroom baguettes.

The event goes off spectacularly—the writer, Stephen, reads from his book and answers questions about it, the food is widely praised, and my friends mix well with Molly's. But since his book is about growing up in group homes and becoming addicted to drugs, no one feels too primed for romance. Still, it's one of those gatherings that no one wants to leave. Helen says that as a party ends, you should be gathering everyone to go to a "pre-chosen supper place" afterward, but everyone's full from our appetizers, and the party has led straight into the after-party. Looking around the room, I know that Helen would deem it a success.

Shortly after that, in early February, my friend Shari and I commit to launching a book-editing company. We've both taught writing and have had people approach us over the past few years for help editing their books. I've always done it a bit haphazardly, spontaneously deciding on my fee and trying to help in the best way I can. But if we band together, we decide, we can make it official: have set prices, a specific way of editing, and possibly even share clients. We come up with a name and design a Web site and, before we know it, people are hiring us. While brainstorming ways to make our business stand out from the competitors, we land on the idea of hosting a reading series so that our clients can have a chance to read their work aloud alongside well-established writers we know. Plenty of editors can help aspiring writers with their material but how many can offer them the chance to experience one of the major rites of passage of professional writing? The reading party that Molly and I threw gives me the confidence to challenge the voices in my head that tell me that what we're planning probably won't work and that the last thing New York City needs is another reading series.

Amazingly, everything comes together: I ask my friend Jeremy if we can hold the readings at Birch, his hip, new organic coffee shop attached to the Gershwin Hotel, and Shari comes up with the idea that we have masseuses on hand to give guests back rubs before, during, and after the readings. The first Readings & Rubdowns event is packed—standing room only—and we plan our next one for two months down the road, committing to doing them every couple of months thereafter.

Even though I live in New York City and people hold readings, not to mention mythology seminars, not to mention naked clown classes, not to mention many other things far more bizarre and industrious, every day I marvel at the fact that I've had the gall to help start a reading series. Looking around on the night of the first event at those listening attentively, sipping their drinks, and chatting between readings, I can't quite believe how easy it all had been to pull off.

It's not quite an "if you build it, they will come" *Field of Dreams* moment but I still marvel at the fact that I've transitioned from being someone who talked about doing things—who passed a pottery studio and mentioned how much she'd like to take a class, who told her friend they should start a business together—to someone who actually does them. By pushing myself to follow Helen's instructions for living, I've discovered just how simple it can be to change who I always thought I was.

This motivates me to go back to working on myself.

The mouth is where the words come from, but the eyes tell the story," Arthur says. I nod and hope my eyes aren't telling Arthur a story they shouldn't—like about how uncomfortable I am when I look at someone who's gazing directly at me. "When we make eye contact," he continues, "it changes the sound of our voice because we've created a visual relationship." The whole time he's talking, he doesn't take his eyes off of mine.

I'm meeting with Arthur because of one particular passage in *S&SG*. It was in a chapter devoted to how to be sexy and contained this seminal sentence: "If you squeak or squawk, are thin or reedy . . . or are decidedly nasal, consider a voice revise." I once would have once breezed by such a statement, confidently assuming I was in the clear. But a few years ago, after I gave a talk in front of a large group of people, two men from the audience mentioned separately—and quite matter-of-factly—that they'd enjoyed what I'd had to say but that it was difficult to listen to because of my voice. I wasn't sure which was more surprising—the fact that two different people would say such a thing to me, or that they did so in a way that presumed I would of course know what they were talking about.

I would have considered this an isolated incident—two intonation-obsessed men or perhaps a particularly shrill day—but that was around when I got my first call to appear on TV. I had been writing for entertainment magazines when someone from VH1 called and asked if I'd be interested in coming on the network to talk about celebrities. This led to a CNN appearance, which led to the *Today* show. And when I started writing first-person pieces about sex and dating, the television opportunities multiplied, and I suddenly found myself as the relationship expert on a show called *Attack of the Show* on the tech network G4. And this new career had led me to a joyless but addictive new hobby: reading people's not-always-pleasant reactions to me, usually on message boards that a person who liked herself more would probably avoid. I knew better than to buy into the general negativity, but what I read about the way I spoke was specific enough to have stuck with me. "Anna David has a voice made for print," one person wrote. A woman chimed in on Twitter that listening to me made her want to "stick hot pokers" in her eyes. And while of course it doesn't make sense to put a lot of stock in the words of an overreactive stranger (how that person handles the existence of Fran Drescher, we'll never know), I became, if anything, curious about the fact that something I'd always considered at the very least inoffensive could inspire feelings in anyone.

So a few years ago, when I ended up at dinner with Arthur, a celebrated vocal coach, I asked him what he thought was wrong with my voice. "Absolutely nothing," he responded in an unsurprisingly peaceful tone. "You just need to breathe more." That was comforting and logical, and I remembered to concentrate more on breathing the next few times I was on TV. I'd think of Arthur occasionally after that, reasoning that I could justify hiring him if I did more TV work, but that otherwise it would be a petty indulgence. And then good old Helen came along and gave me another reason.

Which is why I now sit in Arthur's lovely home office during a February trip to L.A., looking at him as I come to terms with how uncomfortable I am making eye contact. I don't share this with Arthur, who's now saying that eye contact causes your voice to lower and also to grow stronger and calmer. You don't need to maintain it, he adds, when you're not talking. "But when you're speaking," he says, slowly and deeply, eyes on me, "I want *you* to have the power and control."

Arthur next tells me that I should try to "see" a period at the end of every sentence I say. "I see a period," I say, envisioning a period at the end of that sentence.

"No, you don't. Try again."

"I see a period," I repeat. This time, as I say the word "period," I imagine myself digging a pencil into a piece of paper.

"Better. Again."

And so we continue, with me picturing deeper and darker

pencil marks as I speak. On about the fifth or sixth attempt, I notice that the ends of my phrases are actually starting to loop downward and finally really understand what he's talking about. A period is very different from a pause or from lowering your pitch, Arthur explains, because it communicates "authenticity" and "gives you more colors to tell your story."

While I like the idea of having the entire ROYGBIV color palette at my vocal disposal, the longer we talk, the less I'm able to focus on what I'm saying because I'm devoting all of my energy to *how* I'm saying it. I'm speaking at a fraction of the pace I tend to, which is simultaneously inspiring and disconcerting. People always tell me that I talk fast, so in a way it feels nice to slow down. But at the same time, I like my vocal speed because it makes me feel smart and thus miles away from the little girl who thought she was a raving idiot. I tell Arthur that I think speaking quickly indicates a fast-working mind—picturing periods at the end of every sentence—and he nods but says that speed makes a voice go higher, which isn't good.

Then Arthur tells me that I drag out the ends of my phrases and that this can be perceived as elitist. "No," I say. "Really?"

"No, not 'no-o,'" he repeats, clipping the word off at one syllable, keeping it quick and sharp. "Can you repeat that?"

"No." I try to imitate his sharp delivery. I'm stupidly flattered by the notion that I sound elitist. "I always think of myself as sounding so uncultivated compared to the rest of my family. I always assumed I sounded, if anything, a bit Valley girl. I know that I say 'like,' 'um,' and 'you know' too much."

"Oh, that's true, too."

This is disappointing; I'd been hoping Arthur would refute that point. "It is?"

"Is," Arthur responds crisply. "Not 'i-is.'"

This time, I force myself to copy him precisely. "Is," I repeat, finally getting what he's saying when I realize that I've been treating "is"—and God knows how many other one-syllable words—like it's feet, as opposed to inches, long. Arthur had asked me before I came to meet with him to think about how I wanted to be perceived; intelligent and calm, I'd told him. Speed talking and word dragging out clearly aren't helping me to give off either of those things.

"When you speak, I want you to repeat in your head, 'I need to be aware with a silent and loving breath,'" he says now.

I nod. "I need to be aware with a silent and loving breath."

"Exactly. I want you to think about crafting how you want to be perceived the same way you would think about crafting the arc of a sentence or book. And I want you to hold very positive thoughts about yourself in the back of your head when you're speaking." I promise I will, even though I'm not sure how I'm going to be able to think about how wonderful I am, repeat sentences about breathing in my head, put periods at the end of my sentences, make sure my words don't drag out at the end and still come up with original thoughts to express.

Arthur continues talking—about how I should try to release the tension in my jaw and how the strongest muscle in the body is at the base of the tongue—and I commit to tape recording myself talking and doing a vocal exercise that involves reciting a poem first clothed and then unclothed. I'm saying all of this slowly and there are periods at the ends of all my sentences, but I have to imagine that even Helen might find nude poem recitation to be a bit much.

. . .

So what exactly do you think is wrong with your voice?" Jason asks over the phone one night.

I'd met Jason because, during one of my sporadic visits to Match after returning from my most recent trip to L.A., I'd noticed a "You've captured someone's interest" e-mail from a guy with gorgeous photos and a smart and witty profile. At first I'd thought it must be a fake—something Match put up there to keep the women on the site from canceling their memberships, or at least a real profile with phony photos. But when we met for lunch, the high cheekbones, almond-shaped eyes and almost obnoxiously in-shape body I'd seen in his pictures was evident. And the combination of these looks with his playful sense of humor succeeded in pushing the fact that he was a currently out-of-work commercial actor to the back of my mind.

"My sentences loop up at the end," I explain, picturing a period as I say the word "end." "They sound like they lack authenticity. And I drag my words out in a way that seems elitist." He doesn't say anything. "Don't you see what I mean?" He still doesn't respond so I tell him about the blistering criticism my vocal cords have received from the Internet community. I briefly wonder if I should be sharing the fact that people think my voice is annoying, not to mention that I read about myself on the Internet, with someone I've only been out with three times, but he laughs.

"I like the way you talk," he says. "It's unique." A feeling of pleasure burns through me at the compliment. "Although the way you say 'well' is weird."

"Really?"

"You go, 'Wulllll.' It's cute." This way of saying "well"

doesn't seem grating and I like the idea that I have a word I've made my own, not to mention that a guy I'm so attracted to appreciates it. "I don't think you need to change your voice."

"But I like tweaking myself," I object. On our second date—a few nights after we'd met at lunch—I had told Jason about Project Helen and he'd appeared somewhere between bemused and confused by the concept. "I believe life is about self-improvement."

"Maybe," he responds. "Or maybe it's about self-acceptance."

"But this isn't about not having self-acceptance," I say, a little too quickly. "It's about making me into the best possible version of myself so that I'm able to live the best life I can."

I don't tell him, but lately I've been a little worried that I may be setting myself up for failure with this project. I'm proud of what I've done—not just the external strides I've made but also the way that I've become someone who challenges herself, who makes things happen, and who's willing to risk looking or feeling stupid. Still, when I ran into an acquaintance last week who had heard about what I was doing and wanted to know if I'd "found a guy yet," I panicked. It didn't help that she'd just announced that she was pregnant with twins. Helen warns of "pressure groups" who "dig at you like chiggers" over your single status; she suggests that we use "cunning" and "fortitude" when we're in these situations, but I used neither and merely snapped that I wasn't on a manhunt so much as I was attempting to live in a world where everyone thinks you must be on a manhunt if you're single.

She nodded and surely wished she'd never inquired while I wondered how many more of these types of queries—not to mention looks of pity—I'd receive if I followed every last one of Helen's recommendations and still didn't end up with "the one." Later that day, I stumbled on the blog of a woman who'd been determined to find a guy in a year. The year had ended and her final entry was the most unintentionally depressing thing I'd ever read—a post about how she'd, yet again, gone on a date with a guy she liked only to never hear from him again. She'd made every effort to dress up her desperation as optimism but I saw through it and quivered at the thought that I was doing the same thing. After all, despite what I've defensively been telling people, a part of me really is seeking out a man who will complete me—and, arguably even worse, doing a whole lot of work to make myself worthy of him. Right now, Jason's around, but who's to say if he'll stay? I somehow feel like I keep having to convince him that I'm worth it—like if I don't say enough clever or witty things or look sexy enough or do a succession of impressive somersaults and cartwheels, then he might fix his beautiful, almond-shaped eyes on someone else.

But right now he's still here. "I'm just saying that I like the way you talk," he says.

"I like the way you do, too," I tell him. I had asked him over e-mail before we met if he still had a Southern accent since he is from Louisiana, and he had told me that it only surfaced when he was drunk or angry. I haven't seen him either but I hear the accent every time he speaks. I've never noticed if his sentences have visual periods at the end of them or not.

A few days later, I'm back to feeling enthusiastic about living my life the Helen Gurley Brown way. Who cares, I reason, what the other people have to say? These past eight months have given me more confidence and courage than anything I've done since getting sober. I used to think self-esteem came from receiving a certain amount of accolades out in the world, but relying on that to feel good meant that I pretty much believed I was worthless if I wasn't receiving any praise. Thanks to Helen, I've learned that self-esteem actually comes from doing estimable acts—like working on myself. With that in mind, I decide to focus on some of her recommendations for being sexy.

Scanning *S&SG*, I spy an easy one: watching the 1960 movie *The Sundowners* because, she writes, it features Deborah Kerr at her sexiest. So one night, after cooking for Jason—the same chicken, broccoli, and Caesar salad combo that David got—I tell him that I've rented a classic movie I'd like us to watch. He looks like I've just informed him that I think we should study and recite words out of the *Oxford English Dictionary* and, quite frankly, the movie description on the Netflix sleeve makes me feel sort of the same way. "It's about sheep farmers in the Australian outback," I say, trying to act like this is a good or even exciting thing. "Supposedly," I add, "Deborah Kerr is incredibly sexy in it."

Now he looks intrigued, possibly picturing Ursula Andress in her gold bikini or Marilyn Monroe in *Some Like It Hot*. "I could do it," he says. "But the sheep farmer thing sounds really boring. Can we turn it off if we're completely bored?"

"Absolutely."

So we sit on my couch on a freezing March night with a blanket draped over us and await sexiness. What we see instead is Deborah Kerr playing a long-suffering wife of a hard-drinking sometime sheep farmer played by Robert Mitchum, who seems to only want to live in a tent and sing off-key in saloons. Kerr spends most of the movie nagging him—rightfully so, in my opinion—about finding them a place to live that doesn't require zipping a panel closed or washing with a bowl of filthy water. There's nothing remotely sexy about what she's doing, unless picking up a jar and complaining about the lack of money in it is sexy in a way I don't understand. I try to keep Jason intrigued by mentioning that the movie was nominated for five Oscars but the truth is that I've sort of had it with the film myself. Still, I'm determined to stick it out until we get to the part where Kerr becomes sexy so I suggest that we turn down the volume and put the subtitles on to make the experience more interesting. He agrees but that's when I start to fall asleep.

"What's happening now?" I ask after dozing for a minute. I open one eye.

"She's losing it and he's like, 'Woman, let me go sing my ridiculous song in the bar,'" he says. I laugh and then laugh even harder when Jason imitates the singing.

When I tune in to the movie again, Kerr's cooking for a whole bunch of men—Mitchum has apparently transitioned, mid-career, from sheep farmer to sheep shearer and he now has all these other guys who appear to work for him. They keep praising Kerr for being able to prepare and serve so much food and for, in general, being such a long-suffering wife and I continue to try to figure out what Helen could have possibly found sexy about this. Kerr's undoubtedly beautiful, but slinging hash and faking an Aussie accent doesn't bring out the va-va-voom in anyone. If anything, she's sexy because she's nurturing and understanding—an

Earth Mother who will support her man but is also somehow strong. This reinforces much of Helen's message—that be-your-own-woman-but-also-cater-to-a-man concept she preaches. Perhaps she was responding to the themes rather than the actual visuals.

Around when Robert Mitchum enters a sheep-shearing competition, Jason leans toward me. We'd kissed after our second and third dates but we were at my doorstep both times, so this is the first time our lips are colliding while we're inside and leaning against each other. I open my eyes and see that his are clenched tight, providing me with a perfect view of his long lashes. They're quite pretty. But after working so hard to get to a moment like this, I make the conscious decision to stop thinking and simply surrender to the way it feels, just like I surrendered to the waves in the Dominican.

The Sundowners night turns out to be quite sexy, after all.

I still want to try some of Helen's other recommendations for sexiness, so one day when Jason and I are walking his dog, I decide to put her instructions for flirty eye contact to the test, figuring that this way I'll be doing both what she said as well as following Arthur's advice. Helen's suggestions on eye contact are quite specific: "Look into his eyes as though tomorrow's daily double winners were there," she writes. "Never let your eyes leave his. Concentrate on his left eye . . . then the right . . . now deep into both."

"Come on, Rudy—it's time for you to go," Jason says to his cocker spaniel and then he pretends to be his dog talking back. "Okay, Jason," he screeches in a tired old man's voice that doesn't sound the way I think Rudy would if he could talk but which nonetheless always amuses me. "I'm coming. But you put so much pressure on me!"

Trying to maintain eye contact while laughing and also while Jason is focused on getting his dog to go to the bathroom is almost impossible. Still, I make an effort, craning my neck so that I'm gazing at Jason from a little below him as he watches Rudy lift his leg and pee. "You look weird," Jason says, glancing at me. "Are you okay?"

I nod and decide to wait until we're sitting down to continue the experiment. Once we're at a nearby outdoor café, Rudy crouched covertly beneath our table since dogs aren't allowed here and this dog is all too familiar with how to help his owner get away with breaking the rules, I fix my eyes on Jason. He's scanning the menu, not looking up. "Are we eating a meal now or having a snack?" he asks. "Because we're going to eat later, right, after the party?"

"I think we should just have a snack," I say, eyes still on him, thinking about how nice it was to hear "we're going to eat later": I am, for the moment anyway, a "we" with someone I want to be a "we" with. Jason and I have been taking each other to various events—he even brought me to his ex-fiancée's birthday party—and we're a good team in that way: because he's attentive, I feel comfortable in his world and I appreciate the way he can just jump into conversations in mine. Having someone I like come with me places also makes me see just how tired I was of either being on my own or dragging a friend along as my plus-one.

After we order hummus and pita bread to share, I realize that I've completely lost focus on my mission, so I wait for Jason to start telling me a story. It doesn't take long—I knew it wouldn't, the guy's a storyteller for sure—and as I listen to him talk about how he got in a fight with a guy at Starbucks over half-and-half, I look from his left eye to his right.

"The thing is, this guy was a real douche bag," Jason is saying. "You know the kind of guy I mean? The three-piece suit, the cell he's of course talking on, not even realizing that no one wants to hear about his plans to go to Southampton that weekend? And he probably wasn't even going there—or even going to work, the suit was probably for show. He was just one of those guys who wanted people to think he was, you know?"

Jason doesn't notice that I'm trying to look at his eyes like they contain winning lottery ticket numbers.

"So before we even start arguing about the half-and-half, this guy thinks, for some reason, that I've shoved him," Jason continues. The waitress drops off our drinks and he takes an enormous gulp of his iced tea, draining it to the middle of the glass. "I was still, like, five feet away," Jason continues, "so I don't know if it was someone else or if he was out of his mind and looking for a fight."

He keeps talking but I'm so focused on trying to gaze deep into both of his eyes that I lose track of what he's saying. I'm picking up the fact that the tension with the suit wearer escalated but I'm not sure exactly how or why because, God darn it, I'm trying to flirt with Jason with my eyes and he's totally oblivious. He's talking and I'm not listening and I'm looking and he's not noticing and I wonder how many romantic situations—how many human interactions—are like this. Does Helen understand that eye focus in this specific way isn't great for paying attention to the content of the conversation? Or maybe it isn't as distracting once you get used to it? Perhaps she doesn't think listening on dates is that important.

Jason is still telling me what happened that day—at this point in the story, he and the cell-talking, suit-wearing, Southampton-visiting stranger have taken their argument outside of Starbucks—and I'm beginning to understand that the guy I'm dating is telling me a story about how an inter-action he had with a stranger escalated into an argument in the street that sounds like it got physical and that this is po-tentially very bad, indeed—as in one of those red flags I'd promised myself I'd start noticing. But I don't like the idea of Jason getting into fights with strangers over half-and-half, so I assume that I must be misunderstanding the story.

And I don't really have time to think about it anyway because I'm instead contemplating the seven most disturbing words in *S&SG*: "knowing how to sit still is sexy." Now, I've never, as long as I've lived, known how to sit still. Being anywhere for more than an hour makes me ridiculously restless. I'm always the one signaling to the waiter for the bill. I knit in movies because it helps me to stay put for two hours, and tend to break a solo Netf-lix-viewing process into three or four parts over a period of a few days. But sitting here with Jason, I order myself to not suggest that we get the bill, not sneak glances at my phone, not do any-thing but fight the ADD-like tendencies that run through me. As we continue to chat—eventually moving off his Starbucks fight and onto a girl from his acting class—I realize that noth-ing makes sitting still harder than telling yourself you need to sit still. I focus on having eye contact with him to distract myself.

Then I think about a few more of Helen's proposals: not talking too much about your family or boss, laughing at jokes, and applauding bravery. While I used to tell dates far too much information about my family—thinking, I see in retrospect, that confessing private details could establish instant intimacy with them—I've gotten much better about that in the past few years, and Jason has told me far more about his family than I've told him about mine. And since I don't really have a boss, I'm also in good shape there. Furthermore, laughing at his jokes is easy since I find them funny. But maybe, I think, I should try applauding his bravery. I'm not sure if the Starbucks story counts as an example of bravery but when he moves on to telling me about a movie he likes, giving pitch-perfect imitations of the dialogue, I reason that it's brave to speak in an accent that's not your own and tell him as much. He gives me a funny look before continuing with the plot summary.

By the time we get up, I'm exhausted. Trying to be the sexy, charming flirt Helen wants me to be doesn't leave much of a chance to engage with the man across the table, not to mention allow him to engage with me. When Jason grabs my hand and asks me if I want to walk or take the subway to the party, I conclude that I've clearly done a decent enough job of flirting with him or we wouldn't be in the position we're in. For the moment, I put Helen's flirting recommendations on the shelf.

A few weeks later, Jason and I go to Montauk, where I have a meltdown and yell at him for not being interested in anything I say, which inspires him to tell me that he thinks we got too serious too fast and should probably slow things down, which makes me feel rejected so I snap that I could never have taken him seriously in the long term since he's an out-of-work commercial actor.

The drive back is horrible, and that's before Rudy covers the entire backseat with vomit a color and consistency more disgusting than anything I would have ever thought possible. The good-bye that follows is even worse.

Even though I know that everything I said is true—I never did feel that he cared about what I was saying—I'm horrified by how I handled the situation and become immediately despondent.

While we were dating, a part of me had been aware of the fact that we probably didn't have a long-term future together. But being around a guy I was attracted to who also made me laugh, someone I could sit across the table from and talk to on the phone and watch movies with and sleep next to, was like drinking a cool, refreshing glass of water after a 10-year hangover and the loss of it feels, at first, like a crucial part of me—a lung or limb—has been suddenly and violently removed.

Because the whole time I was telling myself that I couldn't take Jason seriously, another part of me was saying the opposite. It was offering up thoughts like, Why *not* him? It was working overtime to shove the less-than-appealing facts about him—the debt he mentioned, the lack of future plans, the Starbucks fights—to a deep recess of my brain so that denial and fantasies could blossom. It was allowing me to pretend that I didn't feel like I had to do handstands in order to keep him interested.

A few nights after the breakup, I'm relaying all of this to Shari. Helen says that when going through any form of heartbreak, we should "lean hard" on girlfriends, going "over and over and over the story as long as it gives you any solace to talk about it." Right now, Shari is the victim of this.

"The truth is," I say as we sit down at a bar, "I miss him. A lot." A sob gathers in my throat. "And it was idiotic—not to mention cruel—to say what I did about him being an out-of-work actor. It was a low blow and I only did it out of vengeance." I start to tear up. "Do you think I should ask him if he'd take me back?" I know I sound pathetic but right now the pain of being with someone who isn't a wise long-term choice seems preferable to the pain of not.

"Take you back?" she asks as the bartender hands her a martini.

I nod. "He had said he wanted to slow things down—not stop seeing each other—but then I jumped to thinking it was over." I rest my head in my hands as a new distressing thought occurs to me. "But when someone says they want to slow things down, they always mean that they don't want to see you anymore and just don't want to have to say it, right?" I have a vague memory of answering this question on television for someone, and shame that I can give advice I can't seem to access or put to use in my own life momentarily drowns out the shame I feel over my behavior with Jason.

"I don't know," Shari says. "But I'm not sure I'd want to be with someone who didn't really want to be with me."

I know that what she's saying is true—I'd, in fact, said the same thing to Roger in therapy that morning. Still, for a split second, as I look at Shari's cleavage-revealing dress and her martini—and then think about how much younger she is than me—I'm intensely jealous. The hedge fund guy, who turned out not to be a spy after all, had sent her a dozen roses that week.

A few minutes later, I tell her that I'm tired and should go. Once home, tears of self-pity flowing, I call Nicole. "I know it's not *him* that's making me sad," I say. "I dated him for less than two months. But it still *feels* like it's him. So realizing it's not him—that this is some age-old pain that's just been triggered by his leaving—doesn't make me feel any better."

"I get it," she says. "Same pain, new face?"

Her sympathy elicits more tears. "I can't even make a casual dating situation work," I wail, adding dramatically, "I destroy everything!"

"It seems like that needed to be destroyed," she says gently. "And I don't think you did anything wrong: it probably didn't work because he's a self-obsessed actor. Sometimes men suck."

While a part of me is comforted by her words, the other part thinks that it's easy enough for her to say that since she has a boyfriend. A fresh sense of self-pity oozes from me as I lament, "I just think I'm past my due date and should give up." I suddenly realize I'm complaining and therefore, according to Hugo, putting scenarios out in the world that will later come and hunt me down. This only makes me feel worse.

Nicole sighs. "I hope you know that if I was saying that, you'd tell me how absurd I was acting."

"I guess." I wipe tears off my face. I know I'm being mean to myself—making up stories that I'm then believing—but I can't stop. Sometimes, I feel like my brain is a hyper-critical roommate—one who won't shut up about how useless and pathetic I am—and once I go there, clawing myself out is almost impossible.

"Look, I get it," she says. I hear a voice in the background and suddenly understand that Tim has been at her place the whole time we've been talking. This makes me descend to an even lower emotional state: I'm the pathetic spinster friend in New York calling to be saved from my thoughts while she's trying to have a nice night with her boyfriend.

"I should let you go," I offer.

"Okay," she says. "Just promise me you'll at least try to be nicer to yourself."

"I promise to try."

Once we hang up, I make an effort to follow through on my word. I stare at my Karlstad couch, my thick wall of curtains and my half-steel, half-glass bookshelves and try to think about how good I feel about having made my living space so nice. Then I consider Helen's recommendation that I shred an old towel, throw beanbags against my fireplace, or have a tantrum to get over a breakup. But I'm too practical to shred a towel and don't have beanbags or a fireplace; besides, I feel sad and not angry.

It suddenly hits me that I'm back in the mentality I was in before I started following Helen's advice—back to telling myself that I'm going to be alone forever. But I'm not the same person that I was then. I've started to live the "rich, full" life Helen told me was possible for a single woman. I've challenged myself, grown as a result, and only plan to keep growing. I have everything I need; now all I need to do is be as nice to myself as I would to whatever man I hope to one day share it with.

Within a few minutes, it occurs to me that what I'm

experiencing isn't the most unbearable, painful experience imaginable, but simply the hurt that comes with rejection—and that, what's more, this is a good thing because it means I've at least taken a risk. I was out on the board, riding a wave, and it knocked me down. And that's okay; I used to just stand on the shore. With surprise, I realize that this was really the first time I've let my guard down with a man since I've been sober—aside from with Will. For the past decade, I've kept everything under control—including my willingness to open myself up. Which means that no matter how gut-wrenchingly awful this is, it's far better than standing on the sand, wondering if the water will ever get less scary.

By the time I get into bed, I feel much better. And right before I fall asleep, I consider the idea that perhaps I've leaned too far in the serious direction and need to have a bit more fun.

Part Three

CHAPTER NINE

The Don Juan, the Younger Man, and the Married Man

The single woman . . . has a better sex life than most of her married friends. Her choice of partners is endless.

—*Sex and the Single Girl*

I meet Nick because I'm determined to meet Nick. Or at least I am the late March day a friend shows me his picture and then a link to brilliant, amusing, and titillating erotica he writes under a pen name. I've all but abandoned my Match membership by this point—not, I tell myself, because I think all the men on there will hurt me the way Jason did but because none of them appears to be even the slightest bit sexy. While I'm still determined to meet men who would make appropriate long-term partners, I also want to enjoy my life as a single woman. And Nick looks like he could be quite enjoyable, indeed.

After finding him on Facebook, I try to come up with the best way to propose a union. "I love your writing and the way you look and think I'd like to kiss you all over" would be the most honest approach. But, aside from all the obvious issues with a missive like that, I don't even know if he'd be horrified to find out that strangers knew he was the author of the erotica.

So I tell a white lie—something I feel certain Helen would condone in this particular case—by sending him a note that I'm a writer and would love to take him out for a cup of coffee to pick his brain about the Internet marketing his company does. I'm hoping, of course, that he'll see through this flimsy excuse and understand that I just want to meet him.

A week later, Nick responds. Since the soft ruggedness of his photos and intellectual sensibility of his writing suggested that he wasn't exactly the kind of guy who spent his days coming up with new status updates or poking people, I figure this may be the first time he's been on Facebook since I contacted him. Still, his response doesn't exactly leave me with the impression that he can't wait to make my acquaintance. He says that his schedule is quite busy but that I should e-mail him the following week because he could possibly work something out with me then.

I e-mail him the next week. He writes back that his job has gotten even crazier but the next week could maybe happen and I should write again if I feel like it. I'm frustrated that he appears to be immune to all the charm I'm making sure to infuse my e-mails with but also know that I can't expect him to drop everything in order to meet. Again, I e-mail when he suggests I do, and this time we make a plan for a midday coffee.

That day, I change my clothes about six times before settling on the same Sass & Bide leggings and black shirt with the asymmetrical zipper I'd put on initially. But when I e-mail him to confirm our plan, he writes back, *So sorry but I got torpedoed with an afternoon meeting so I'm not going to be able to make it. Let's try again soon.*

This time, I'm hurt. Which means that I respond passive

aggressively. *Dear Nick,* I write. *If this is a plan you can commit to and stick with, let me know. Otherwise, don't worry about it.*

He doesn't write back.

I mostly forget about him over the next few weeks, during which my sadness over Jason dissipates almost entirely and I relish finding contentment in my friends, my work, and my life in general without needing to have a guy around to make it all feel complete. But one day, when I'm discussing Project Helen with my married friend Colin, he asks me about the various ways I've been meeting men.

"Oh, the usual," I say. "Through Match, through friends, through sheer determination."

"I don't know why you're not trying to find single men you admire and then e-mailing them to ask if you could meet," he says. "Men love that kind of thing. And it's all too rare."

"But I already tried that! And it backfired."

I tell Colin the Nick story but he only shrugs. "So write him again," he says.

"Again! But I wrote him and then wrote him again and then wrote him *again* and he acted like I was a complete nuisance."

"No, he didn't. It just sounds like he was busy."

I consider that. I have a black-and-white mind that often only sees extremes: a guy is either madly in love with me or else finds me completely annoying. "I guess he didn't so much make me feel like I was pestering him," I admit. "He just didn't pick up the ball I dropped in his lap. I wanted him to somehow become attracted to me, and then want to meet. Isn't that what an erotica writer is *supposed* to do?"

"That's just not how these things work," Colin explains.

"You reached out to him so you need to continue to be the aggressor. You can't change the rules mid-game."

Later that night, I consider the Rollerblades I've worn, the ceramics wheel I've sat over, the French classes I've survived, and the windsurfing board I've stood on and determine that I'm far more capable of putting myself out there than I think I am. *It's okay*, I think, *to be seen making an effort*. With that in mind, I e-mail Nick again.

This time he writes back quickly, apologizing for his past flakiness and suggesting that we get together that week. I'm so surprised that I don't quite believe our plan will happen, and on the appointed day at the appointed meeting place, I half believe he won't show.

But suddenly he's right in front of me—the golden hair, mischievous smile, and pouty lips I'd seen in his photos on full display—acting charming and sweet and asking me thoughtful questions. And it's clear from his manner that he considers this a personal, and not a professional, meeting. Over a late lunch, he tells entertaining stories, makes obscure literary references that somehow don't sound pretentious, and talks openly about the erotica he writes so that I'm free to confess how much I like it. He manages to strike the perfect balance between talking and asking questions and I'm feeling like all my stalking of him was well worth the effort.

Then he mentions that he has a girlfriend.

I react cavalierly, the way I think I should to save face about having hassled a happily coupled-off guy into meeting me. I move on to the next topic slowly enough to make it look like this information doesn't throw me off in the slightest and quickly enough to indicate that I don't think we need to dwell on it, either.

Then he mentions that they have an open relationship.

It's not like I haven't heard about open relationships before. I've even speculated that they might be the ideal solution to the problems that seem to plague most partnerships, allowing people the freedom to act on impulses they might otherwise have to repress and help them to not codependently rely on their mate. But I've never actually known anyone in one.

I ask him what that means and he explains that he loves the woman he's with but she's not willing to give up her live-in boyfriend so he sees her regularly but is free to engage in whatever else he wants to. Her boyfriend accepts the fact that she's also dating Nick, and the two men hang out sometimes. Nick instantly shifts, in my mind, from a potential boyfriend to someone I need to stay away from. I therefore don't make any effort to appear cool and blasé about this type of modern-day arrangement and instead turn him into sociological study subject by peppering him with questions—all of which he gamely answers. I even tell him about falling for Will, and we bond over what it's like to love someone you can't really have the way you want. Afterward, he insists on picking up the bill and walking me to my train. Then, as I'm about to descend the subway stairs, he says, "Next time, we should get together for a drink."

I think, *He said next time. He said drink. Does he think I'm not fazed by this open relationship business?* Not sure what to respond, I say, "I don't drink."

"Oh, okay." He shrugs, his smile mischievous as he hoists his backpack up higher on his shoulder. "A beverage, then."

I nod and smile and hug him good-bye, not saying yes but not closing the door, either. Once I'm alone and can process what happened, I feel a familiar sting of disappointment—all my pursuit and it turns out he has a girlfriend—but remind myself that I can't expect to reach out to one man and have us fall for each other.

The next day it occurs to me that Nick may know magazine editors I could contact about publishing an erotic section of a novel I abandoned long ago. I e-mail and ask him. He writes back that he doesn't—he publishes his for free—but suggests that I let him read what I wrote and, in exchange, he'll give me his latest piece. *I'll show you mine*, he writes, *and you show me yours?*

The trade happens and I don't have time to think about how he's reading the most graphic piece of material I've written because I'm too distracted by how turned on I am by what he sent me: a story about a man who uses his neckties to attach girls' wrists to the bedpost before he has sex with them. Just as I'm finishing reading it, I get an e-mail from him that reads: *So, are you going to send me any of the photos?* I smile; in the material I'd given him, the female character references some sexy pictures she had taken.

What I sent you was fiction, I remind him.

I know those photos exist, he responds.

Hell, no, I write which, translated, means: *Yes, these photos exist—I was, after all, a bit of a wayward youth—but no, I'm not e-mailing them to you.*

He asks me what he can do to get me to change my mind with such brazen confidence that I stop acting coy and just say that there's nothing a guy I'd met once could say that would motivate me to send him my naughtiest photos.

What if he offered to bring you dinner this weekend? he writes.

My fingers linger over the keyboard. "This is a bad idea," I say out loud, not certain if I'm talking about showing him the photos, the fact that he's in an open relationship and is therefore not available, or both. Then I think about the different categories Helen breaks men into—Married, Divorcing, Younger, Homosexual, and the Don Juan—and consider her assertion that no girl is really ready for marriage until she has "weathered the rigors of a romance" with a Don Juan. Nick isn't a classic Don Juan—as far as I know, those guys pretend to be available only to leave you wailing into your pint of Ben & Jerry's when they've moved on to their next victim—but the fact that he's already in a relationship does give him some of the characteristics of one. He's actually a better choice than a genuine Don Juan, I reason, since he's being straightforward about the fact that I'm not the only woman. *Saturday?* I write.

When he shows up that Saturday, the dynamic feels familiarly unfamiliar and I can't tell if that's because he's one of the tortured artist types I've always dated or because he immediately makes himself at home, scooping homemade Indian dishes and sauces out of plastic containers and onto my plates like it's something he's done 100 times here.

It turns out that Nick is a terrific cook. And, I learn when we finish dinner and he begins casually rubbing my shoulders, one hell of a masseuse. By then, my admittedly flimsy boundaries have disintegrated and the shoulder massage turns into a full-body massage, which turns into an opportunity for me to discover that Nick's mouth is as soft and supple as I'd fantasized it would be. Kissing him is like submerging myself in a delicious and long-desired hot bath. And something about the enthusiastic and highly focused way he runs his tongue over my body makes me feel like he's giving me something rather than taking something away, a sensation I don't realize until that very moment is the exact opposite of what I tend to feel in sexual situations. I'm usually very conscious of the way I behave and how far things go in bed, but with Nick, I can't seem to think about anything except how good the trail his tongue is making over my body feels. When he gets to my most sensitive spot, I can't summon up the voice to tell him he shouldn't. So instead I try to direct him—to tell and show him what I like and how—until he orders me to be quiet. That's when I learn just how good being ignored can feel.

Late the next day, Nick e-mails to ask me if I think he's earned his photo. I smile but know I shouldn't be e-mailing a nearly naked photo of myself to any guy, let alone this guy. But I probably shouldn't still be relishing in afterglow, either.

He e-mails again a few minutes later, telling me what he'd do if he had one of these photos, and the description is steamy enough for me to become the girl who does, indeed, e-mail scantily clad photos of herself to a man she's met twice. I can hear Helen in the back of my head telling me that exploring my sexuality is fine but that the path I'm on isn't going to get me what I want. Still, I reason that it's easier to get a job when you have a job, and this same philosophy surely applies to sex and romance. Because my fickleness, arbitrary prudishness, and occasional pity parties of the past few years, I've been the furthest thing from sexually satisfied and it would be better to search for my potential future mate if I was already having good sex. Besides, the risk of my becoming obsessive with someone new would diminish if I had a Nick in my life.

When he asks if we can meet up the following Thursday, I immediately agree and even offer to cook.

But Nick's rigorous schedule intercedes yet again and he ends up having to reschedule for the following week—when I then have to go away; by the time I'm back, Nick's left town. With all this time to consider the matter, I remember that I can't be giving the universe mixed messages. In short: I say that I want to move to the next stage, to get married and have a baby, and feeling Nick's tongue on my inner thigh, however delightful it may be, isn't getting me any closer to that. And I can somehow perfectly imagine 10 years down the line all too well: I'm still sleeping with Nick, who's still sleeping with his girlfriend, who's still sleeping with her boyfriend. When Nick proposes another get-together, I tell him that I now have a boyfriend so I can't. And this isn't altogether untrue; it's just that instead of an actual boyfriend, I have something very different: a boy toy.

D id I tell you how old I am?" he asks one late March night, smiling. He, in this case, is Max—a tall, willowy, pale-skinned guy who couldn't be anything other than a model.

I shake my head. This guy's young—that much I know. But it's not like I haven't veered into younger territory before. "How old?" I ask.

He smiles again, his bedroom eyes doing what bedroom eyes do. "Twenty."

I know that I should scream, "Twenty?"—at least in my head—and then excuse myself, stop whatever it is I think I'm doing here, and go find someone who isn't nearly half my age to entertain myself with. But men—boys—who look like this have never paid much attention to me before. If this is what putting more Helen-instructed care into my appearance nets me, I'll keep researching "face saving" machines until I find one. In other words, there's no way I'm shutting down this opportunity before it even becomes a real opportunity. "Come on," I say instead, engaging in the sort of serious eye contact that both Arthur and Helen would approve of. I would have put him at 30, or maybe 25 but *20*? Do they even allow 20-year-olds in places where I go?

"Just turned," he says. "My birthday was in February."

Jesus. A month ago, he was a teenager. Still, there's nothing in *S&SG* that says flirting with someone his age is unacceptable; on the contrary, Helen writes that a "junior" can "be a wonderful date" because he can "keep you on your toes and swinging."

Cougar is such an ugly word: you say it and instantly your mind swells with the image of sunburned, age-weary cleavage popping out of an animal print dress. But I'm somehow able to eradicate all distasteful connotations of an older woman with a younger man and instead channel some version of Demi Moore or Madonna. Which is convenient since, before I'm even fully aware of what's happening, Max is leaning in to kiss me.

To elaborate on the kiss: within several minutes of his lips meeting mine, we're engaged in a full-on make-out session. To elaborate on where this is taking place: at the Boom Boom Room atop the Standard Hotel during a *Details* magazine party. Two factors about this are relevant: one, that we're sitting in front of what is, without a doubt, the most stunning view of New York City that I've seen, and two, that I write for this magazine—am working on a story for them as this 20-year-old's tongue enters my mouth—so I'm essentially engaging in the sexiest kissing session in my recent memory at a work party.

This bothers me for about 10 minutes of our roughly hour-and-a-half-long public marathon. Luckily we're sitting on booth cushions below the main level so the only people who can truly see what we're doing are those who are gathered next to the window. One of them is my friend Ari, and the fact that one of the reasons we have a platonic relationship is that I deemed him, at 29, to be far too young for me, is an irony that isn't lost on me as I bite the 20-year-old's lip.

Between kisses, Max tells me that he's only been modeling for a month and, when prodded, admits that he's already working for all the top designers. He also says that he just got to New York last week and lives with nine other male models in Long Island City, that he's only had sex with two women, and that he doesn't believe in cheating. He strikes me as funny and smart and shockingly worldly but as I kiss him, I wonder if he's lying about the only-two-women part and if I'm just telling myself that he's funny and smart and shockingly worldly because I'm in awe of his six feet, lanky build, and perfect cheekbones. But I'm really too distracted to be able to come up with answers. Besides, a new question has started floating along the periphery of my mind: how on earth did I get lucky enough to attract this perfect specimen?

At a certain point, the party ends and I have to figure out if

I'm bringing him home with me or not. Because I try not to do things I'm going to regret, because it isn't a good idea to bring strange men, no matter how beautiful, inside your apartment, because even Ted Bundy was supposedly attractive and charming, I settle on the next best thing: plan a date with him for a few nights later, then let him walk me home and stop me for spontaneous make-outs along the way.

Y ou realize, of course, that the way you handle these things is bullshit," Molly says as she shakes her head, morning sunlight making her blond hair glisten.

It's the day after the magazine party and I'm exhausted after having woken up at dawn, completely panicked that I was out of my mind for having all but mauled and been mauled by a near-child at an event that was populated with editors I need to maintain proper, professional relationships with, and further panicked that even being attracted to a guy that young indicated that there was something terribly wrong with me. I knew that Molly was the one I needed to talk to. While I have other friends who can have sex without attachments, she's the one who relishes it, who tells stories about nightlong, multiorgasmic experiences, and who regularly informs me that I've forgotten how to just have fun with sex.

"What was I supposed to do—bring him inside and have sex with him last night?"

"Yes! He's 20! What else are you going to do? Date him?"

"He's very mature!"

"Mature? He can't even have a legal drink!"

"And for that reason, I should have had sex with him the night we met?"

"Yes!" She stands up, green eyes ablaze. "Instead of recognizing an opportunity for wanton sexual pleasure without any complicated entanglements, you did your usual thing."

"My usual thing?" I ask, even though I know exactly what she means. The fact is that I tend to be a tease, always grappling with how to follow my natural desires and still feel like the man I'm following them with will respect me afterward. Helen, like Molly, disapproves of this type of behavior, writing, "As for not going quite *that* far and merely teasing your young man to the jumping-off point while you turn your own feelings on and off like a gas jet, you can get your responses so out of whack you'll never get them straight again."

"The game you're playing doesn't even work," Molly rants. "You spend all your time trying to manipulate a guy into wanting you to be his girlfriend when what you should be doing is enjoying yourself and then later figuring out if you even want *him* as a boyfriend."

"Maybe you're right." With Nick, I hadn't worried about keeping our sexual interplay innocent and the result was an extremely pleasurable experience. Besides, I know in my heart that a good guy who's available and not just looking for a challenge doesn't lose interest in a girl because she lets him move forward physically. What I've been doing has really just been a pointless game where I pretend I can make a man fall for me by controlling what happens in bed. In *Sex and the City* terms, I've been behaving like Samantha before deciding at the final moment that I'm Charlotte. "I just don't think I know how to break the pattern," I confess.

She smiles at me from over her teacup. "Oh, honey, it's easy. Forget this whole 'I'm not going to go all the way' crap. Sex is sex. Who's to say that actual sex is a bigger deal than writhing around in a bed together?"

I nod and think about how in college and my early 20s— back when I felt like I understood how men worked and never analyzed what I should do in order to get the result I thought I wanted—all of the decisions I made about sex and romance came so naturally that they never even seemed like decisions. Does everything just get more complicated as you age? Or have I overcomplicated something that's actually quite simple? "So what should I do?" I ask Molly.

She shrugs. "You just fuck him."

Here's what I learn about being my age and telling people you just had sex with a 20-year-old.

They love it.

And I don't mean they love it in a "you go, girl," semi-indifferent way. I mean that people get extremely excited. These are the same people who, if they heard me say that I was sleeping with a 25- or 30-year-old, might nod with some resignation and either say out loud or just think that it was sad I couldn't accept my age and find someone more appropriate. I'm not sure if the age 20 simply shows I'm not taking myself and everything else so damn seriously or if the sheer ridiculousness of the situation suggests that I must have tapped into some otherworldly justification. Potentially the men who hear about it just think it must mean I'm some kind of a nymphomaniac while the women correctly assume that we must be talking about one extremely hot guy. The result is that explaining that I'd spent the previous night in bed with a 20-year-old—something I hadn't planned to tell anyone besides Molly—immediately garners me all sorts of praise and admiration.

My night with him had been, I must admit, spectacular. He'd come over a few nights after the *Details* party and introduced me to the concept of no refractory period: he'd just pull off the filled-up condom and ask, "Again?" He'd held me tightly while we slept and then, in the morning, cooked me a breakfast of Texas toast and served it to me in bed.

Now, hours later, I'm discovering that, apparently, having sex all night makes you look better. While this isn't surprising— Helen, after all, wrote that liking men and enjoying sex makes women sexier—it isn't an experiment I've done with any sort of regularity. The last time I was having lots of sex, I was either drunk or high, not to mention a good 15 pounds heavier than I am now. Point being: I never had people rushing up to me and requesting my beauty secrets. But three days after the magazine party, one day after my romp with Max, two different female friends ask me for the name and number of whoever's been doing my Botox. Because I'm a chronic confessionalist, and also because I like to brag, I explain to both women that I haven't had anything injected into my face but have instead met a guy who can do it multiple times in a row. Their wide-eyed looks fill me with pride.

But as I'm explaining this—and taking note of my internal soreness, light arm bruising, and chapped chin, semidelicious sex injuries I'd long forgotten could occur—I can't help but notice that the guy I'm talking about isn't contacting me. He'd been texting constantly in the days and hours leading up to our romp but now he's gone quiet.

I see two options: I can have a delightful memory of a relatively perfect experience—a trip down an otherwise untraveled road that I could conjure up from my future rocking chair as evidence that I'd once had body-slapping, sweat-drenched sex with a guy who would get hard about two seconds after coming and whose years of teaching yoga had left him with something like 0.01 percent body fat.

Or I could try to do it again.

Before I make my decision, I torture myself a little over the fact that I haven't heard from him, rereading the earlier texts he'd sent and concluding that embracing the Molly way of doing things had, indeed, left me feeling rejected and licentious. I call Molly and ask for advice but she's confused by the fact that I'm taking his silence personally. "Honestly, you and I are just so different about these things," she sighs. "I'm really not sure what to tell you."

When I get a text from him later that night—perfunctory, dull, with nary a mention of our spectacular night—I become conscious of the fact that I have more control in these situations than I act like I do. My reaction to seeming indifference has always been to feel offended, react with bravado, retract whatever feelings I may have started to develop for the guy, and then resent him until I forget about him altogether. But Helen has helped me to see that I'm a powerful, strong single woman. What's more, in this particular scenario, I'm the one with the life experience—not to mention apartment. I can figure out what I'd like and then let him know whatever I want to let him know about it; he'll either be on board or not and if he's not— well, I've lived several decades without knowing this guy, so I'll surely be able to handle his absence.

When I text him the next morning that I'd like to see him but could use a little more enthusiasm from him, he writes back immediately and enthusiastically—declaring after a few more exchanges that he'd very much like to see me again.

That's a nice idea, I respond.

He writes: *Then invite me over.*

Me: *Now?*

Him: *Why not?*

I stare at my phone. I look at my computer. It's the middle of a workday and I've always taken workdays very seriously, writing for at least as many hours as your average workaholic spends at the office.

On the other hand, this isn't an opportunity that comes up every day.

About a half hour later, the 20-year-old is shrugging and going, "Again?" while holding out another condom, and I realize that there isn't a person on earth that I'd like to trade places with at the moment.

Still, the equilibrium of such an arrangement cannot hold. The fact is that no matter how advanced he is for his age, how much we genuinely connect, how lean and strong his body, we just have no future. He's the one to bring this up first, falteringly revealing after another daytime escapade that he's going to be moving to Europe soon for his modeling career and he can't go there with any obligations. He adds that he's starting to develop feelings for me and that scares him; I wonder if he's claiming this so that I won't be hurt, and my first instinct is to take what he's saying as a full-fledged rejection. But it's more like an urge to move a phantom limb than an actual feeling and

I can't summon up the energy to let my mind really go there. I'm perfectly aware of the fact that he and I could never have a real relationship and, for one of the first times that I can remember, I don't try to convince myself that we do or beat myself up for not being alluring enough to make him want to be my boyfriend despite the fact that it would never work. It occurs to me that one of the reasons I've wanted sexual escapades to turn into relationships in the past is that I've felt guilty for having had sex with someone I didn't love. But Helen's philosophy that you can have "as many men as you want" has fully infiltrated my system and I don't have even a smidgen of guilt. He asks if we can still be friends and even though this type of question in this type of situation has tended to offend, annoy, or enrage me, I realize that I'd actually like that. I end up giving him my Razor scooter—something I never ended up using because everyone who saw it laughed and told me that they were only for kids.

The same week that the 20-year-old disappears, Nick resurfaces. *I saw a woman who looks like you at the gym*, his e-mail reads. *She was bending over and I had somewhat torturous thoughts. How's your relationship?*

I reread the e-mail with the understanding that the universe is offering me yet another opportunity for wanton sexual pleasure without any complicated entanglements. Before I can talk myself out of it, I write, *I'd like to hear some of those torturous thoughts. Or maybe you'd prefer to show them to me?* All he responds is, *Wednesday, 8:30 p.m. I'll come over.*

That Wednesday, Nick doesn't even say hello; he just pulls my clothes off with one hand as he shuts the door with the other.

"Lie down," he commands. I want to want to defy him—there's no way I should let a guy, let alone a guy with a girlfriend, order me around—but I'm so turned on by the way he's simply walked into my apartment and taken charge that I simply follow his instructions. I walk over to my bed and get on it. "Face down," he adds. As I turn over, I watch him remove his tie.

"So your piece wasn't fiction, either, was it?" I ask.

He laughs and tells me to be quiet as he walks toward the bed. "I'll let you know," he says, "when you can talk." He takes my two wrists in his hands and fastens them to the bedpost with his tie while I curse how wet I'm getting. *Is what turns me on really this masochistic and twisted?* I wonder as I watch Nick remove his clothes and then reach into his bag and pull out an eye mask.

"You're a bad girl," he whispers as I watch him walk back across the room.

"Why? You didn't tell me I couldn't watch you."

"But I did say not to talk and what are you doing right now?" I don't say anything but think, illogically, of my voice lesson, wondering briefly if my last sentence had a visual period on it. "This mask stays over your eyes," he says after putting it on me, his face now so close to mine that I can feel his breath. "Are you okay with that?"

I nod. I'd played around with this kind of thing before—usually with boyfriends when we thought it might spice things up if we got a little risqué—but those experiences always left me feeling like we were both silly sexual dilettantes who didn't really know what they were doing.

Nick knows what he's doing.

"I'm going to give you a safe word," he says once he's slipped the eye mask on my face. Part of me wants to jump up and dance a jig—*I have a safe word! I'm really living now!*—while the other feels certain I should be more alarmed by what's happening. "Yellow," he continues, and I'm just the slightest bit disappointed. I don't know what I'd been hoping for but "yellow" sounds a little cheerful and hokey for wanton sexual adventure. I wonder if this is his standard safe word or if he's come up with it for the occasion.

I don't have much time to ponder the matter, however, because Nick is now trailing his tongue over my body in much the same way he did the other time and the fact that I can't see and that, what's more, I'm entirely at his mercy is causing me to wriggle excitedly—a fact that doesn't escape Nick's notice. "You're sopping," he whispers again and then suddenly his face is down at my wettest spot, soaking it up. A few seconds later, he's gone—and not just from that particular spot.

"Nick?"

No answer.

"Nick?"

I hear him walk toward me from the entryway. "I thought I told you not to speak," he says.

"But—"

"If we're going to do this, I'm going to need you to follow the rules." His voice is stern and I'm suddenly grateful for the sweet little safe word.

I know what a sensible girl would do in this situation: she would say that enough was enough, ask this obviously unhinged, power-tripping individual to untie her, and never speak to him again. But I stay quiet, feeling more turned on than I perhaps ever have, as I listen to the unmistakable sound of a condom wrapper tearing. Next thing I know, he's inside me—but almost as soon as I've grown accustomed to it, he's pulled out.

"Come back," I whisper. I can feel him lying next to me on the bed, one of his legs resting against mine.

"Uh-uh—no begging," he says. Then he smacks my ass. "And no talking, either." The bed shifts as he stands up.

"But—"

"If you continue to beg, I'm going to leave," he says. "And not just the room. I'll leave your place."

"Without your tie?"

"Yes, without my tie, sweet girl," he says, suddenly leaning in to kiss me. I can't tell exactly where he is now but think he's standing next to the bedpost by the window. He pulls away abruptly, and as I reach my face forward for another kiss, he says, "That counts as begging, my dear."

By the time he unties me and we have sex, I feel like he's released something in me I never knew existed—an inner sex goddess far more audacious and less graceful than the one I'd periodically tried to act like. Before he leaves, he coaxes me into e-mailing him another picture.

*L**unch tomorrow?* Nick's e-mail reads.

Lunch, in the past few weeks, has come to mean a specific time in the mid-afternoon when I take the two trains required to get to Nick's apartment and he walks the block and a half from his office to meet me there. He tends to greet me at the door by shoving me against it and while sometimes we make it to the bed, we usually end up on the floor. The tie and eye mask have long since been abandoned because, I assume, we've both realized that we don't need to get any more turned on than we already are.

Having determined that the best outfit to wear for Nick is the one that's the easiest to remove, the next day I put on a short dress Kendall would definitely not approve of and head over. The sex is as satisfying as usual and, as we lie together afterward and he tells me that he doesn't have very long because he has a shrink appointment ("Not the shrink shrink but the one who gives me my meds"), I think about what a relief casual sex can be. In a standard dating situation, the fact that Nick went to a shrink for medication would be something he'd probably tell me, haltingly and with hope that I wouldn't judge it, somewhere between our third and sixth dates. But when you don't have to worry about whether the person you're sleeping with is trying to assess your potential as an appropriate mate, you can say whatever you'd like whenever you'd like.

"What time?" I ask.

He looks at his clock—an antique, nondigital one that I'd assumed until now was a decoration and not an actual device that told time. "I have another half hour," he says, smile rakish as he gestures toward his erection.

"Well, we should make good use of that." I slide down between his legs, thinking about how I've never been able to make him come from oral sex and suddenly wanting to remedy that. As I start to put him in my mouth, however, he pulls away a little bit. I look up. "Are you okay?" I ask. "Would you rather I stop?"

He shrugs indifferently. "If you want."

"If I want?" I say, hurt. "I'm not detecting a lot of enthusiasm from you."

Nick slides an arm behind his head. "Well, there are certain things I like to save for her," he says, not unkindly.

I lie back on the pillow and pull the covers tight around me. "Save for her?" He'd never mentioned anything like this before—he almost never brought her up—and until this point, he'd always been eager and excited. "What does that mean?"

He gets out of bed. "It just means that while I don't mind receiving oral sex," he says as he stretches, "I really only let myself go from it when I'm with her." His smile is innocent, as if he'd assumed he was telling me something I already knew.

I nod, trying not to be hurt by the news that I've been spending time trying to arouse a guy who's been fighting me on it. *It's just sex*, I tell myself. *You're not allowed to be hurt.* But I don't seem to listen. "That's a little weird, Nick," I say as he walks, naked, into his bathroom. I raise my voice so he can hear me. "I mean, given the fact that she's living with her boyfriend, it's probably safe to assume she's not saving anything like that for you." I can't tell if I'm hoping to hurt him or just telling him the truth—or if, in this case, they're the same thing.

Nick comes out of the bathroom and kicks the door closed. He's still smiling as he says, "Well, that doesn't matter. I do it more for me than for her." I look at him—the golden hair now in a sort of sweat-induced Afro, the body pale in certain spots and splotchy in others—and search for some evidence that he knows how odd this entire conversation is. But he looks cavalier, like he assumes that everyone talks about how they save their oral sex orgasms for the primary woman in their open relationship. "Don't forget," Nick adds as he sits down on the bed, "I'm not in this situation by choice. I only want to be with her."

I nod since that's pretty much what he'd told me from the beginning but also start to wonder what the hell I'm doing in an apartment in the middle of an April day listening to a man I just had sex with tell me to my face that he doesn't really want to be here—and, even worse, assuming I won't mind. He leans over and kisses my foot, bringing my toe up to his mouth in what I imagine is an attempt to cushion what he just said. "Besides, I like that this is all about bringing you pleasure," he says, adding a growl, but the sentiment and even the way he's sucking on my toe feels forced. He's definitely brought me an enormous amount of pleasure. But, unlike him, I *am* in this situation by choice. And it occurs to me as I remove my foot from between his teeth that I'd rather choose someone who would hesitate at least a little bit before telling me he has to meet with the shrink who gives him his meds.

I don't reach out to Nick and he doesn't contact me and before long, the only evidence of our affair are the e-mail exchanges I still have saved on my computer. But while I'm grateful to have had the purely carnal experience of sex without commitment since I'd always assumed I was someone whose guilt and shame wouldn't allow her to live with that, I don't really have any desire to see him again. Soon after, I learn when I'm reporting a sex story for a magazine that "yellow" is a common safe word. "It's code for 'slow down,'" says the person I'm interviewing. Slow down. And I am.

Yet not having Nick or the 20-year-old to focus on makes me nostalgic for Will again. It's been over nine months since we met and I'm still feeling the aftereffects—still believing he's the most intelligent, insightful, cool, and loving guy I've ever met. But I have more perspective now and can thus acknowledge that he can't be the deity I've made him in my head. And yet I keep thinking that, like the bruise that's just one day gone, my feelings for him will disappear—that I'll wake up some morning and wonder how I could have thought I fell in love at first sight with someone I was only around for a couple of weeks. But it never happens. The bruise has healed and yet I remain just as convinced that my feelings were and are real. I wonder how long that will last or if it will stay with me forever.

While I'm still hanging on but determined to let go—trying not to play the songs that remind me of him, stopping myself from reflecting on what could have been—I notice that I've somehow begun attracting other married men. They're suddenly, for the first time in my life, all around me, making overtures. And almost as if the universe is determined to test me on this one—*are you going to be a home wrecker or not?*—they've started to come in increasingly attractive packages. One is an editor who never acknowledged me during my decade-long crush on him but now wants to get together for candlelit dinners, another a man whose books I devoured in my 20s. And it's not just coming from those wearing rings; men with girlfriends also start asking me out while explaining that what they have going on with "her" is very undefined. Not all of these guys are handing me hotel keys or begging me to embark on affairs but it's clear that I could engage, at least emotionally, and I wonder if learning firsthand that not all married men are as blissfully happy as I'd sort of blindly assumed they were is causing me to emit energy that I'm game for an adulterous affair. But since the best possible thing—some version of love—happened during my one adventure in this territory and it made me miserable, I run from every last temptation.

The most surprising part of it all is that this kind of thing never happened before. The other-woman role is one I was literally born to play: I always felt like the other woman in my parents' marriage because I often felt like my dad treated me like I was, and I used to be nervous that my competitive nature and drive for attention would somehow cause me to accidentally end up trying to seduce my friends' boyfriends. Even though I never did—I was far more likely to consider the guy an intrusion on my relationship with my friend—I somehow never trusted myself in this way.

As I'm thinking about this, a male friend I'd confided in about Will asks me if I'm aware of the fact that what I did with him was essentially an act of violence. "This is someone with a wife and kids," he says, "and by doing what you were doing with him, you were taking him away from that, giving him the promise of something else, and thus actively hurting his family." His words stick with me. How much of my getting involved with Will, or interacting with any married guy, is me trying to exact revenge on all those women who looked so well-adjusted by getting married in their 20s? Am I trying to get back at them for all those smug "You haven't met anyone yet?" remarks I'd endured? In a way, flirting and being flirted with by other women's husbands was a way to prove that, despite what my mother and society and Nora Ephron movies had said, I'd made the right choice: *I may not have your children or mortgage but I can attract your husband.* Of course, being able to tempt a conflicted married man is about as difficult as luring a starving person into a three-course meal. But it never feels like that at the time. It usually feels like the opposite: that it must mean I'm special because I'm worth the risk. Maybe that was true with Will but I have to believe that when it comes to the others, the reason I'm being targeted isn't that I'm special but that I look like I may say yes.

Helen doesn't get into any of this in *S&SG* and even says that married men can be used to "add spice to your life." And maybe they can for some women. But they can't for me anymore, not because I think I owe it to womankind but because I feel like I owe it to myself.

CHAPTER TEN

The Eligibles

You ought to have about 30 men to keep you from feeling
like you live in a manless world . . . these are the men you
could marry, maybe. They are single, reasonably attractive
and introduceable to your friends.

—*Sex and the Single Girl*

In April, it occurs to me that, despite my recent bout of rampant
sex, I may well be living in what Helen would call a "manless
world."

It's not that I don't know a lot of men. I do. But aside from
the romantic prospects that dip in and out of my life, the only
ones I'm close to these days are gay. Nicole, Shari, Elizabeth,
Molly, and almost all my other female friends are chummy with
straight men. But while I hung out with a lot of straight guys in
L.A., I don't here in New York; over time, gay men have simply
replaced them.

This could be a sign of growth. After all, my old pattern was
to manipulate a boy into friendship if I didn't feel attracted to
him and then use him for whatever validation or companionship I wasn't getting from whomever I *was* attracted to. And my
selfishness wasn't the sole issue. The truth is that those relationships could only go to a certain level; if I shared true sadness or

pain with one of these guys, it often seemed to terrify or con-
found them. Gays were easier: consistently ready with a quip,
usually willing to analyze every last emotion, far more prone to
compliments, generally lacking ulterior motives, and, perhaps
most importantly, often quite available. Helen writes that a girl
who's afraid of marriage will be drawn to gay men because she
"feels safe with them and they in turn with her" but another
reason I'm close to so many men who love men is that they're
slightly less likely to get married and start procreating; in other
words, they help me to deny the fact most everyone else my age
has coupled off.

Right now, however, it's time to get back in touch with the
straight guys I know—my future husband, after all, could be
one of them. According to Helen, the best way to figure out
your options is to make a list of your "eligibles"—all the men
you're acquainted with who could be potential partners. (She
also, bless her, has a subcategory called the "eligibles but who
needs them"—"the weirdies, the creepies, the dullies, the snobs,
the hopeless neurotics and mamas' darlings.") The roster, she
says, is meant to include fathers, uncles, brothers, cousins, family friends, clergymen, doctors, dentists, butchers, accountants,
brokers, hairdressers, and the husbands of friends; the only men
you're supposed to leave off are bus drivers and bartenders. According to her, you should have about 30 in all.

While I don't want to defy Helen, putting my dad, brother,
and any other family members on my list gives me the creeps. I
also don't have a butcher or clergyman and don't see how I could
include my accountant or anyone else I communicate with but
have never met face-to-face. Going through my address book

operating by these rules, I hit the number 30 while only on the C's ; feeling pretty good, I continue to add names until I get to the Z's. Grand total: 178

At first I'm excited. Look at all the men I know! Helen would be so proud to learn that one of her disciples is such a terribly social creature! I think back to when I read *The Tipping Point* and examined Malcolm Gladwell's list of 250 last names taken randomly from a New York phone book with the assumption that I would of course know people with most of them. Alas, my number was far below the average of Gladwell's acquaintances, forever shattering my image of myself as a potential "connector." But here I've passed Helen's unintentional sociability test with flying colors.

After a few minutes, however, this actually seems a bit tragic. Look at all the men I know and I still can't find one I want to be with who wants to be with me. If there were only 30 on the list, at least I'd have an excuse. Not wanting to be dragged into a depression over this, I do calculations to try to figure out who are legitimate eligibles and determine that 58 are married or in serious relationships, 28 are gay, 18 are work contacts, 16 are people I've already dated, and five have major drinking problems. But this still leaves 58—nearly double the number that Helen thinks should be the total. Discouraged, I consider the fact that I've known too many men, been on too many dates, and weighed too many possibilities to even know when a real one comes along.

So I make more incisions to my list and, after crossing off the men that are unrealistic (no matter what happens, it's safe to say that my shoe repair guy and I are not going to be walking down any lovers' lanes together) and the ones that I'd be interested in but I know aren't interested in me, I'm left with 10. I spend some time considering each of those and then ponder a lifetime of waking up alone, and the last scenario is the most appealing. Then I wonder if my expectations are simply too high. Am I still clinging to the notion that a perfect man is going to come along and sweep me off my feet when I should just be grateful for the opportunity to have 10 potentials? Maybe, I think, the guy I'm holding out for doesn't exist.

The next step becomes clear: I need to open my mind to the men I come across who I don't think are my type. The recent oats I've sown have helped me to see that what I'm intrinsically drawn to tends to leave me feeling empty or alone. Besides, the more I've liked or loved someone, the more handsome he's become to me. So why not start considering those who don't initially excite me and see if an attraction can grow?

When I meet Ryan at a party in mid-April and suggest that we get together for lunch, I'm not entirely sure what my intentions are. I'm intrigued by his job as a TV production executive and surely consider, at least in the back of my mind, the fact that he could be a great contact. But my motives aren't always clear, even to me, so all I know when I'm sitting across from him at the restaurant is that I find him intelligent and appreciate his take on things. I don't in any way want to tear his clothes off, to run my fingers through his long, curly hair or writhe against his pudgy-looking body, but when he suggests we go out that Friday night, I think that this could be a chance for me to see if a spark could build.

At first, dinner is pleasant—easy conversation at a trendy new place. Convinced, perhaps, that my new mature attitude has also caused my palate to grow up, I agree to split foie gras with him even though I don't like it. A major food critic Ryan knows stops by our table and the whole scene feels like it could be out of *Sex and the City*. When the critic walks away, however, Ryan and I fall silent. I tend to think of myself as a good first date—someone who knows how to keep the chatter lively. But for whatever reason, my repertoire falls flat and the threads I want Ryan to pick up are left dangling somewhere beneath the foie gras we've both abandoned. That's when I lean back on an old safety: querying him about his family.

"I'm really not in the mood to talk about them," he responds with a sigh. I nod and try to come up with other topics. During our lunch, Ryan had questioned me enough about my sobriety to suggest that he knew quite a bit about alcoholism so I ask him how he came to be so informed. He looks annoyed, shrugs, and says he doesn't feel close enough to me to share that. "You're really intense," he then says. "Do you always need to go there—to the painful stuff? What about a conversation about—I don't know—hobbies?"

My face flushes. I *am* intense, I think. Why can't I be a bubbly girl who discusses the latest *New York Times* headlines or at least whatever blockbuster just came out? Then I'm angry: who is *he* to shame me for being myself? I can hear the defensive hostility in my tone as I ask Ryan if he has any hobbies but I don't think he can because he just starts talking about how much he loves skiing.

When he tells me that the view from his roof is amazing,

I'm still clinging to the notion that my fresh mental outlook is the solution to my singledom so I agree to let him show it to me. The view is indeed amazing but when he asks if I want to join him under the blanket he's brought up, I don't have it in me to force what I think I should be forcing. He walks me to a cab and we have an awkward cheek kiss. I know we won't go out again and the thought is a relief.

I learn that eligibles can resurface out of nowhere when I'm leaving an Upper East Side French bistro one night at the end of April and a preppy-looking guy walks up to me. "Is your name Anna?" he asks. "Because I'm with someone you know and he sent me over to make sure it was you." He gestures to a nearby table, where my old friend Aaron is sitting.

Aaron and I met because we were in the same restaurant almost two decades ago and the people we were eating with knew each other. We'd occasionally get together after that but one night he hit on me and when I told him I thought we should just be friends, he said he understood but afterward became increasingly acrimonious. Eventually I began either ignoring his attempts to get together or wishing I had when he'd fling subtle barbs my way.

Once I'm sitting at his table, however, I feel something different between us. The edge of hostility is gone. And he looks good: the rest of his face seems to have caught up to a nose that used to seem too big, he's discovered glasses that work well with his slightly square face, and his hair is still thick and dark. We talk about his life in L.A. and mine in New York and confirm that we're both still single. When he tells me that he's in town for his friend's birthday party the following night and then invites me to come along, I accept.

At the party, I feel the crackling of potential, which inspires me to be truthful and tell him that it often seems like he's trying to put me down. To my shock, he admits that I'm right, adding that he thinks he does it out of the mistaken conviction that he'll eventually feel like he's gotten back at me for rejecting him.

I'm impressed by his honesty and he's the first thing on my mind when I wake up the next morning. I tell him as much in an e-mail and he responds: *I like that you were thinking about me while you were in your bed—I just wish I'd been there, too.* For some reason, this e-mail—more than what he'd admitted the night before, more than the disappearance of his previous animosity—makes me feel like he's a real possibility. He'd never been so direct with me before and I found it sexy. And the idea of him in my bed is a surprisingly nice one. Since he's leaving town that day and I'm going to L.A. the following week, we make a plan to get together there.

Over dinner in West Hollywood, I'm more vulnerable and honest with him than I've been before and when he leans in to kiss me on the cheek, I'm thrilled to feel an unmistakable glimmer of attraction. I picture myself telling people how we were friends for years—until the one day I saw the light and then it was happily-ever-after. In my fantasy, I'm smiling beatifically and saying that I never realized "the one" was right in front of me the whole time.

But we're taking things slow—merely discussing our potential as partners without making any move toward that. We talk and e-mail over the next two weeks and then he's back in New

York again so we make another dinner plan. For whatever reason, this feels like the occasion we've been building toward: if Aaron and I are going to happen, tonight is the night.

An hour before he's scheduled to pick me up, I get a work call that ends up taking longer than it should and leaves me with a headache and no time to get ready. I pray that Aaron will be late but instead he shows up 10 minutes before he's supposed to. Since I've always been terrible at keeping my emotions hidden, I know that my irritation about his timing—as well as my stress from the past few hours—is obvious as I let him in. When he greets me with "I always like to come early to see how people handle it," my annoyance only grows.

And at dinner, the energy between us is different than it's been lately: the passive-aggressive undertones are back. When Aaron signals for the check, he says, "You know, you haven't smiled once this whole time."

I immediately feel the same shame and defensiveness I did with Ryan. First the shame: Now I'm too intense *and* dour? Dear God, I used to know how to date! What the hell has happened to me? Then the defensiveness: Stop telling me what I'm doing wrong! Just let me be who I am at this moment! "I haven't?" I ask him. "Are you sure?"

He nods. "Trust me, if you're sitting across from a girl who never smiles, you notice."

I want to point out that we spent most of the time talking about formative-years experiences that had left us emotionally scarred and that isn't the sort of thing that makes a girl want to break out in a grin. But I keep the thought to myself. Still, this is when I know that Aaron and I aren't going to work out. I'm not sure if it's because he's made me aware of the fact that he doesn't really make me smile—Duchenne or otherwise—or if I just see that I'll never be able to stop feeling judged by him, but my fantasy about us dissipates more with every passing second. I want to get it back, to feel safe and accepted and enthusiastic again, but the balloon has been popped, or may already be floating somewhere in the sky.

Despite my discouraging encounters with Ryan and Aaron, I notice when sharing these tribulations with my friends that I'm not hoping they'll save me by saying whatever will help make everything better. And I'm not jealous of the fact that Nicole is still with Tim, Shari's continuing to see the hedge fund guy, and Molly has just returned from the Caribbean with her new fashion photographer boyfriend. I'm not sure when, exactly, but along the way I've become more self-reliant and less convinced that because something good is happening to a person I know, it can't happen for me.

Yet I also see that I'm hardly "surrounded" by men the way Helen thinks I should be. And this makes me ready to entertain the possibility that the men on Match may not be as bad as I'd thought they were before. Jason was on there, after all, and even though we didn't work out, he proved that the site had viable options. Maybe I'd judged the profiles too harshly and not taken into consideration the fact that most people weren't natural writers. If Match required its members to, say, explain IPOs and stock investments, I'd look like a complete idiot, so it probably wasn't fair to dismiss men simply because they didn't share my skill set.

I'm not, however, throwing all requirements out the window. As I look at the site, I continue to pass on the men over 55, the ones who write things like "I'm telling the truth about my age (unlike MANY OTHERS on this site) and smoke but never in a house or in front of women"—an actual excerpt from a message I receive—and anyone who looks overly Republican, sexist, racist, or terrifying. But I overturn my previously established no-emoticon rule, concluding that a person who gets involved with the sort of men I have has no business not considering a guy because he writes "LOL" or uses a smiley face in an e-mail or text.

My new attitude yields a few new possibilities. In early May, I have coffee with a guy who looks like a younger Paul Newman in his photos but who can't seem to form complete, cohesive sentences in person. I meet another who tells me that he's put all his money into a lemon powder that's going to render the use of real lemons in drinks obsolete. As a testament to my fresh, unbiased approach, I even go out with someone who's checked the "3 or more" kids box on his profile. None is a love connection.

I then start exchanging e-mails with a guy who lives in the Hamptons and isn't wearing a shirt in his main photo. The shirtless picture is typically an automatic never but times when I'm prying my mind open by hook and crook aren't typical. Besides, he's not flexing or standing in front of a Harley or doing anything equally disturbing—just lying in a clean, white, billowy bedroom. I give him a hard time in an e-mail about the photo and he takes it, explaining that he mostly put it up as a tongue-in-cheek response to all the other guys with shirtless photos on the site. I reason that being cheesy or clichéd with full self-awareness is almost like not being cheesy or clichéd at all and, after a few back-and-forth exchanges, he and I make a plan to meet in the city later that week.

He texts me to suggest the Ace Hotel and I respond that it tends to be mobbed in the evenings so we should first locate each other at the coffee place attached to it. He writes back: *Just wear something sexii and I'll have no trouble finding you.* Horrified by the cheesy spelling of sexy but reminding myself that I need to be less critical about the things that don't matter, I write: *Sexii with two I's? Interesting,* a communiqué that's about a hundred times less judgmental than I feel.

His comeback is instantaneous: *Yes, one for you and one for me. Wink wink. I'm good, aren't I?*

I stare at the phone, knowing that I can accept only so much. This is no mere emoticon, no LOL followed by a series of exclamation points. This is a grown man who writes the word "sexy" with two I's followed by two winks followed by a sentence declaring his pride over his cleverness. In a sense, I feel like I've gotten what I deserve by corresponding with a guy who puts up a shirtless photo. I contemplate different responses—the honest one where I say that I really don't respond well to that way of communicating, the fake one where I pretend not to be as snobby as I am and still meet up with him, and the one that's right in the middle. The middle wins: I text him that I'm not going to be able to get together after all. I don't hear back.

Not ready to give up, I continue poking around the site and discover something I hadn't seen before: a "favorites" button that allows you to pick the people you find most appealing—something they can then see. I love this idea: it's like the grade school approach of getting your friend to tell the guy you like him so, if he's interested, he can go in with full confidence that you'll respond.

I put six men on my favorites list, and one, Kevin, contacts me. These odds don't seem terrible, and his message thanking me for picking him as a favorite and telling me that he likes how my profile makes me look like "an overly serious hard ass" is funny. After a few more exchanges, though, he stops writing back.

That's when I consider revising my Match profile. Kevin's "hard ass" comment, while a joke, wasn't the only response I'd gotten to what I'd written on my page—a couple of other men had sent me messages that said I seemed negative or conflicted about being on the site. Reasoning that this had once been true but the new, positive me doesn't feel that way, I go through the cringe-worthy process of reading what I'd originally written in my profile.

While I understand that what I typed up is a direct, slightly wry summary of my thoughts and feelings, I have to admit that, if I didn't know me, it could definitely be interpreted as the musings of someone who felt uncomfortable Internet dating and who brought up things—like the fact that she wasn't looking for a "meal ticket"—that most would rather leave unsaid. So I delete what's there, replacing it with a paragraph about how I can't fake laugh or lie, how I think all kids and animals are amusing but "not in some Mr. Magoo or Mary Poppins kind of way," how I love pulling lint from the dryer, and how my favorite moment is when I discover that a man is a good kisser. I figure this is honest, sweet, not too earnest, and just the tiniest bit playful.

A few days later, I hear from Ben, a tall, bespectacled writer who manages to have long hair and still be sexy. We meet for coffee, and in person he's sweet, funny, self-effacing, and—best of all—asks me to have dinner with him the following night. We go out a few more times and while I like him, I don't feel the obsessive need to hear from or see him the way I usually do when I'm interested in a guy. I wonder if this is what dating is supposed to be like—having fun with someone you occasionally kiss good night. Usually, both the guy and I jump in headfirst and start spending every minute together. But after a few weeks, Ben tells me that he suffers from anxiety and that our relationship is triggering it. He'd gone on Match, he explains, to start casually dating people and hadn't expected to find someone he wanted to see on a regular basis. He adds that meeting me has made him see that he needs to go back to therapy to deal with his anxiety issues and he'd love to get in touch again after he does.

When I share this with Molly, she sighs and tells me he sounds like "a piece of work." Yet I respect his straightforwardness and self-awareness, relate to his issues, believe everything he's saying, and have the all-too-rare feeling that he's someone I'd like to stay in touch with no matter what happens. I tell him that I understand. And I do. But I also see that Match is only going to take me so far. I want more dates. And the way I'm going to get them, I decide, is by widening the net.

By most people's standards, I'm a social creature—primarily because staying in and watching TV or reading a book all evening is pretty much out of the question for me since I don't sit still for that long. It therefore doesn't really take any effort whatsoever to keep showing up at book readings, parties, dinners, media mixers, friends' performances, salons, literary magazine events, and whatever else is going on. But none of these seems to be introducing me to any new, exciting men.

So I consider some of Helen's suggestions for encountering fresh bait. Deciding to test her claim that a pin with a message printed on it will inspire interaction with the opposite sex, I wander into a store that sells pins at the Farmers' Market in L.A. when I'm there in May and buy one that says "California State Fair" on it. I figure that since it says California and I'm from California, this will be an excellent conversation piece once I'm back in New York. When my friend John comes and meets me, however, he objects.

"That's a total old lady pin," he says. "Only an octogenarian would say anything about it. And an octogenarian wouldn't be able to see it since the writing's so small."

We return to the store and I exchange my state fair pin for one that features the New York postage stamp with the famous Love sculpture on it. I'm excited by the switch—not only is this one far more youthful-seeming but it also projects exactly what I'm seeking. I attach it to the top of my shirt and prepare for commentary.

Nothing happens.

Undeterred, John and I sit down for coffee at Monsieur Marcel, a French café in the middle of the Farmers' Market, both of us eyeing a handsome, light-skinned black guy sitting by himself, and communicating through eye signals that we think he's an ideal candidate for the pin test. Sensing our stares, the guy looks up and we both grin at him. He smiles, nods, and glances away.

"Just give him a minute," John whispers. During that minute, the guy turns around so that his back is facing us. "He's probably just unfriendly," John adds. I nod but then we watch the guy initiate a conversation with a girl in workout clothes who's walking by. She laughs at whatever he says to her and they keep talking.

Not wanting to let go of the dream of the conversation-inspiring pin, I turn to the waiter as he approaches us to pick up our dishes. "What do you think of my pin?" I ask him.

He glances at it and shrugs. "It's fine," he says. He looks more closely. "Actually, it's kind of weird. Why does it say eight cents?"

"It's modeled after a stamp," John pipes in. "That's a famous sculpture in New York."

The waiter nods warily and asks if we'd like anything else. We don't. When we leave, he comes running after us and at first I think he's going to confess that he reconsidered the matter and thinks my pin is terrific but he's only returning the sunglasses I'd accidentally left behind.

Our next stop is the Apple Store at the Grove, where we ask a 20-something employee what he thinks of the pin; he also finds the eight-cents part weird and seems equally uninterested in the Love sculpture. He does, however, mention that if I were someone he thought might buy a computer, he'd without a doubt tell me he liked it.

While my pin doesn't attract any suitors on its own, there's no denying the fact that it helps me to interact with men I otherwise wouldn't. It occurs to me that even when Helen's suggestions seem like they're not working, they actually are.

"I think you need something louder," John says as we make our way through the Farmers' Market back to our cars. We're walking by Monsieur Marcel when I notice that they sell T-shirts with French sentences displayed on them.

"Wait a minute!" I exclaim. "Helen says that the pin should contain a message—an actual sentence. She had one that said, 'I have gray hair, brown eyes and a black heart.'"

John stares at me. "Are you serious?"

I nod and point to a shirt that declares *La vie est belle chez Monsieur Marcel*. "This is what I need. The pin is too subtle. This is bigger—and it's an actual statement. And it rhymes! Plus it doesn't say something ridiculous, like most statement T-shirts. It's sophisticated. It tells people that I speak French."

"But you don't really speak French."

"I know. But the people seeing the shirt don't. Maybe it will even make them think I *am* French."

He eyes me. "And why would you want that again?"

There's no stopping my enthusiasm now. "Because that's a true conversation piece! Someone might stop me and say, 'Oh, are you French?' And I could say, 'No, but I just took a French class. *Est ce que tu parles Français?*' Or really, '*Est ce que vous parlez Français?*' since he'd be a stranger and I wouldn't want to use the familiar *tu*."

John looks from the shirt back to me. "I like how the words will be right on your breasts," he finally says.

As it turns out, John's lack of encouragement may have been prescient—or perhaps just perceptive. Once I'm back in New

York, I don the shirt optimistically, darting around the streets of Manhattan waiting for a Frenchman or curious stranger to ask me what it means or why I'm wearing it. But aside from a few quick glances that may well have been glances at my breasts and not at the words displayed across them, the shirt makes no impact on the men who see me. Without a friend to help me make my special addition into a conversation piece with strangers, this method is fairly ineffective. I conclude that Helen's thoughts about displaying words from our clothing had to have been more relevant at a time that predated the "I'm with Stupid" shirt.

Or am I just trying too hard? Helen also claims that simply walking around by yourself is a good way to meet men, which inspires me to begin embarking on solo journeys sans special T-shirts or pins. Of course, living in New York and simply getting where I need to go requires plenty of solo journeys, but frenetically rushing to make the 1 train doesn't exactly scream, *Please approach me* in any language that could be appealing. I love the regular walks I start going on along the West Side Highway and Highline but only encounter aggressively gay men, serious runners, or happy couples.

So I return to the drawing board—*S&SG*—and read that Helen also recommends having "the maddest beach towel you can lay your hands on," such as one with a checkerboard print on it. I go online and—voilà!—find that exact towel, which also comes with checker pieces. Who cares that I don't remember how to play? The towel is adorable.

But the men on the beach in Montauk—where I faithfully trot out my towel several different weekends in May that I go there—feel differently. Or I should say: they don't seem to feel anything about it at all. I wonder if checkers is simply too dated a game, or too associated with childhood, for anyone to gravitate toward it; today you probably need to have a towel version of an iPhone application to attract anyone's interest. Or perhaps no one who has the option of staring at or going in the ocean wants to play a game of checkers on a towel. Not wanting to give up, I chat with a surfer one morning while we're drinking coffee next to each other on the Ditch Plains beach. Spreading out the towel on the sand, the checker squares on full display, I use my limited windsurfing knowledge to ask him about the day's waves. While he's happy to talk surf, he doesn't appear to be at all interested in me—let alone my towel.

Back in the city, I brainstorm new ideas and stumble on one I'm surprised Helen didn't recommend: the pet as mating facilitator. While, as a cat owner, it's almost impossible for me to wrap my head around the notion that an animal could do anything to improve a person's dating life, everyone I know with a dog ends up meeting people as a result. Surely a dog is a better conversation piece than a pin, shirt, or towel? My friend Tom agrees and, better yet, agrees to let me borrow his chocolate Lab, Charlotte, one bright May afternoon; he drops her off at my place and suggests that I walk her from my apartment to his— about 10 blocks away—and then we take her together to the dog park at Washington Square.

At the first stoplight, Charlotte nuzzles up to a man standing next to me, and he pets her and tells me she's really cute. Good dog! Alas, he appears to be in his 70s and is clutching a woman's arm. While Charlotte doesn't respond to anyone else during our walk to Tom's apartment, I Duchenne smile at every person in the vicinity. Then, as we reach Tom's block, Charlotte finds a friend—a cute miniature bulldog—and they start sniffing each other. The man at the end of the miniature bulldog's leash has a buzz cut and pretty green eyes. Eureka! "What's your dog's name?" I ask. I don't know if it's the fact that I'm wearing a Dana-approved dress and Bee-directed makeup or if I'm just growing more confident all the time but I feel very much in control.

"Bandit," he says, neither friendly nor unfriendly. Bandit? Miniature bulldog? Maybe he's gay. Bandit's owner eyes our two sniffing dogs warily. "Yours?"

"Charlotte." A pause. I'm certain there's some dog-related question I'm supposed to ask next but am not sure what it is. "Good dog?" I finally ask.

He gives me a nervous look. "I'm sorry?"

Concluding that my question has the unique distinction of being both idiotic and a conversation killer, I ask him what his name is as if that's what I'd originally inquired.

"Steve," he says. "Yours?"

I tell him and then we nod at each other as Bandit stuffs his nose in Charlotte's butt. I think that Steve could be a bit nicer given the action my temporary dog is giving his but maybe when two dogs are having a moment, engaging with the other owner is inappropriate—sort of like trying to get it on with the father of your teenage daughter's prom date. Charlotte starts barking and Bandit barks back and I think they're showing excited affection but then they're growling at each other and I'm not sure what the etiquette is here but Steve doesn't seem concerned so I don't do anything. That's when I notice Tom standing behind Steve, grinning in a way that makes it clear he's been here the whole time, observing my inept attempts both to act like a dog owner and to flirt.

"An appropriate question might be, 'How old is he?'" Tom says in a loud stage whisper. I have no idea if Steve notices or hears Tom. I ask Steve how old Bandit is as if I haven't been instructed to right in front of him.

"Seven." Steve's nervous smile persists as Bandit reinserts his nose in Charlotte's behind. Steve probably thinks I'm from a nearby asylum that allows patients to interact with animals and Tom is my male nurse. Still, he gamely asks, "How old is Charlotte?"

From his perch a few feet away, Tom holds up five fingers. "Five," I answer. Tom gives me a thumbs-up with his other hand and I assume it's another finger. "I mean, six." Tom puts his thumb down, shakes his head, and points to the five fingers he's still holding up. "I mean, five." Embarrassed, I add, "And a half." Steve looks like he wants to be anywhere but here.

I decide to put him out of his misery. "Well, Charlotte and I should probably hit the dog park," I say as I tug on her leash. Bandit looks sad that his nose will be losing its temporary dwelling space but his owner's relief is palpable.

At the dog park, Tom sits on a bench while Charlotte and a terrier start fighting with each other. Still holding on to her leash, I hover around like an overprotective parent until the terrier's owner, a guy with shaggy red hair and Ray-Bans, looks up from his cell phone conversation to suggest that I take Charlotte off the leash since, he explains, leashes not only make dogs in dog parks angry but also cause the other ones to pick on them.

I nod and release her, noting that all the other dogs are running and sniffing and playing freely and that by walking in here without letting her free, I've revealed myself to be the impostor dog owner that I am. Charlotte and the terrier immediately cool it and Charlotte embarks on a tour of the park's dog butts. As she scampers from dog to dog to dog, I scamper after her. After a few minutes of this, I notice that all of the other dog owners are sitting on benches and socializing. Tom, for example, is now lounging and laughing with a pretty blond girl. They appear to be enjoying their conversation so much that I don't want to interrupt but eventually I conclude that I don't have anything else to do now that I understand you're supposed to be watching and not chasing your dog.

After introducing me, Tom explains that they've been talking about how funny it is that I'm using his dog to try to meet a man. I smile gamely, pretending I don't want to kill him for spreading this information around the dog park and as if I'm not humiliated by how amused they are. "When I saw you running after Charlotte, I knew something weird was going on!" the girl says and they both howl. Before I can sarcastically thank Tom for explaining appropriate dog park behavior to me ahead of time, he suggests that I look for a man I think is attractive and join him on his bench. The pickings are slim here, and attractive seems to be out of the question, so I settle for the next best thing—a man. I sit down next to a 50-something guy reading the paper but he ignores me. I pull out my phone to check my e-mail and when I look up again, he's gone.

I return to Tom and the girl, now getting along even better than before. My escapades here may not be netting me any action but I think they could be doing wonders for Tom. "Go up to that guy," Tom says, motioning toward a greasy-haired rocker type standing with a thin, tattooed brunette. I have the vague sense that I've become Tom's guinea pig.

"But he's with a girl!"

"No, he's not. They're just two dog owners talking."

As I'm about to make my approach, the rocker guy and tattooed girl kiss. "Well, he moves pretty fast," I say to Tom as I collapse on his bench. "Or dogs are even better for hooking up than I realized."

I f you want to meet a good guy, you need to go where the good guys are. And the good guys, it occurs to me on my way home from the dog park, are helping others.

My motivation to do this isn't, of course, solely man-related. I've fed the homeless, danced in senior citizens homes, and even choreographed *The Wiz* for a group of newly sober ex cons at one of the first free rehabs in Los Angeles. Yet throughout all this, I'd never considered the fact that it might introduce me to the right kind of man.

At an orientation meeting I attend for a New York community service organization, however, the group of 50-odd people is made up of at least 45 women. The team leader giving the introductory talk is male but his warm-up jokes—or really just one joke since it's many variations on the idea that he'll have to throw things at people who fall asleep while he's talking—suggest that he's not for me. In between his renditions of that joke, he explains how we can sign up on their Web site to do every-thing from serve food at soup kitchens to help rebuild commu-nity gardens to take underprivileged children to the zoo.

The following Saturday, I commit to serving breakfast at a church that feeds the homeless. I figure that even if this activity doesn't turn up any possibilities, at least I'll be doing something for other people and perhaps gaining perspective on how com-paratively minor my problems are.

When I arrive at the church, I'm surprised to discover that the group of volunteers gathered is mostly male. Maybe all it took was a little selflessness to land me in single-woman heaven! I start introducing myself but can't help but notice that it's not the friendliest crowd. Assuming that people are probably tired from being up this early on a Saturday and perhaps a bit solemn because of the sobering activity we're about to engage in, I don't take it personally and continue to search for solidarity; eventu-ally I find and talk to a lovely girl who's also volunteering here for the first time. We meet some of the guys standing around and I discover that they're almost all in their early 20s and from a church group outside Philadelphia. The most attractive of the bunch, a blond named Tony, is shocked when I tell him that I live in Manhattan. "That's amazing," he marvels with a shake of his head. "When we came in last night, I kept wondering how anyone could live amongst all this filth." That's pretty much the end of our interaction.

A woman wearing a hairnet and apron appears in the din-ing hall and announces that she needs six people to help with eggs. Only one or two raise their hands—a fact that in retro-spect I should have paid closer attention to—and I agree to go along with them because it seems like the right thing to do. This leads to me spending the next several hours bent over a portable griddle, cooking 12 fried eggs at a time, while several stern kitchen volunteers shout, "More eggs! Egg people, please cook faster!" The seminary student next to me—who's here because she has to write a paper about various forms of community service—tells me she really wishes she'd chosen to read to the blind instead. I attempt to chat with the guy on my other side but he appears to be the quiet type—or at least the must-concentrate-very-hard-on-egg-frying type—because he only offers one-word responses.

I'd been hoping to interact with some of the people we were cooking for but whenever I glance at those in the dining room, one of the kitchen people barks that we need more eggs. Not ready to give up on this experience as a potential way to mingle with good-hearted men, I smile at the one or two male volunteers who don't seem to be a part of the 20-something outside-Philly church group. "More eggs!" one shouts at me while the other looks away.

I emerge from the church smelling like fried eggs—a scent that doesn't leave the clothes I'm wearing until I've washed them several times—and feeling like I've just endured a trial-by-fire introduction to life as a line cook in a diner. The orientation leader had mentioned during his introductory talk that when he was walking home after the first time he served food in a homeless shelter, he'd felt connected to the city in a way he never had before. But I, quite honestly, am simply relieved to not be frying eggs.

• • •

When I tell Nicole about my experience at the dog park and church, she asks me why I'm not going to places where I know I'll find single men. "Like a prison?" I ask.

"No, like a singles' night somewhere. Like one of those speed dating things."

"Speed dating?" My mind is already conjuring up an image of uncomfortable-looking people wearing name tags and looking traumatized. "Aren't those things creepy?" I ask.

"You mean creepier than trying to meet a man on the street or while feeding the homeless?" she asks, letting this sink in before adding, "At least you *know* these guys want to meet someone. It's like Match, but you don't have to bother with looking at profiles or e-mailing."

"Since when are you advocating something that's like Match?"

"I'm not. It's just that if you were willing to do Match, this doesn't seem all that different."

Not sure if I should be depressed or inspired by her words, I think about Hugo Cory's belief that the best way to get through something you're scared of is to evoke and then gaze at your fear of it. "I guess if I tell myself that only pathetic and desperate people go to those things, then that will be my perception of it," I say. "But maybe I could think something different." If, to Hugo, the imagination is like a Hollywood studio, maybe what I see as a horror movie could actually be a romantic comedy.

Nicole is, of course, safe suggesting this, seeing as she's 3,000 miles away and I therefore can't beg her to accompany me. So I call Shari and try to sell her on the idea. She's silent. "Look," I say, "speed dating has always been one of those things, like solitary confinement or tightrope walking, that I've been happy enough to avoid. But maybe it would be good to do what I consider to be the most humiliating thing on earth. And since you have a boyfriend, you'd just be sort of auditing the experience as my wing woman."

To my surprise, she agrees and together we look over options on a speed dating Web site I've found. After passing on Size Matters (for tall men) and The Bald and the Beautiful (where, thankfully, only the men have to be bald), we settle on one for nonpracticing Jews. "They'll all probably be smart," I offer. "And funny. And maybe they'll make us feel better about being bad Jews." She laughs, and I buy the tickets before she can change her mind.

The night of the event, we arrive at the Soho bar where it's being held and give our names to a girl standing at the front with a clipboard. She curtly hands us each a sheet that explains how the evening is going to work: women will be seated at various tables around the bar and men will travel from one of us to the next in three-minute intervals. As we make our way to our booths, I try to channel Hugo Cory and not judge the nervous, conservative-looking, and not terribly alluring people around me.

A cheerful guy who would be quite appealing if his eyes weren't so close together walks over and hands me a sheet of paper; he tells me that after each man leaves, I should write down his name and a few identifying characteristics and then check a "yes" or "no" box to indicate whether I'm interested in him. These notes, he explains, are just for me. The real decisions will come after the event is over, when I log on to the speed dating company's Web site to mark who I want to go out with and learn who wants to go out with me.

First to sit down at my table is Alberto, a short, squat, and friendly guy who proudly explains that he's half Puerto Rican and half Bolivian. I ask him if that means he's not Jewish— an ironic question coming from potentially the worst Jew in America—and he admits that he's not but says that his friend who runs the speed dating company asked him to come since there was a shortage of men. At the end of our three minutes, Alberto asks for my number.

"But I thought the whole point of this is that you don't do anything now—just log on to the Web site later," I respond, stalling. Guy number two, who bears a striking resemblance to Tom Arnold if Tom Arnold's hair was white and stuck straight up, hovers in the background, waiting to take his seat.

"I'm not on the Web site, though," Alberto says, rising slowly and hovering over the table as the Tom Arnold guy slides into the seat hesitatingly. Alberto and I look at each other awkwardly and, not knowing how else to fill the silence, I smile at the new guy and say, "This is Alberto! He's not Jewish!" They give each other an uncomfortable look and I marvel at how I've somehow managed to channel George Costanza's mother. Alberto walks away.

Tom Arnold is named David and he's harder to tear information out of than a mobster on the stand. Then comes Gary, a fedora-wearing Long Island music teacher who urges me to take piano lessons and sing, even when I tell him that I'm tone deaf. Next is Joel, a 50-something guy who informs me that my necklace is "very odd" and then immediately launches into a diatribe about how judgmental women are. "They don't seem to understand that attraction is something that can build," he says. "And New York women are the worst."

"How long have you lived here?" I ask, thinking that if he'd just come from a small town, the adjustment to city ladies might be jarring.

"Since 1984." I glance down at the sheet where he's been keeping track of the women he's met so far and notice that he's checked "no" next to all the names that preceded me. Eventually the bell rings. Was that three minutes or 30?

Richard is tan and has nice dimples and, he tells me, really likes concerts and dressing up in costumes. "Nothing creepy," he adds with a laugh, and then proceeds to walk me through every one of his Halloween outfits of the past two decades. Even though he's young—my guess is about 22—he's clearly taken a leadership role tonight. "There was a guy in the bathroom before this started who was freaking out because he didn't know what to say to anyone," he says. "I tried to calm him down." I point to Joel, now torturing the next woman, and ask if it was him. It was not—or at least Richard isn't admitting as much. Richard is sweet but I don't really need another experience with a guy who's young enough to be my son.

The next guy, Matt, has a name tag that's unnecessary since he's also wearing a Best Buy uniform T-shirt that has the same name sewn into it. Influenced, perhaps, by my conversation with Richard, I tell Matt that the Best Buy shirt is a great costume. He looks confused and tells me he's not in costume but actually works at Best Buy. "I'm a regular here," he explains, gesturing to the bar, "and when I came in tonight, the owner—a buddy of mine—said the event was short a few guys and asked if I could help out." He's not Jewish, he adds, but he does know how to install TVs. He confesses that most of the women he's met so far have asked him for iPad discounts.

Matt is followed by Todd, who has longish blond hair and tells me that he's a voice-over actor—a somewhat difficult fact to believe because his voice is rather squeaky and difficult to hear. I contemplate recommending that he contact Arthur but then he says he doesn't care about his voice-over career anymore because he's transitioning into stand-up comedy. Unprompted, he begins his routine, which seems to be focused on the behavior of food delivery people in New York. "You know how they always hold the elevator so they can get out of the building as fast as possible?" he asks. I don't but tell him I do and when he laughs, I understand that this was meant to be the funny part.

Abram, Zev, and Adam follow. Of the three, Yanni-haired Adam has the most interesting story: raised Orthodox, he decided last year that he didn't have faith anymore but hasn't yet told his family. I feel bad that his poor Jewish mother is going find out this information after a woman who only knew her son for three minutes.

Zev, who's balding and Santa-bellied, tells me that he's just returned from the Rainbow Festival in Pennsylvania, which, he informs me, is like Burning Man except that everything—including the drugs—is free. "That means free mushrooms and acid!" he exclaims, causing me to feel bad for two Jewish mothers in a row.

I meet a nearly seven-foot-tall copy machine salesman and a trainer who offers me a discount on sessions if I buy in bulk before the event is declared over and Shari is standing at my table. I've never felt happier to see her. "Now the people who are interested in each other are supposed to hang out and drink at the bar," she says, gesturing to a side door. We make our escape before anyone can stop us.

Once home, worried that my experience may send me spiraling into a post–speed dating depression, I decide to make a list of the reasons why I'm glad I went.

1. I can't say I haven't tried everything.
2. I never have to go again.
3. It made me see that I still have hope.

I stop writing, pen dangling in mid-air. Right there on the page of my Moleskine notebook is tangible evidence that I haven't given up. After the Match dates, the pin wearing, the towel displaying, the dog walking, the egg making, and the speed dating, I both feel good about being on my own and still believe I can have what I want. In a certain way, I'm more optimistic than ever. Because somewhere along the path of evoking and gazing at my fears, I came to understand that I don't need to believe in them anymore.

According to Helen, an airplane is an ideal place for potential romance because of how "sexy" it is to be "almost as close to a strange man as a banana to its skin from 20,000 feet in the air." It's a sentence I spend a great deal of time pondering since I've sat next to plenty of men on planes and certainly felt like I was squished as close to them as a banana to its skin, but never noticed anything remotely sexy about it.

But one Friday night in May, when I'm flying to Miami for the weekend, I'm seated next to a tan, square-jawed, blue-eyed guy who definitely qualifies as sexy. I'd noticed him when we were boarding, had heard him talking on the phone to someone I'd theorized was a woman from the tone of his voice.

"Hi," I say as I slide in next to him. The fact that we've been randomly placed together and that it's a two-seat row assures me that breaking those mirrors didn't do anything to destroy my luck.

"Hi." He gives me a friendly smile and goes back to reading his magazine. Then he looks up. "What's your name?"

"Anna. Yours?"

He holds out his hand. "Darren." We shake; his hands are soft and his handshake firm. He watches as I put my backpack under the seat in front of me. "I saw you at the gate," he says. "You were having some trouble with your boarding pass?"

"Oh, yeah." I'd accidentally printed out the itinerary instead of the boarding pass, which had caused a brief but stressful interaction with the woman behind the Delta counter. I smile, grateful that I'd been calm and not IKEA-customer-service rude about it. "I saw you right before we boarded," I tell him.

"Really?" I watch his eyes crinkle as the corners of his mouth turn up and, for the first time since I learned what it is, I'm positive I'm gazing at a real, live Duchenne smile. Then he sighs. "Did I look like I was desperately trying to get off a phone call?"

"Actually, you seemed quite happy to be on it."

He laughs. "God, no. I was talking to a girl I used to date

who borrowed and then broke my car while I was gone. So I was listening to her explain that I'm coming home to a convertible with a top stuck at half-mast."

"Yikes." I try to subdue my excitement over hearing the girl referred to in the past tense.

"Borrowed my car *without asking*," he adds. "She told the valet guy at my building that I had said it was okay."

My smile grows: car stealing had to qualify her for *permanently* past tense. I continue to rein in my reaction.

Just then, the pilot announces that our plane is last in line for takeoff so the flight is going to be delayed—a situation that has, in my history of experiencing such situations, annoyed or even enraged me, but right now sounds delightful.

"I have to start making better choices," Darren says with a smile. "I think my picker's broken."

I laugh at the expression. "A broken picker? I relate."

Our eyes connect and I have the distinct impression that Darren thinks mine do, indeed, contain tomorrow's lottery numbers. "Does that mean," he asks, "that you're single?"

By the time we've landed, I've learned that Darren is a doctor who often travels to third-world countries, and we've made plans to have breakfast together the next morning. Breakfast is followed by a day of lolling around in the Miami sun, and before I leave, we've shared a few kisses and already decided that he's going to come visit me in New York the following weekend.

He arrives late that Friday night and I have to be up early on Saturday for a work obligation so I tell him to keep sleeping. The whole time I'm gone, I imagine crawling back into bed with him, falling asleep in his arms, and then rising together in the afternoon for a perfect sexual experience followed by a leisurely late brunch.

But when I walk into my apartment, Darren is already up, eating a bowl of Frosted Flakes he either went out and bought or brought with him. I'm aggravated but don't want to be: here I have a real, live man in my apartment, a man who's kind and smart and successful and interested in me—in other words, exactly what I've been seeking—and all I can notice are the slurping sounds he's making, the soggy cereal, and the fact that my fantasies, even the ones I just had five minutes ago, are so very different from reality.

I fight through my discomfort, telling myself that it's remnants of fear that are still, despite the work I've done, influencing my behavior. And for some of the time over the weekend, this internal pep talk works. Darren and I share meals, take walks, and hold hands. But something is missing and I'm not sure what it is. He's not closed off or defensive or tormented. He's sweet and thoughtful and brought me presents, for Christ sakes. He's inarguably attractive in every way and yet I'm not attracted.

Perhaps, I theorize, I don't like myself enough to be able to respect a man who actually seems to like me. Maybe that Groucho Marx quote about how I'd never want to be in any club that would have me as a member is simply how I feel when it comes to men. Or could I just be too controlling, too set in my ways, to actually be able to welcome another person into my orbit? I'd once heard that Jack Nicholson, when he married the mother of his children, moved them into the house next door, and I'd always thought that sounded rather ideal: the white picket fence without having to share it. What if I'm one of those people who simply isn't capable of companionship—who has too many fears and anxieties and justifications and excuses and issues bouncing around her head to actually be capable of having a true partnership with another human being?

Could I be beyond Helen's help?

Part Four

CHAPTER ELEVEN

Honing In on the Issues

You need a quiet, private, personal aggression . . . a refusal
to take singleness lying down.

—*Sex and the Single Girl*

"Is Darren available?" Roger asks.

"Yes."

"Was Jason available? Nick?"

"No. And no."

"Is Will available?"

"No."

"Are *you* available?"

I know this is the real question. The others have been give-
aways, the equivalent of college gut classes, but here's the one
that the entire grade, the entire semester, the entire life rests on.
"I guess . . . no."

He folds his arms and leans back in his chair, victorious—
albeit in a bittersweet way. "Exactly."

"But at the same time, I *feel* available," I insist. "I want to
connect. I want to be intimate."

"So what happens?" he asks.

"I don't know." I glance at his bookshelf. "It's been so long since I've been in a relationship with someone I love that my memories about what it's like feel fake, or like they're scenes from a movie I saw. And I don't remember how to go from point A—meeting the guy—to point B. Or even, really, what point B would be."

Roger takes his glasses off and wipes the collected dust away by flipping the cloth against the lens. "I think you need to look at why you're so terrified to be dependent on someone."

"I don't think it's that," I object. "I just think I've forgotten how to let myself be open to love. My old yoga teacher used to say that we're born able to do all the asana poses but years of living eradicates our ability. And that's how I feel: unable to do something that was once, and should be, second nature."

"When was the last time you really depended on a man?"

I'm irritated by the way he's focusing on dependency but gamely flip through a Rolodex in my brain. "I guess it was Brandon," I say quietly, adding, "The guy I lived with in L.A."

"I remember who Brandon is."

"But I feel stupid talking about a relationship that was over 15 years ago."

"Maybe that was the last time you trusted yourself with someone."

Annoyed, I snap, "This isn't about how I don't trust myself. It's about figuring out why I feel suffocated by a great guy who seems to like me but drawn to the ones who don't. It's about trying to understand why my fear that I'm going to be alone forever is, when I meet a good guy, immediately replaced by a fear that I'm going to be stuck with him forever. It's about determining why men who have one foot out the door bring on that transformative, electric, and overpowering high I associate with love, but the good ones don't."

"That high isn't love. It's obsession."

"Intellectually, I understand that," I say. "I get that mature relationships don't cause colors to be brighter, sounds to be sweeter, and the air to always smell like perfume. But I still think a man must not be right for me if my entire body doesn't alight when I get a text message from him. And if I don't feel that way, I can't seem to just go with the program; I'm either all in or all out."

"Has it occurred to you," Roger asks, "that Brandon was also at fault?"

Now I'm exasperated. "This doesn't have to do with Brandon! Besides, he *wasn't* at fault. I was a monster. I deserved to be left. Trust me, I would have left me, too."

"Really? Because it sounds to me like you were frightened— like you gave up your whole life for someone, moved to a strange city, and wanted reassurance that you'd done the right thing. That seems perfectly understandable. He could have given that to you."

"I'm telling you, he was right to leave."

"Did you go to couples counseling?"

I think back: while I was in therapy at the time, Brandon wasn't and, in fact, had told me he thought it was silly. "No." A forgotten memory surfaces. "He actually made fun of me for having a therapist. He'd always ask me how my 'inner child' was afterward."

Roger sits up straighter. "He did," he says.

"He did."

"And for 15 years, you've been beating yourself up for driving him away?" I nod and fight back tears that want to come out. "At any point in these 15 years," Roger says, "have you gotten angry with him? He abandoned you in a city where you didn't know anyone."

"Oh, come on." My aggravation resurfaces. "My problems today are caused by a failed relationship from over a decade ago? Please." Roger was always prodding me to "get in touch with" my so-called rage: we'd devoted many sessions to how the way my family laughed at my sadness set me up to deny my feelings and blame myself; this was why, Roger thought, I was never mad at Will for what Roger called "emotionally seducing" me. "And now all I need to do is break through and realize it wasn't my fault? Please. This isn't *Good Will Hunting*."

"I didn't say it was."

"Look, I *am* angry," I vent. "But I'm angry at myself for being as old as I am, doing everything I can to prepare for a relationship, and then running away from the first real possibility. I'm angry that I can't figure out why I'm this way." My eyes settle on him. "And I'm angry at you for not being able to fix me."

Roger doesn't seem fazed; therapists are surely used to being the recipients of misplaced furor. He says, "If you allowed yourself to get mad at Brandon, maybe you'd also be able to get angry at Will and Jason and Nick and the others who have let you down. Then maybe you'd stop blaming yourself." He smiles wryly. "And me."

For the first time all session, I don't feel annoyed with Roger.

"I just wish you could tell me exactly what to do so I could have what I want," I whisper.

"I wish I could, too. But you know there are no easy answers when it comes to this kind of thing."

I nod; for just a second, I'd wanted to believe that he—that Helen, that someone—had the precise solution for me. "I do. But I really wish there were."

Later that afternoon, skimming through *S&SG*, I stumble on a passage I'd never noticed before: "Possibly you learned as a child that to get on with Mommy and Daddy, you'd better keep your voice down, your anger contained, tears contained."

I close the book and think about the tantrums of my youth and how crestfallen I used to feel when my family would laugh. Then I reflect on what happened with Brandon. While I definitely expressed my anger at him at the time—it is, in fact, what made him leave—it's true that my rage shifted from him to me as soon as he was gone. When I think back on our relationship, I cast him as the innocent victim and me as the evil tormenter, an ironic summary since I'm always telling people how a breakup is never only one person's fault.

When I got sober, a few years after Brandon and I broke up, one of the first things I heard was that anger was just sadness directed outward. I'd been infuriated a lot of the time up until that point and I suddenly saw that when I lashed out at other people, I was usually trying to make them feel as bad as I did. I've learned to control that impulse since then—figured out how to pause and consider the idea that the would-be recipient of my acrimony probably isn't at fault and then channel my feelings more appropriately. But maybe I've swung too far in the other direction. Possibly it's been easier to blame myself than to get mad, close the door, and move on. Perhaps I need to learn how to express anger not just at myself and my therapist and IKEA customer service representatives but also at the men who have disappointed me.

Then a new thought occurs to me: what if my not responding to Darren isn't a sign of how incapable I am of being in a relationship but simply an indication of the fact that I, for whatever reason, just don't like him? What if it shows that I'm being honest with myself and am not willing to go along with something just because I should, so that I can tell the "pressure groups" that my project is working and know for certain that I never have to expose myself to Match and speed dating again? Potentially both are true: I can allow myself the freedom not to respond, to take Brandon—and maybe Will, too—off the pedestal, and then, hopefully, move on to someone who, for whatever inexplicable reason, does make me light up.

Then I think: If I've only just now become aware of the fact that it's okay for me not to like someone I feel I should, I probably have some other false and unhelpful beliefs about relationships. I probably need to replace the old concepts that haven't worked for me with some new ones that do. And the way I'm going to start doing that, I decide, is by observing happy couples in action.

At my friend Amanda's birthday dinner, I notice her husband, Seth, walk around the table with a camera so that he can take photos of Amanda with each of her friends; another night when I'm at their apartment, I see him rush in and, after checking on their two kids, excitedly pull out an array of gluten-free desserts for his sugar-loving, wheat-allergic wife. The more time I spend with her, the more I notice that the texts or calls that really make her laugh are from Seth. And when she talks about what he does for a living, it's clear that she thinks he's the best in his field for what he does; I have no idea whether or not this is accurate, but it obviously is for Amanda.

One weekend in Montauk, I watch my friend Vanessa rub her husband, Craig's, head while talking to other people and hear her say with pride to those who don't know him, "Have you met my husband, Craig?" The two of them, both successful, bounce between L.A. and New York with sometime stints in Hawaii; they're living, breathing proof if ever there was any that married life needn't be dull and predictable.

I observe a couple that live in my neighborhood who walk around holding hands but not talking to each other. Part of me is envious and inspired by them, the other part judgmental and discouraged. Have they run out of things to say? Or do they represent true contentment—companionship without having to utter a word?

I talk to my dad's stepsister Barbara, who didn't get married until she was 44, doesn't have kids, and always seems blissfully happy. "I never wanted to get married but always thought I'd have children," she tells me. She says that every time she got into a relationship, she'd envision herself crossing a street with the man while a car barreled toward them. "I'd try to visualize if I would be the one to protect us from imminent danger or he would," she says. "And in my mind, I was always the one who pushed us out of the way."

Unlike me, Barbara was in a series of long-term relation-ships but wasn't ever with someone she missed when he wasn't around until she met her now-husband, Paul. "With the men before him, it would always be something," she says. "I'd hate his laugh or that he smoked, or that he draped sweaters over his shoulders. Really what I was saying was that it wasn't right. People, especially my family, used to tell me that I'd always be single because what I was looking for didn't exist, but I believed it did. And if I'd accepted what they said and just married who-ever was there at the time, without a question I would have ended up divorced."

Her words feel like a soothing bath. *People used to tell me that I'd always be single. If I'd accepted what they said and just married whoever was there at the time, I would have ended up di-vorced.* While for the past few years, a part of me has felt that I'd rather have been married and divorced than just perpetually single—that it would at least make me seem and feel somehow less suspect—I've also always known that I'd do anything to avoid ending up divorced the way my parents and grandpar-ents were, and that the reason I was never interested in making that kind of commitment in my 20s is that I wasn't sure I could spend 40 or so years with the same person. I realize while talk-ing to Barbara, however, that I've grown so accustomed to the idea that my single status is all my fault—that I want something that doesn't exist, that I can't commit, that I have intimacy is-sues—it had actually stopped occurring to me that I could still be holding out for the right thing and that my decisions, or non-decisions, were possibly the right ones.

Even though Barbara could have had kids with Paul, she

didn't in the end. "I was enjoying my life and career and for whatever reason, I never got around to it," she says. Paul had two full-grown children by then and she now feels like she gets all of the benefits and none of the drawbacks of parenting, adding with a laugh that she once saw a bumper sticker that seemed to be very appropriately about her: "If I'd known how great grandchildren were, I would have had them first." Maybe, I think, I'll be like Barbara—convinced I want something but perfectly happy without it?

When she and I get off the phone, I log on to Facebook and notice the status update of a guy I just met at a party. It says: *My friend in Seville is looking to do an apartment trade with someone in New York for most of the month of August.* I read it again: yes, the universe is potentially offering me an opportunity to spend time in a city I loved more than any other I've ever visited. The fact that I'm seeing this just after talking to Barbara about accepting my single life feels like a sign. *I'm on the path I'm meant to be on.* I instantly e-mail the guy, saying that I want to do the trade—that I don't care what his friend's place is like or need any more details but just want to commit *now*, before someone else with a better Manhattan apartment comes along and makes the same offer. He puts me in touch with Raquel, the woman in Seville, and we start making our plans for the following month; I will away all the negative thoughts that are starting to pop up—about how I can't afford the plane ticket, about how I'll probably miss a slew of amazing career opportunities if I leave the country for an entire month, and about how lonely I'll get if I'm on my own for that long.

During my period of planning this solo journey and observing couples in action, I suddenly start encountering all these people who are miserable with the path they've chosen—and they make me increasingly grateful for the fact that I'm not shackled down by an oppressive relationship and have the freedom to take off for a month. A friend of a friend tells me how lucky I am to be single because her husband is emotionally abusive and she dreams of the day she can get away from him. A married guy I know confides in me that he doesn't think marriage works—that it only made sense when we only lived to be around 40. An acquaintance who I always assumed was a single mom because I never heard her talk about a husband mentions a guy one day; when I ask her who he is, she says, "My husband" with an eye roll before telling me that while she doesn't love him, she's grateful to him for giving her a child.

When I was younger, it had never occurred to me that I might enter my prime childbirth years and not have some sort of a plan for kids in the works. But during these past few years of smiling, waving, and cooing at other women's babies, part of me accepted the fact that my body was maturing faster than my emotional state and I realized I was open to the idea of adoption—that the goal was to raise a child and not necessarily have it come from my womb.

I've always been an impulsive decision-maker. Rather than looking, then jumping, I just jump. As I call the airline to book my plane ticket, I wonder, is this my problem with romance? Because I don't weigh the pros and cons, don't really assess how good a choice I'm making, but instead allow myself to be led by some inner whim, do I always put myself in situations that will end up later causing me to get hurt? But at the same time, this just feels right. "I need a ticket from JFK to Seville, Spain," I hear myself say.

Project Helen has forced me to become clear about my life—to really see what I have and what I want without hiding any of the less-than-palatable truths from myself. And with this greater clarity has come even more enthusiasm about the idea of adopting. I'm always coming up with new reasons why I might not want to go through pregnancy and delivery: the nausea, a state that makes me feel like I literally may be dying and need to be hospitalized; the hormonal mood swings, a terrifying thought to someone who can find herself crippled by emotions under normal circumstances; the body destruction. The notion of being able to save a child who might otherwise grow up under less-than-ideal circumstances has also become increasingly appealing. Still, I know that I'm also telling myself these things in order to cushion the increasingly likely news that it really may be too late for me by the time I feel truly ready.

Of course, pregnancy is hardly the only daunting aspect of the process. As a lifelong commitment-phobe, I can't help but wonder how I'll handle the one commitment you can never get out of. There's no telling your kid things got too serious too fast or suddenly realizing he or she isn't the one that you want. I tell myself that I won't make any of the mistakes my parents did, but that doesn't mean I couldn't wreak havoc on tiny psyches in altogether original ways. Surely I won't laugh when my child cries but what if I do something equally—or more—damaging?

And what if I get one of those undeniably nightmarish kids? Walking down the street the other day, I saw and heard a little boy wailing in a way that I can only describe as sounding like he was begging to be despised. As I got closer, I noticed that his mother seemed to be doing everything she could to comfort him, but he simply refused to allow her to help. What if I got one of those—and was then stuck with him for the rest of my life? Even worse, what if my mothering skills were so poor that I took what would have been a perfectly delightful child and then turned him into one of the shrieking monsters? I think about how hard I am on the people I've hired over the years to help me with accounting, my Web site and various other work projects. With them, I tend to be impatient, demanding, and ever ready to point out errors—essentially, I expect perfection at every turn and am utterly disappointed when I don't get it. Of course, I'm kind and grateful when all goes well, but still, is this what I'm going to be like when my child makes mistakes? How, in other words, does the aggressive, demanding career woman I've become mesh with the mommy who kisses boo-boos?

Elizabeth, meanwhile, is handling her pregnancy with more grace and ease than I have when not pregnant. She's hired a baby nurse to help her in the beginning, has done every bit of research possible, and talks casually about potential ways to make the transition easier—having her family come to town to pitch in or renting a place in the Hamptons for one of the first few months in order to escape the city's heat and crowds. If she's terrified and overwhelmed, she's doing a damn good job of hiding it. But I still don't feel remotely convinced that single parenting is for me. I've tried to picture myself in my apartment with a newborn and then an infant and then a child, imagined the Single Mothers by Choice meetings, thought about the concept of hiring a babysitter so I can go on a date, and the entire scenario chills me. No matter how often I hear about celebrities who land the guy *after* adopting a kid (Angelina Jolie, Calista Flockhart, and Michelle Pfeiffer, not that I'm obsessively keeping track), I just can't imagine it for myself. That isn't to say that I never will; for the past year or two, I've thought that maybe when my career seems more secure or I feel the clock ticking to the point that I can't hear anything else, I'll welcome the idea. But one day when I'm in a cab with Elizabeth and noticing that pregnancy has only made her prettier—her protruding belly is adorable, her hair has grown long and luscious, and her face has blessedly stayed the same size—I wonder if that day will ever come. What if instead I wake up one day to find it's too late, that the possibility of motherhood has swept me by while I was staring into another unavailable man's pretty eyes?

I decide to make an appointment with my gynecologist.

A chipper woman, Dr. Graham is thrilled when I mention that I want to talk babies. I remember when she broached the topic last year how quickly I shut her down because I didn't want to talk about something that still felt so out of reach. This time, however, I'm enthusiastic. I tell her that I'm interested in finding out how fertile I am and she says she thinks that's a wonderful idea. She's not nearly as discouraging as I expect her to be—she's full of stories about patients in their 40s and beyond who have gotten pregnant and gives me the general impression that if this is something I want, it's well within the realm of possibilities.

Still, she does press the idea of my doing artificial insemination now. I explain that I'm just not interested in single motherhood at this point but tell her I want to find out about the possibility of freezing my eggs. What I'd learned about the process already was somewhat discouraging—both in terms of how many babies have been born that way and how expensive the process was—but I'm still open to the idea. She nods and writes down the name of a fertility doctor.

There's a nervous vibe in the air when I walk into the Upper East Side fertility clinic. Women, only one with a man by her side, frantically scan their phones or flip magazine pages without appearing to take in a single word. The waiting room is bright green: the walls seem to scream fertile. Are all fertility clinic waiting rooms painted this shade?

I continue to scan the crowd: it's affluent and I spy a lot of wedding rings. We're all probably the same age but I feel a lot younger and I get the sense that everyone else knows exactly what they're doing here while I'm still not sure. *I'm just checking out my options*, I plan to say if anyone asks, but no one looks like they will. We make the people sitting in regular doctor's waiting rooms, where some may potentially be waiting to find out if they have fatal diseases, seem comparatively peaceful. Whenever a woman's name is called, she jumps up; when it's the one who has the man with her, she forgets all about him as she follows the nurse to a room down the hall. He trails behind, looking confused by the fact that he's become an afterthought.

Once she's gone, I look around again and determine that this isn't the sort of environment that welcomes conversation. I'm guessing that's because anything we could possibly talk about would feel too invasive for a chat with a stranger; we have too many unanswered questions to be able to handle any more.

As we stare at but don't read magazines, Beyoncé sings in the background.

Eventually I'm led back to an examination room, where I change into a gown and am given an ultrasound. The nurse, who has a heavy but difficult-to-place accent, shows me my uterus on the machine. "It looks how a uterus should look," she says.

"Well, that's good." I grin. "Certainly better than *not* looking how a uterus should look."

She gives me a thin smile; the fertility clinic is clearly no place for levity. "You're going to have to keep coming back and having it measured," she says.

"Really?" I ask. "I just want to check my fertility. Why would I come back?"

"The doctor will explain it to you," she says brusquely and leaves the room.

Another woman enters, inserts a needle into my arm, and starts taking my blood. "Is this your first cycle with us?" she asks.

For the second time in five minutes, I'm confused. I say the same thing I did before, that I just want to check my fertility. She gazes at me oddly—it's clearly unusual to be here for this—and tells me to go back to the waiting room. I do and from where I sit, I can hear her talking about me to someone I assume is the doctor. "She doesn't want to get pregnant right now," she says. Then something I can't decipher. Then: "That's why there's a question mark on her file."

To my left, a youngish-looking woman smiles at me. Her left hand is hidden and I have a sudden and strong feeling that she might be in the same situation as me: single, relatively ignorant about this entire process, and just hoping to find out about her fertility possibilities. We start chatting and after a few minutes, I ask if this is her first time here.

"Oh, no," she says, and as she begins raving about her doctor, I see her wedding ring. I don't catch the doctor's name but it's not the one I'm here to see. "He immediately found out all the things that were wrong with me and I got pregnant right away," she adds with the fervor of a Scientologist, explaining that she's back for more. I don't ask what was wrong with her.

When her name is called, she rises and wishes me good luck. Now, I have a problem—an entirely ridiculous problem—with people wishing me good luck; I hear it as patronizing even when I know it's not meant to be. For all she knows, I have six babies at home so she surely doesn't mean it in an I-have-kids-and-you-don't-so-you-need-luck way. "Good luck" in a fertility clinic is probably just what "Break a leg" is in an audition waiting room. I smile and wish her the same.

Soon I'm led into a room to discuss egg freezing with a kind woman who tells me about how it's done, where the eggs are stored, and happy stories of women who've had babies this way. The process of talking to a professional about egg freezing helps me to see that I'm just not interested in putting my eggs on ice. I know that I may be missing my last chance, but a strong part of me believes that everything happens the way it's meant to and that having eggs scraped out, hoping they survive the process, freezing them, and then going through IVF is defying this faith. I say as much to the kind woman, who looks a bit discouraged by my response but tells me she understands.

Back in the waiting room, I think about people's decisions

to have kids. We're all sort of conditioned to instinctively feel sorry for the women or couples who don't become parents—we imagine the emptiness they must feel for never having heard the pitter-patter of little feet or ponder the horror of not having anyone to care for you when you reach old age. And I was certainly one of them. In fact, until I spoke to Barbara—and started thinking about Helen—it had literally never occurred to me that people might be *happy* with these circumstances.

Yet it seems like so many couples have children because they believe that's just what you do—the next item on the to-do list— after you get married. I wonder how many of them consider the big picture: everyone seems so focused on the getting-pregnant part, or the having-the-right-stroller part, or the getting-the-kid-into-the-right-preschool part. Do they think about toddler tantrums and teenage sullenness, not to mention the concept of bringing someone into this world and then having to someday watch that person endure stupefying, incapacitating pain that they might not be able to ease? What if that's more than they can bear? I know how hard it is for me when my mom is depressed. How do people withstand seeing something like that in their kid?

I don't come to any conclusions before my name is called again. This time, I'm led to see the doctor, a petite, rather adorable woman who gazes at the X-ray of my ovaries and tells me they look good. "There are lots of follicles," she says encouragingly before letting me know that she'll call me with my blood test results later.

For some reason, that doesn't make me nervous; being in the waiting room and feeling entirely clueless about something I should surely know more about shook me but I'm not scared to hear the news. I just believe I'm fertile—an entirely ridiculous statement to make but one that is nonetheless true. When the doctor and I speak later and she says that my FSH—follicle-stimulating hormone—is 8.4 and that this means that I'm fully capable of getting pregnant since below 10 is normal, I'm nevertheless relieved. But I also know that pregnancy is certainly no guarantee—I could still have all kinds of things wrong with me like the woman in the waiting room. Besides, I'm aware of the fact that fertility can be about as fleeting as an unavailable guy's declarations of love. The doctor confirms as much. "Remember, this could change in a month or two months or six months or 12 months," she says. "But," she adds, "usually drastic variations don't happen overnight."

In order to acclimate to the notion of motherhood, I ask Elizabeth if I can go with her to a childbirth class. "Sure," she says. "But the only one I have left is breastfeeding." I figure that any topic is as good as the next when you're as ignorant as I am, so we make a plan to meet there later that week.

Of the 20-odd people gathered in the Tribeca clinic, about half are men; one is wearing pajamas. Water bottles abound and most of the women chug with abandon, waddling over for refills from the cooler as soon as they're empty. A lactation consultant hands out packets and then lectures from the front of the room: we learn that there's milk in the breasts from the third trimester on, that babies usually feed between eight and 12 times in a 24-hour period, and that these feedings should take between 20 and 40 minutes.

The facts keep coming: Oxytocin is released when muscles

around milk-producing cells are squeezed! Babies are born with reflexes that help them to nurse! Pain is a sign that something isn't right! I'm the only one taking notes, which I have to assume is because all this is common knowledge by the time you're as close to delivering as these women look. We watch a short movie, *Follow Me Mum*, which is narrated by an Australian woman and shows an endless succession of mothers breastfeeding. "Is that the most nursing any of you have ever seen?" the teacher asks as she turns the lights back on.

"Most I ever want to see, that's for sure," Elizabeth says under her breath. I think pregnancy has made her funnier.

As the lecture continues, I see a woman reach for her husband's hand—a notable occurrence because it's the first sign of physical affection I observe. I'd gone in assuming that Elizabeth would stand out as a brave single mother—the sole woman who had the strength to go through this process alone—and that I'd feel proud of her but also a bit protective. Yet none of the women who have men next to them seem any better off than those who don't; the guy in pajamas, in fact, looks like he may be enough of a handful that he's given his partner all the preparation for motherhood she needs. That's not to say that these guys appear unenthusiastic; many, in fact, look so interested that you'd think they were going to be lactating and feeding the babies themselves.

Unfortunately, I can't maintain their same focus and, after about 90 minutes, I'm restless and whispering to Elizabeth that I don't think I'll be able to make it through the next few hours of this. She says it's fine if I sneak out, that people have done that throughout the previous classes. I smile with gratitude, knowing that another viewing of *Follow Me Mum* might send me over the edge.

I feel a similar restlessness when I go to California soon after to visit my family and spend time with my two-year-old nephew—a gorgeous, bright, adventurous kid who doesn't stop moving until he falls asleep. Because he's potentially the cutest child on earth, seeing him running, tumbling, or scampering is so adorable that you feel like you could watch him forever.

And yet I learn, when I accompany my parents and sister-in-law to the playground in the mall, that I can't. In fact, I tire of it after about an hour. Helping him onto a new part of the jungle gym and then seeing him scoot right off in order to then run around the playground and the area outside the playground is, it turns out, not all that fascinating. Buying him balloons and then watching him release them into the sky also grows old quickly. Why, when Helen suggested that we "borrow" children, did she not mention that the activity could be incredibly dull?

My parents, stepsister, and I fall into what feels like a well-established routine where one of us runs around after him while the other three sit on a bench and watch; during that time, one of the bench dwellers, maybe two, mentions how cute he is. Then another of us takes over chasing after him and the pattern repeats itself, the only difference being that the comment about his cuteness alters slightly, usually by becoming more specific.

At a certain point it becomes clear to me that this is meant to go on all day, and what's more, that my family is happy to do it that long. When a promotions woman from Macy's approaches us with postcards about the spectacular sale the store is having, I yearn to follow her inside. But I feel guilty, like I should be just as intrigued as everyone else is by my nephew and that if I were really as determined to be a mother as I say I am, then I, too, would never tire of sitting on a bench and watching him dart off various pieces of playground equipment. But I can only fight my natural urges so much. "I'll be back," I say to my mom as I get up and walk toward Macy's. "Soon."

Elizabeth's baby shower brunch is the day after I return from California. It's an event I've been anticipating with trepidation, since baby showers can be traumatic. I'll never forget my first one; sitting among the other girls, decorating onesies and toasting our pregnant friend, I pretended to be comfortable, acted like I knew exactly what my future mothering plans were, let alone what a onesie was—the whole time feeling like a child who'd wandered over to the adults' table and been mistakenly assigned a seat. I think I was the only woman there who didn't have a husband or boyfriend and, after a half hour or so, suffocating myself with a onesie seemed preferable to sitting and listening to the chatter about double dates and where to get the cutest maternity clothes.

Afterward I saw that I hadn't done enough mental and emotional preparation for the event—hadn't acknowledged that celebrating my first pregnant friend was going to bring up feelings about the fact that I wasn't at that stage and didn't know when I would be. I'd just gone in thinking that it would be a fun party and that I'd probably get to eat some delicious cake.

I'm determined not to make the same mistake this time so I tell myself before Elizabeth's shower that falling apart just because the conversational focus will be on mommyhood isn't an option. But when I enter the sun-drenched private room of an upscale Soho diner, I see that no planning was required. Her family and other friends are lovely and warm and full of chatter about their lives and careers and all sorts of topics that don't have to do with what is or isn't inside their wombs. And right in the middle of it all stands Elizabeth, looking resplendent and like she may well burst before the eggs Benedict is served.

Although the focus does turn to babies when we start eating, there isn't an iota of detectable sanctimoniousness. The "pressure groups" and "digs" Helen has taught me to be aware of simply aren't here. Leslie, a single movie producer on my left, confesses that she froze her eggs—"Years ago, back when the storing part was cheaper"—but she doesn't know if she'll use them. "I'm still holding out for the partner," she says. Elizabeth's doula, who's seated on my other side, nods. She has a husband and child and also helps women through deliveries, but spends as much time at brunch talking about the Ph.D. in English she's in the process of earning. The former advertising executive across the table from me has two kids but speaks mainly about how hard it is to reenter the working world after taking so much time off to raise them. Rather than seeing the mothers as the haves and we nonmothers as the have-nots, I understand for perhaps the first time that issues about relationships and career and kids plague all women and that many of us, if not all, speculate that we may not be making the right choices.

I talk about my willingness to adopt, half joking that in many ways I think I'd be doing my future kid a favor by not passing along some of my more emotional or tortured genes. The movie producer laughs, but that's when the adoption horror stories surface: one girl talks about her friend who takes anti-depressants and therefore couldn't adopt a baby from China, another tells a story about the hurdles a woman she knows had to go through, and a third mentions two friends of hers—a couple in their 40s—who simply gave up after running into so much age discrimination from adoption agencies.

The last story makes my heart sink: I'd blindly believed that adoption was a realistic option—something I could do if I jumped through the right hoops and stayed determined. But maybe it was another possibility that had slipped from my grasp while I was off trying to convince myself that yet another unavailable man was really available. But I halt my fear spiral before it can really take hold by telling myself that this conversation is just another wave I'm riding and that I don't need to let it pull me under. It's a choice to let my mind conjure up an image of me weeping as the 37th adoption agency I've contacted says no. Just breathe, I think, and let it pass.

"Hey, Kelly Preston is pregnant and she's 47," the movie producer offers cheerfully. Another mentions that she thinks the writer Susan Orlean had a baby at 50. A third talks about the world's oldest mother, who gave birth to twins at 70. Someone makes a joke and we all laugh. The wave recedes and I finish my cake.

Elizabeth delivers the week before I leave for Spain. I visit her in the hospital, and find her just as calm and cheerful as she's been the past nine months. "Hey, there!" she says as she nurses a tiny blue-eyed blob, putting to use all that she'd gleaned from our never-ending breastfeeding class.

She starts telling me about giving birth: the contractions, the vomiting on the cab ride to the hospital, the realization once she was there that she was dilated enough to have gone in at least 10 hours earlier, the fear and pain of the pushing. I hear about the suction cup that had to be placed on the baby's head so he wouldn't slide back in and about placenta stuck in the womb and about stitches, and I'm enthralled but also wondering how on earth she and every other mother is strong and courageous and insane enough to endure what sounded to me like the most hellish experience a person could have. And then, 24 hours later, to sit and calmly talk about it while nursing! She doesn't even look tired.

I ask if I can hold him and, after cautioning me to not let his head fall, she places her baby boy in my arms. I make eyes at this creature that looks more like an alien than a child and marvel at the notion that she believes I'm up to the task at hand. The youngest baby I'd ever held before was at least six months old, and it seems impossible that I'm rocking something that was in her womb the day before. How does Elizabeth, someone very similar to me, someone whose "husband bed" next to hers remains a receptacle for baby present boxes, feel so certain not only that she won't drop him but also that she'll be able to do everything else required so that he grows up healthy and happy? How does she have this confidence that I'm only now getting as a result of all the guidance I've gotten from Helen?

"What was your first night like?" I ask.

She shrugs. "It's funny; I don't know where the time went," she says. "I only slept a few hours. I didn't watch TV. I guess I was just tending to my little man."

"And what are you going to do when you go home?"

She smiles. "We'll see. I have a baby nurse who will be with us temporarily. I'm going to do my best not to work but hey, I was sending some e-mails this morning." She laughs at herself. "I'm sure I'll figure it out."

I wish I could say the same thing with such confidence.

CHAPTER TWELVE

The Rich, Full Life

Living dangerously lengthens and strengthens your life.

—*Sex and the Single Girl*

"*¿Hablas Inglés?*" I ask optimistically as the sun beats down on my skin. I'd been walking for a good half hour without seeing any signs of humanity so I'd allowed myself to fantasize that the women I'm posing this question to will be able to help me. But they both shake their heads brusquely before returning to a conversation so fast-paced that it could surely only be understood by Spaniards who were either incredibly quick or just very drug-addled.

I was crazy to come here. Who goes to Spain in August? More specifically, who goes to the hottest part of Spain in August? And even more specifically than that, who goes on a solo journey to the hottest part of Spain in August for over three weeks when they don't speak Spanish whatsoever and have recently proven to themselves that they have absolutely no affinity for languages?

A crazy person—that's who, I think as I make my way over one of Seville's many bridges.

It's not like I hadn't been warned during the month before my trip. It seemed like everyone with functional vocal cords felt the need to offer up what was wrong with my plan. But I'd fought down every objection, explaining that there was no such thing as too hot for me and pointing out that New York City wasn't all that cool in August, either. I'd laughed off those who said that Spain was one of the few places in Europe where you really needed to know the language. I'd reminded people who'd asked me why I was going by myself how much I loved being alone. *I'm a very independent, self-sufficient person*, I'd said, sometimes feeling like I was speaking the truth and other times wondering who the hell I was kidding.

I step off the Triana Bridge and onto a street called San Jacinto where I note that everything, absolutely everything, is closed. There isn't a person in sight. Could all the Spaniards have fled? If so, I didn't blame them. Though I was loath to admit it, my naysayers had been right about the heat. It was unrelenting. And I hadn't encountered a single English speaker since I'd arrived over 24 hours ago, and I was lonely as hell. Plus that glorious perfume smell—the blooming, I'd learned, of the city's orange blossoms—wasn't remotely detectable in the summer. I think about comparatively cool New York, where the stores and restaurants were actually open, where I know how to talk to the people in them, where I have friends and a life, and then of the Spanish family living in my apartment there. I wanted to reach out and shake my former self, the one who'd held on to some ancient, romantic notion that I was meant to come back here. Could I endure 20 more days of this?

Then I try to get myself to appreciate where I am by staring at the bridge I'd just walked over. There's no denying the beauty

of those three arches composed of cast-iron circles above a glis-
tening river. But couldn't I just be marveling at a photo rather
than standing by myself in the stifling heat next to it?

Screw Helen and the way she'd gotten me to see that I never
really traveled anywhere. Screw Helen and her talk of saving
for a "European jaunt." Screw Helen for writing that going on a
trip like this by myself would be "single-girl heaven." And screw
me for buying into all that and believing that the best way to
celebrate my singlehood and independence and the changes I've
made would be to jump on a plane and come to the city I'd
glamorized for all this time. I curse myself for having committed to this plan without entirely thinking it through.

As I look past the bridge, however, a tiny part of me alights
with hope. Off in the distance, I spy a restaurant that appears to
be open and a smiling man standing in its entryway. Maybe, I
think, he'll speak perfect English and will be able tell me where
everything is, especially the secret, off-the-beaten-path places
that other tourists never get to see. Perhaps he'll even become
my friend and come with me on his days off to climb the Giralda
tower of the cathedral and tour the Alcazar gardens. I begin
walking toward him. But the closer I get, the more my expectations dissipate: his smile, I begin to see, is actually more of a leer.

"*Linda,*" he says as I approach. *Linda*, I'd learned in the
Dominican Republic, was a compliment: pretty, it meant. You
weren't, however, meant to take it as praise so much as an indication that you might not be in a safe place—a clue that this
would be a good time to walk in the other direction. But desperation makes a woman do funny things.

"*¡Hola!*" I say warmly. "*¿Hablas Inglés?*"

His face freezes in a mild panic and I realize I'm interacting with a man who probably utters *linda* at every passing lady and has never, in his history of employing this method of seduction, seen or even expected a response. I do not let my epiphany deter me. What's the worst that can happen? Surely it's too hot to bother with rape.

"*¿Hablas Inglés?*" I ask again, friendly smile intact.

He shakes his head. Then he sticks out his tongue and wiggles it in a very specific way—a move so singularly disgusting and distinct that I instantly know it's meant to indicate the oral sex he'd like to be performing on any female who would allow it.

A woman, even a desperate woman, can only be so open-minded while attempting to forge her way in a new environment. Turning quickly and stepping back onto the Triana Bridge, I comfort myself with the thought that by tomorrow, I'll only have 19 more days left.

We'll pick you up at eight, the e-mail says. I close my computer, content for the first time since I arrived. It's Monday morning in Seville and I have a plan. Thank God I'd asked Raquel, the woman I'd traded apartments with, if she had a friend I could contact if I ran into an emergency. Raquel had passed along the contact information for Sofia, who was sweet enough to offer to take me out for tapas with her husband tonight. How bad could things be?

As I emerge onto the street, I know the answer: not bad at all. The temperature is at least 10 degrees cooler than it was the day before. And the streets are bustling: people are dashing into shops and standing at counters and tables, drinking coffee and eating thick slabs of bread dipped in olive oil and covered with mashed tomatoes. No one had fled; everything had just been shut down yesterday because it was Sunday. An excitement builds in me as I enter the fray: this is the Seville I had been seeking. Coming here wasn't a mistake but a decision to act on a small, quiet voice inside of me that had been telling me to return. I stop at a café for a coffee and, as I sip, I unfold the map Raquel had left for me in the apartment. I'd resisted grabbing it at first, having reasoned a long time ago that I was someone who simply couldn't read maps; I rarely understand which way is north and which way south, not to mention east or west, and had long ago come up with a tangible disorder to explain this: *I have directional dyslexia*, I'd say with a smile every time a kind person offered to show me where something was on a map. But I don't have that luxury here so I spend a half hour studying the map and discover that nothing about this activity is remotely complicated. I had been on a street, or *calle*, called Avenida de la Constitución. And now I'm on one called Triana—which leads back to the bridge. I walked here via a street that the map claimed connected them. Where had I gotten the idea that this was so hard?

Glancing at my notebook, I see where I've scrawled the address I'd found for a local gym, as well as the location of a spa I'd agreed to review for a spa trade magazine. My goal for the day, I decide, will be to find the gym. Tomorrow's objective will be to locate the spa. A smile grows from inside me. My to-do lists at home tend to be filled with so many tasks that a team of superheroes couldn't accomplish them in a week, even if they went without sleep. But all I'm going to do today is find the gym. Actually, scratch that: all I'm going to do today is *try* to find the gym.

Roughly an hour later, I do. And this isn't some gym that's easy to locate or on the main drag but an unmarked place that's tucked onto a side street three roads off of San Jacinto. There was no way I should have been able to find it. And yet I did. I went where the map indicated I should, looked around, and then, through a series of interactions with friendly strangers, elaborate hand gestures, and liberal use of the word *gimnasio*, attained my goal. Maps aren't hard, I realize; communicating with people who don't speak my language isn't all that difficult, either. The challenge is that I tend to be late or aggravated—usually both—when I'm attempting these activities because I'm simply trying to do too much. Maybe, I think, this is a metaphor for my life. I somehow believe I need to do everything I can to be the best writer and friend and daughter and sober person and citizen that ever existed. And that means that I rarely take the time to feel good about any of it—or simply to stop and breathe and take in the scent of the orange blossoms. It's probably no accident that my quiet inner voice has led me to a country known for its siestas.

Pride over my accomplishment keeps me giddy for the rest of the day and later, when I get another cup of delicious coffee from the café where I'd read the map, I think about the many tiny achievements I make over the course of a month or week or day in New York that I never give myself any credit for. I smile at the waitress giving me my coffee, then take my to-go cup and walk outside—where I immediately spill the coffee down the front of my white dress.

Now I've spilled plenty of coffee in my time—once, during

a brief and misguided attempt at waitressing, an entire pot onto the lap of an understandably irate woman—and so I'm familiar with how I respond: essentially, after confirming that there are no burns, I mutter, "I'm a fucking idiot" repeatedly either aloud or just in my head, whether Hugo Cory would approve or not. But out here on Calle Triana, my first thought is that it's no wonder I spilled since I'm balancing so much at once: I'm in a strange city where I don't know how to speak the language or count the money or where I'm going. Walking home, I wonder what's happening to me; instead of the zero-tolerance-for-mistakes policy my head usually employs, I'm treating myself with gentleness and empathy.

Entering my temporary apartment, I turn on the computer and see two e-mails—each from different men I went out with a few times before I left for this trip. The two guys are entirely different—one is a 41-year-old restaurateur and yoga enthusiast who loves to travel, the other a 31-year-old writer who tutors kids. I've kissed them both and have no idea what's going to happen with either. Hearing from them reassures me that I'll have something—someone, or in this case, two potential someones—to return to and I'm about to respond. But then I decide that I'd rather stay focused on what's going on in Seville right now and not what may go on in New York when I get back.

I turn off the computer and let myself out onto the apartment's enormous terrace, suddenly overwhelmingly grateful to be here—and for my life in general. I love the changes I've made and the way I've confronted my fears. As I gaze at the view, I'm fully conscious of how thrilled I am to have rejoined the world and put myself out there, even though it meant having my heart broken a bit. I take in the sunset, and then my doorbell rings, so I go downstairs to meet Sofia in the sweltering Spanish night.

Floating on my back in the ocean, I gaze at the various couples in various stages of *flagrante delicto* both in the water and on the sand. There's no doubt about it: Spaniards maul each other—all but dry hump—at every given opportunity. I've heard that it's age-old rebellion against the reign of Franco, but all I know for certain is that I've grown accustomed during my time here to watching gorgeous people constantly go at it.

Exchanging slobbering kisses over bowls of gazpacho or lying on top of one another on the beach, Spanish people make love look so easy. Everyone's so beautiful and young—somehow even the old seem young here—and romance looks like it's one nonstop celebration: Just find someone and start making out! they seem to be saying with every embrace. Kissing and touching feels good! At home, I'm far more likely to see a couple on different cell phone calls as they sit on the beach together, and I'm certainly no different than my fellow countrymen. Maybe, I think, I need to adopt the Spanish attitude about love and relationships.

Returning to the shore, I towel off and then begin walking back to the beach house that I've been staying in for the weekend. Raquel's friend Sofia had turned out to be a gold mine in every way—sweet, funny, friendly, and, perhaps most relevantly, eager to practice her English whenever possible—and, as a result, my life has been jam-packed since the night we met. Essentially, she and her equally friendly and sweet husband, David, decided that I would be their project and so they've insisted on including me in every last thing they do.

One night, we wandered down by the Guadalquivir River, the same one that had captivated me when I came here in college, and they told me about their city, pointing out every last site and explaining the history: the Triana Bridge was designed by Gustave Eiffel of Eiffel Tower fame, Sofia would say. The Gold Tower was built in the 13th century and used to act as protective entryway to the port, David would then explain. I tried to imagine bringing them around New York—or my real hometown of San Francisco—and shuddered when I considered how unable I'd be to tell them about the history or sites. I haven't even been to the Statue of Liberty, so I certainly couldn't conceive of bringing foreigners there and telling them about it. They were so proud of their hometown and their country— their eyes would alight when they talked about local soccer players and bullfighters and even the sites—and it occurred to me that I'd moved around so much that it had never crossed my mind to have any sort of city or even state, let alone country, pride.

As we walked through Barrio Santa Cruz, the Jewish Quarter, Sofia explained to me that most Sevillianos want to stay in Seville their whole lives; she told me that they live at home when they go to college and, even as adults, go to their parents' house for lunch and let their mothers do their laundry. I thought about how I picked a college as far from home as I could possibly get while still remaining in the same country, and wondered what this restlessness was inside of me that caused me to resettle in different cities rather than just stay put. Was I continuing to seek something that didn't exist, convincing myself time and again that I needed to change my external circumstances when I should simply sit still and find someone to kiss like the Sevillianos do?

We sat in restaurants, surrounded by loud, raucous crowds, eating crispy patatas bravas (spicy fried potatoes) that Helen would most certainly not approve of and mouth-watering chorizo that, I told myself, she probably would because of the high protein content. They schooled me in how to savor pan con tomate—crusty bread rubbed with smashed tomato and garlic, then drizzled with olive oil — and directed me to the store that sold the best olive oil in town. We lounged in Alameda de Hercules, an enormous open plaza shrouded by trees, and savored ice cream from a parlor that had more varieties of chocolate than I'd ever seen. We stood in tapas bars where friends they'd known their whole lives came up and greeted them excitedly.

Another night, at an out of the way bar they told me was popular among tourists, one man broke out a guitar, another started singing, and still others began dancing while an artist sketched the entire scene. The musicians, dancers, and artist were all good enough to be professionals but when I asked Sofia if they were, she only laughed. Another day, a friend of theirs took me to the top of the Cathedral of Saint Mary of the See, the largest Gothic cathedral in the world. I was about to complain about having to climb the 30 flights to the top when a Spanish octogenarian whizzed past me. Another time, I went to the Alcazar Castle and got lost in the outdoor maze. Still another evening, Sofia, who'd just started taking salsa classes, taught me a few of the moves and I could manage to do just the arms right and just the feet right but couldn't even conceive of pairing them up.

This weekend we've come to David's family's house in Cadiz, two hours outside of Seville, where they've introduced me to a flurry of friends, cooked me delicious meals, and made me feel far more welcome than a person who's been in their country for over a week and hasn't bothered to learn how to say anything beyond *gracias* and *adiós* deserves. As if the circumstances have been tailor-made for my pleasure, they've even invited along a sexy, soulful, long-lashed single friend of theirs, Rodrigo. He, like everyone else, has been asked to please speak in English so that I can be included, an arrangement that's delightful not only because I can be a part of all the conversations but also because as soon as one of them starts a sentence with "What do you call that thing that" and then follows it with anything, I know that my response—usually something simple, like "wind" or "recycling bin" or "sunset"—will garner a satisfied "Yes, that's right! Thank you!" I quickly become accustomed to automatically knowing the answers to all difficult questions, imagining it's how geniuses get to feel all the time.

Back in Seville after the weekend, I immediately return to the routine I've established, which involves doing a little writing and a lot of exploring during the day and then spending evenings either with new Spanish friends or just at a tapas restaurant by the river with a book. While part of me chastises myself for returning immediately to a routine when I'm supposed to be letting go entirely and forging new experiences, the other part of me can't help but be proud of the fact that I've managed to make myself at home in so unfamiliar a place. In New

York, I imagine I'd feel self-conscious slurping soup at a table by myself with only a paperback for company, especially if I was surrounded by couples shoving their tongues down each other's throats. But in Seville I'm wholly at peace. Despite my contin- ued ignorance about the language, I can't escape the sensation that I've somehow come home.

I also slowly start to notice that I'm putting all the Helen les- sons to use in ways that are entirely mine. I begin to cook for myself but rather than just going to the supermarket the way I do in New York, I shop at an outdoor marketplace where I buy meat from one vendor, fruit from another, and cheese from yet another—and then come back and cook gazpacho and garlic chicken and Spanish omelets in Raquel's tiny kitchen. And, since locating items like 100-calorie packs of chocolate-covered pret- zels is difficult in Seville, I find myself eating far healthier than I do at home. I buy special Spanish creams that I smooth onto my hands and feet and start applying eye shadow in new, inventive ways I'd never tried before. At local shops and flea markets, I pick up floral, vibrantly patterned dresses that Dana, Kendall, and Helen may or may not sign off on, and wear them around town. I buy prints of flamenco dancers and bullfighters without caring if Chris Stevens will approve of them when they're framed and on my wall. And, simply because I'm trying to make sure I'm understood by the Spanish people I meet, I speak far slower than I normally do and make plenty of eye contact.

One day I go to El Corte Inglés department store and use a Helen ploy if ever there was one when I spy an attractive blond guy and inquire, in English, if he knows where the paper towels are. I'm in the paper household product aisle so I realize they must be close but he's tall and has angular features and I figure that this interaction stands the chance of being more entertaining than simply finding them on my own. Turns out I'm right: Gerald is half German and half American and, after he answers me in English, our chatter about paper towels quickly evolves into a plan to get together for a drink the next night.

The day of the date, I marvel at how easy romance can sometimes be. The Match experience requires a series of e-mails, IMs, or other negotiations but in this case, I saw a Brad Pitt doppelgänger, asked him to direct me to some paper products and, within a few minutes, had a date. Is it that people in Europe are just more open or am I behaving differently? I can't tell but show up to meet Gerald with hopes high.

Unfortunately, our drink date isn't exciting—he spends the majority of the hour asking if the fact that he's having wine makes me uncomfortable since I don't drink, which doesn't bother me until he doesn't stop asking me about it. He's also a bit pedantic and negative—factors that make him less attractive to me by the millisecond—and I conclude that our conversation about paper towels was probably the most scintillating we had. But at least, I reason, I'm out there trying. I also continue to spend time with Rodrigo—leaning on him for help with the sort of "pippy-poo" things that come up, like communicating with locals. And yet engaging with Gerald and Rodrigo is simply one of the activities I partake in, like swimming laps at my adopted gym. I'm so busy living my life, in other words, that I'm not waiting to see how I'm being treated by the men in my orbit before determining how I should feel about myself.

It occurs to me that usually, at home, under the surface of everything I do is the sensation of either feeling good about myself if a man I like seems to like me and, conversely, sad if there isn't anyone around to do that. I remember when I first moved to New York and was in the honeymoon phase with a guy I'd just started dating, the joy I'd feel as I walked from my apartment to the hotel where he was staying; when things ended and I, devastated, continued to walk that same path—it was, alas, also my route to the subway—I'd felt almost like I wasn't worthy of being on that street. Sitting on my balcony in Seville, watching the sun set behind the cathedral one evening, tears sting my eyes as I really feel how much I've punished myself for being single: *I didn't think I was worthy of walking down a street* because a guy who'd once adored me didn't anymore. The freedom that comes from realizing that I don't need a man to make me feel worthwhile seems worth the whole trip—not to mention all the work Project Helen has required.

One day, when Rodrigo and I bicycle around Seville's Maria Luisa Park in the hot Spanish sun, it occurs to me that I came to Spain without a plan and yet everything worked out far better than I possibly could have imagined, and that perhaps this means that all the plotting and planning and devising I do when it comes to men is unnecessary. If I'd booked day trips and excursions for my time here, in other words, I wouldn't have been able to take advantage of all the glorious opportunities that have come up. What if, it occurs to me, the more arranging I do, the less room I give the universe to allow the natural order of things to unfold? This isn't to say there's anything wrong with signing up for dating Web sites and walking dogs and going speed dating and doing whatever Helen recommends—just that simply seeing what life has to offer might work better than trying to control it. As I bring my bike to a stop, I vow to let go of the reins of my love life.

If I'm single, I suddenly see, I either obsessively try to change that—basing decisions like whether or not I should accept certain invitations on if I think my Mr. Right might be there, pondering the men my friends know and wondering if I should ask them to set me up—or masochistically trying to confirm my fear that I'm the last single person on earth, scanning Facebook for evidence that people I haven't thought about in years are coupled off and have children. But all this energy I've been exerting on trying to control my feelings about the matter—by either pretending I can arrange a meeting with the man of my dreams if only I concentrate hard enough or by attempting to bring on the feeling that I'm the loneliest person alive—has, I now see, been an utter waste of time. There's so much more than romance in the world: there are friends and food and laughter and sights and smells and sounds and delicious, crispy patatas bravas, and the more I focus on my love life to the exclusion of all those other things, the smaller my world becomes. Besides, it's beginning to occur to me, it's when I let go that I seem to get what I want. The trip to Seville wasn't turning out to be how I'd envisioned it; instead it was turning out much better.

Rodrigo and I approach a part of the park where you can buy bird food that attracts white pigeons that are somehow not frightened to then land on you to eat it. I buy a bag and am immediately living out a scene from *The Birds*, albeit one that's hilarious and not frightening, and which Rodrigo captures in a series of photos. When we bike back home along the river, he turns around and smiles at me. "You know, you're very brave," he says.

"Me?" I ask, surprised. "Really?"

He nods. "It's the middle of a very hot day. Most people are inside. And you're out here, biking around, not worrying about heat stroke or whether or not birds that may have diseases land on you. I think that's unusual."

"Thank you." I beam as I pedal behind him. And I can't deny the fact that he's right: I *am* brave. That morning, I'd booked a plane ticket to Marrakech, Morocco, for the weekend. A friend of a friend had passed along a guy's e-mail address earlier in the summer when I'd mentioned that I was going to Seville, telling me that it was a quick flight from there to Marrakech and I should reach out to him if I decided to go. When I was considering the trip, I'd sent the guy, Kamal, an e-mail asking if he knew of a hotel where I could stay. He'd written, *Yes, you can stay at our riad*, then asked for my flight information and explained that someone would come pick me up at the airport. I didn't know what to expect and speculated that this was probably how people got abducted, but I figured all had gone well in Seville so I had no reason to expect anything different in Marrakech.

When I arrive that Friday, there's no one there to pick me up at the airport. At first, I go into a thorough panic, my worst fears realized: I'm in a foreign country, a third-world country, a Muslim country, by myself and have never met my one contact here. I can't speak the language so I'm probably not going to be able to communicate with a cab driver or even the person at the money exchange booth. Kamal had given me an address but who's to say it was correct—or that it wasn't to a place where the people were going to rob or kill me? What in God's name—or Allah's name or whoever was relevant at the moment—had I been thinking?

But then I reason that I've been in Spain for weeks on my own and have survived just fine, and I don't even speak a smidgen of the language. At least a lot of Moroccans supposedly speak French and, while I may not have been the rising star of my NYU class, I learned enough to get by.

So I get in a cab where I encounter a chatty driver who speaks perfect English and is happy to explain the history of Marrakech and show me where the new city ends and the old city begins. Since I'm going to the old city and cars can't drive through there, he explains that he can only take me to a certain point but that he'll make sure he can find a local to walk me where I need to go. When he drops me off, he enlists a sweet-looking old man who leads me down a few streets, past a series of stands where Moroccans are selling crafts, and eventually points to a door at the end of a desolate path. There's no way, I think, that this could be where I'm supposed to be staying. It looks like the entrance to a run-down slum. I hand the man 200 dirham, the equivalent of about 20 dollars. I know I'm overtipping but it's the only bill I have; besides, I'm beginning to panic about my situation and overtipping seems like a comparatively minor problem.

Instead of being grateful, however, the man glances at another man who has just joined him. The second man, far younger and more robust, grabs the dirham and waves it in my face. "This is what you're offering him?" he asks.

I nod. People in Spain had told me to be wary of Moroccans, who tended to assume that all Americans are both wealthy and ignorant, and often desperately try to take advantage of these facts.

"This is insulting," he says. He spits on the ground. The old man, who, minutes before, had seemed both kind and non-English-speaking, nods morosely.

"I'm sorry, but that's all I have," I say.

"You don't have dollars? Or euros?"

His tone is angry, my math skills suck, and I'm easily convinced I've insulted someone so I'm just about to reach into my purse to try to remedy the situation—write him a check, find my ATM cards and ask him where the closest machine is—when I realize that I may be standing all alone in a foreign country being told I've just done something incredibly offensive, but I'm not an idiot. I just gave a man 20 dollars for walking me the equivalent of two short New York City blocks. I think about Helen, and my journey here, and how I don't need to be frightened. The guy is clearly trying to take me for a ride. "That's all I'm giving you," I tell him before turning toward the building.

I knock on the door and a girl answers. "I'm probably in the wrong place," I say. I will myself to be calm and not to worry about the two men who are still standing behind me. "Someone was supposed to be at the airport," I continue, "but no one was there and all I know is that a guy named Kamal—" She cuts me off with a quick shake of her head, a move which makes it clear she doesn't speak English and has no idea what I'm rambling about. Then she shocks me by saying, through a heavy accent, "Anna David?" I want to throw my arms around her—

especially when she opens the door and I discover that the run-down-looking building is actually a three-floor roofless mini palace with tiled staircases and kilim rugs. (I learn later that many of Marrakech's glorious homes are purposely shabby on the outside so as to put off criminals.) Then a man appears behind her and explains that he's the guide who was supposed to pick me up at the airport but he waited at the wrong gate. I put my bag down and he brings me to an even more glorious riad down the street, where the guide explains to me that Kamal, the guy I've been in contact with, is a young, self-made Moroccan businessman who owns restaurants and hotels throughout Marrakech. Apparently he keeps the one I'm staying in just for friends who are visiting, and I'm the only "friend" in town so I'll have it all to myself. If this isn't an example of the rich, full life I can have if only I can stay serene through the slightly scary parts, I'm not sure what is.

The rest of the weekend is magical. While Kamal is busy working, I enlist his brother Amir, who happens to be visiting from Holland, as my tour guide.

While he's age appropriate, speaks perfect English, and is funny, we have a platonic, rather than a romantic, connection. It's Ramadan, which means that Amir fasts during the day, but that doesn't stop him from taking me to the local restaurants—booths with three or four tables where the food is cooked on a portable grill using meats from the booth across the path and spices from the booth next door—and schooling me on the local customs. As an American, I'm free to walk around uncovered—which is a good thing since the temperature is in the high 90s. Together we explore the medina and the souk, the art museums and local gardens, and unlike my Spanish friends, he's as new to the sites as I am. At the Museum of Marrakech, housed in the old palace of Dar M'Nebhi, we admire the detailed tiling and old Berber rugs and I practice what I learned at NYU since the signs are only in Arabic and French. In the old town shops, he helps me to navigate my way through a series of negotiations with local merchants eager to take advantage of the ignorance of Americans. We go to Djemaa el Fna Square, where I hold monkeys and snakes and am informed, for the second time in a week, that I'm brave. He takes me to a local Hammam, where a blind woman rubs my skin with a black sponge before leaving me on a hot, wet tiled floor—an experience that is somehow one of the most relaxing of my life. One day, we decide to go to Kamal's country club, which is surrounded by what looks like miles of blooming rose bushes and contains a pool about six times as long as any I've ever seen. After swimming, we eat moist chicken that we wash down with cool mint tea, Later, Amir is tired but tells me I should go to Mamounia, a hotel that books rooms for up to $10,000 a night, and which Sofia and David had also insisted I visit. I take a cab over there but before I can even open the car door, a guard in front of the hotel walks up and explains that the hotel only allows people staying there to come past the gates on weekends. I return to the riad, where I explain as much to Amir. "Silly girl!" he says. "You were supposed to nod, get out of the cab, and walk right past him."

"I was?"

His friend, who had stopped by to nap—napping being a popular activity during Ramadan—nods.

"They say you can't go in, but they don't expect you to listen," Amir says.

No matter how brave I'm being, I guess there's always room for more.

On my last day in town, I start petting one of the many wild kittens that roam wild in Marrakech and Kamal spontaneously decides to keep her as a house pet; we bring her back to the riad, where we wash her with my shampoo and feed her fish that we get from a stand down the street. And, after the barbecue that Kamal and Amir throw on my final night, they tell me they're naming the cat after me. Later, Amir creates a Facebook page for Anna the Moroccan cat so that I can keep in touch with "her" and later still, I ride on the back of Kamal's motorcycle, squealing through streets of the old city as we pass men and women in their hijabs. I'm aware of the fact that I may well be risking my life with a lot of what I'm doing here—whether it's blindly trusting these strangers or dragging home wild cats or skidding through the Moroccan streets at lightning speeds— and yet I feel as alive as I ever have.

Epilogue

If you'd like to be loved, then love *yourself*.

—*Anna David*

Back in New York, I vow to hold on to the light and vibrant feeling my trip gave me, and also to go to museums and see all the sights of Manhattan the way I did when I traveled—additionally vowing to make this vow different from all the times I made it after returning from vacations before. I promise myself I'll feel as tranquil and grateful as I did in Seville and Marrakech. And it works—for a couple of weeks.

And then—suddenly, almost violently—I'm stressed, a bit depressed, and not sure why. The girl who was calm and kind when she spilled coffee on herself feels like someone I once heard about but can now barely understand. Eventually I pinpoint what's bothering me: I'd been hoping for something monumental to happen when I returned from my journey to my favorite city after a year of living the Helen Gurley Brown way, a denouement equivalent to Javier Bardem showing up once Julia did all the soul-searching in *Eat Pray Love* or Carrie ending up with Mr. Big instead of Baryshnikov in the final moments of *Sex and the City*. I know that this is my life, not mass-market entertainment, but suddenly this life appears to be shockingly similar to how it was before I ever started my project. Yes, I wear lipstick. My curtains and bookshelves are elegant, indeed. I can roast a mean chicken and don't really swear and put visual periods at the end of some of my sentences and Rollerblade and bike and know I can stand up on a windsurf. But things have petered out with both of the men I met before I left, which means that I don't have a partner I adore—or even evidence that he's on his way.

Then a friend reminds me that just because I haven't met the perfect man by now doesn't mean my project didn't work. "You could meet him next year, and be ready and able to have a relationship with him *because* of everything you did over the past year," she says. But is that even true? And if I do fall madly in love, who's to say I wouldn't have anyway?

No one, of course, can provide solid answers to such questions. But there's still a person I'd like to see try. Alas, my efforts to reach Helen prove depressingly fruitless. While I hear that she continues, at the age of 88, to go to the office every day, my conversations with the various people who answer her phone line at *Cosmo* go nowhere. I'm told to send a letter since "Mrs. Gurley Brown doesn't e-mail," but when I do and then call to confirm that the letter arrived, I'm informed that either it did or did not but I shouldn't expect a response either way. When I get slightly desperate for a response—purchasing a stuffed mouse and a stuffed hamburger, sewing them together, and then sending the creation to Helen's office as an homage to her, the woman who popularized the term "mouseburger"—I realize I may be losing it. At least I hadn't gone ahead with my plan to use a taxidermied mouse for the project—something that, in retrospect, might have come across more like a hate crime than a thoughtful gift.

But somewhere during my process of trying to reach Helen, I realize that I don't have to sit down with her to know that the words she wrote in *Sex and the Single Girl* helped me to come back from being "partially dead." I don't need her to tell me that by embodying the values of the 1960s woman, I found the most important value of all: me.

Because here's what I've come to understand: I used to not really believe I deserved thick, gorgeous panels for my windows or to pull books from a bookshelf specifically selected for my apartment. It didn't occur to me that I was worth cooking homemade chicken soup for or dressing in beautiful clothes. I thought I was half a person because I didn't have a partner but that when I had one, I'd do those things for *him*. Now I see that I'm entirely whole so that if and when I find him, we can be two whole people together, not the person and a half we would have been.

I've discovered something else, too. Before this project, I'd grown more independent and less feminine than I actually want to be. I'd somehow internalized the notion that letting myself be taken care of or primping or doing anything that might be considered overly feminine was somehow shameful. While I'm grateful for all the strides women have made in the past 50 years, I realize now that I don't need to buy into the notion that cooking, taking care of where I live, or leaning on a man make me any less of an evolved woman, or that just because I can build a successful career means I have to focus on it to the exclusion of everything else. Now I see that I can have a fully developed and realized life—one that involves taking more risks, facing more fears, and, in general, treating myself like the special woman that I am.

And just because many other women my age are married and have babies, that doesn't mean there's something wrong with me because I don't, or that I should beat myself up for not being one of them. I'm not too late or the only one still standing during a game of musical chairs. I'm just on time—for me. I finally see that right now, today, I'm not only exactly where I'm supposed to be but also exactly *who* I'm supposed to be. My ovaries may be a year older than when I started and I may still have two cats that make most men wary, but just the same, I now see that I'm quite a catch.

With Helen's help, I've fallen, just a little, for myself.

The best part of all? I don't even need to take myself out to dinner 20 times before roasting up a chicken. I can turn on the stove any old time I'd like.

Acknowledgments

Many people helped me take this book from concept to experience to page. First and foremost Carrie Kania, the best-dressed and most inspiring publisher in town, who first pitched me on the idea of doing something on or with *Sex and the Single Girl*. Then Andy McNicol, who helped me craft the original idea into a fully fleshed-out proposal. But it's really Jen Schulkind who deserves the bulk of my gratitude: I really couldn't have asked for a more dedicated, passionate editor; it's actually quite possible that she cares even more about this book than I do—something I wouldn't have thought feasible—and which she showed with every edit, suggestion, query, and late-night email.

The many people who helped me put this '60s journey to the 2010 test—whether through teaching me something specific I needed to learn or simply by listening and offering suggestions—include Dana Reynolds, Chris Stevens, Bee Cohen, Kendall Farr, Arthur Joseph, Hugo Cory, Vanessa Grigoriadis, Shari Goldhagen, Nicole Balin, Elizabeth Weaver, Barbara Dali, Colin Beaven, Ari Melber, Rex Sorgatz, Kathryn Tucker, Tom Mendes, Dilly Hossain, John Griffiths, Lara Namaan, Amanda Kravat, Jack Murnighan, Natali Del Conte, Bart Gardy, Kathleen Mulligan, Jack Ferver, Teddy Wayne, Eric Anderson, Derek Prince, Rick Isaacson, Alicia Gordon, Sofia Herrera, David Pinero, Raquel Vazquez-Morejon, Rodrigo Elias, Kamal Laftimi, Amir Laftimi, the ladies at Ripplu, and, last but never least, my mom, who handles her role as a character in my writing with far more humor and understanding than I probably deserve.

Writers whose material I read and was inspired by during the year, who influenced what I was doing and informed me in ways far too subtle for me to actually be able to explain, include Tara Parker-Pope, Daniel Gilbert, and Jennifer Scanlon.

Eric Fischer has taken the best pictures of me that exist and generously allowed me to use one of them for this book.

But this book wouldn't exist in any form or fashion if it hadn't been for the wit and wisdom of Helen Gurley Brown. If she hadn't been so courageous and original—and taken those courageous and original thoughts to the page—I wouldn't have the book I do, or be the person I am. Helen, I forgive you for not getting back to me. Especially if you forgive me for mailing you a sewn-together mouse and hamburger.

ABOUT THE AUTHOR

ANNA DAVID is the author of the novels *Party Girl* and *Bought*, and the editor of the anthology *Reality Matters*. She has written for the *New York Times*, the *Los Angeles Times*, *Redbook*, *Details*, and many other publications. She was the dating expert on G4's *Attack of the Show* and has appeared on national television programs including the *Today* show, Fox News's *Red Eye* and *Hannity*, and CNN's *Showbiz Tonight*.

BOOKS BY ANNA DAVID

FALLING FOR ME
How I Hung Curtains, Learned to Cook, Traveled to Seville, and Fell in Love . . .

ISBN 978-0-06-199604-7 (paperback)

Anna David—smart, successful, and single—spends one year following the advice of *Cosmo*'s Helen Gurley Brown, author of *Sex and the Single Girl*, to change her life and either find "the one" or determine once and for all that it's not in the cards.

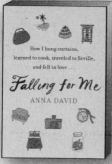

REALITY MATTERS
19 Writers Come Clean About the Shows We Can't Stop Watching

ISBN 978-0-06-176664-0 (paperback)

A collection of hilarious yet revealing essays from novelists, essayists, and journalists about the reality television shows we love, obsess over, and cringe at—and why they, and America, can't stop watching.

BOUGHT
A Novel

ISBN 978-0-06-166918-7 (paperback)

"[David] Simultaneously channel[s] Charles Bukowski and Anaïs Nin . . . with a truly authentic voice that makes *Sex and the City* look like Disneyland."
—Ian Kerner, *New York Times* bestselling author

PARTY GIRL
A Novel

ISBN 978-0-06-137400-5 (paperback)

"Anna David writes with a new strain of relentless, self-deprecating genius that re-casts the worn-down hooves of Prada-wearing demons with spanking new kicks."
—Jerry Stahl, bestselling author